THINK AND ACT.

THINK AND ACT.

A SERIES OF ARTICLES

PERTAINING TO

MEN AND WOMEN, WORK AND WAGES.

BY

VIRGINIA PENNY.

PHILADELPHIA:
CLAXTON, REMSEN, & HAFFELFINGER,
819 AND 821 MARKET STREET.
1869.

PREFACE.

> "He who sneers at any living hope
> Or aspiration of a human heart,
> Is just so many steps less than God."

The bee contributes to the pleasure of the natural palate — the gardener to the sustenance of the physical frame. So the author of this work would contribute to the pleasure of those who find anything good in the few plain reasons set forth in the following pages for the views cherished, and believed to be right. If what is said be the means of making plain the path of duty, or assisting any one in the cause to which it is devoted, it will have accomplished its mission. If the struggles of women engaged in earning an honest living are assisted, it will bless the heart of the writer. I may have occupied too much space in matters of a didactic nature. If so, I will claim it as a failing leaning to virtue's side. Some may think there is more bitter than sweet in the store offered. If so, I hope the bitter may prove beneficial. The nature and substance of the work may, to some of my sex, appear very dry; but I trust it may not prove so to all. It makes no pretension to anything more than it is — a few sober reflections on woman and her business interests.

VIRGINIA PENNY.

BOSTON, November, 1868.

CONTENTS.

OBJECT OF THE BOOK.

THE subject of *Woman and her Work* is beginning to elicit an interest from most noble hearts, both of our own sex and the braver. The subject is one that deserves the consideration of the public, and one to which thinking minds are now being turned, both in our country and in Great Britain. To me it has seemed strange that the subject of women's employments, involving as it does the welfare of hundreds of thousands, should not have received any particular attention, until within the last few years. So far as I can learn, no work setting forth the occupations in which women may engage has appeared except mine, entitled "The Employments of Women." A vacuum on that subject had previously existed in literature. I hear of lectures to working men, and now and then meet with an essay addressed to the working class; but I have not until recently found anything intended especially for working women, except a few small pamphlets issued in London, since the establishment there, in 1859, of a "Society for Promoting the Employment of Women."

Having been much interested for a few years in matters pertaining to woman's labor and compensation, my unemployed moments have been pleasantly devoted to writing out thoughts accumulated.

There is need for a more systematic and harmonious organization of labor in our land. Women suffer from the want of it more than men. Could such an organization be established, numberless women, now destitute and friendless, would be benefited. Besides, the interests of all the higher classes of women would be promoted. Many women have been lost to society by the want of constant employment at fair wages.

We have many books telling us exactly the condition of society, and the need of specific employment for unmarried women, whereby their pecuniary interest and happiness may be promoted, but how to select and engage in an employment, and what employments are open to women, is a subject hitherto neglected, or partially set forth, now and then, in the transient literature of the day.

I wish to see woman's labor properly compensated, and she having free admittance to those employments for which she is fitted. I long to see the condition of the working woman improved, and to see her possessing such comforts and refinements as her station will admit. But to enjoy these privileges she must be trained to some particular field of usefulness. I wish to see girls put in possession of the skill and knowledge of some worthy employment. Then, when alone in the world, they can, with a self-reliant energy, devote themselves to the acquisition of a regular compensation, and lay by something for sickness and old age.

Many and varied are the employments of men. Their physical strength, and more daring natures, open for them hundreds of employments. The out-door exercise of men, and their generally good health, give a stronger, more cheerful, and more uniform tone to their spirits. Scarcely a work of creation exists that man has not explored and investigated. But woman, timid and reserved, has confined herself to the few beaten tracks of labor that custom has assigned her. But now the barrier is being broken down, and woman is entering new avenues of honorable employment. Who does not rejoice that it is so? Many are beautifully adapted to woman's nature, and will serve to render her more useful and more lovely. Let her step in and occupy them. None can or will prevent her. If she meets with scorn and jeers, it will be from those whose opinions are worth nothing; not from the noble and the good.

ORIGIN OF OCCUPATIONS.

A DIVISION of labor in trades may be traced to the talents and tastes of individuals in the early commencement of society. In those days men would exchange the products of the soil for food, or skins for clothing, or such rude articles of furniture as each succeeded best in making. This was inconvenient, from the difficulty of transportation and regulating the value of articles of exchange. Then a circulating medium in the form of metal was fixed on; but the difficulty of weighing it every time a trade was made led to the invention and establishment of coin. Then it became necessary there should be a body of people to attend to the exchange of articles, as it would require all a man's time when there was much to do. This brings us to the origin of traders and merchants. In connection with this, the necessity of a division of labor arose, and, following close after, came the natural sequence of varied employments. The utility of different occupations can not for a moment be doubted by those who have devoted any thought to the subject. "All occupations," says Wade, "however apparently unproductive and trifling, are valuable, if they increase our pleasures, our comforts, and well-being." There are some employments that can be carried on only in large cities. Wants increase with the advance of civilization, and consequently originate new employments to satisfy those wants. "It is a fact well known that the vast machinery of industry, so necessary to civilization, is chiefly set in motion by the wants of man to satisfy his appetite, far more so than by the want of protecting his body, or the necessity of clothing and housing."

We copy from Dr. Edrehi's work a description of the

origin of occupations and guilds, as derived from the works of Von Hommer and Evlia: "Thus we find that Adam was the first tailor, builder, and sawyer, and took his hints from swallows and beavers. He was also the first writing master. Hawa (Eve) was the first bathing woman, in imitation of the ducks and geese of Eden. Cain, the accursed, instructed by ravens, was the first grave-digger, and Abel the first shepherd. Seth was the first button maker and wool stapler. Enoch was the first weaver and scribe. Noah was the first shipwright. Saleb and Hud were the first camel-drivers and traders. Abraham was the first barber and milkman. Ishmael and Isaac were the first hunters and herdsmen. Joseph was the first watch-maker; he is also represented as a most expert carpenter. Moses was a shepherd and cowman, and his brother Aaron a vizier, or deputy. Lot invented chronographs and chronology, and Tip Kepl was the first oven-builder, though Adam has the merit of having been the first baker and cook. Daniel was the first interpreter. David occupied himself in forging coats of mail and helmets; and it is generally believed throughout the East, even by tribes which have not received the tradition from Mohammedan doctors, that the psalmist was a blacksmith and farrier by trade. Solomon employed his leisure hours in basket-making. Zachariah was a pilgrim and joiner. Jeremiah practiced surgery. Samuel was a soothsayer and astrologer. Jonah was a fishmonger. St. John was a sheik, or preacher. Mohammed was a merchant. Our Savior was a traveler. Moslems also believe that our Savior occupied himself in making wooden clogs or pattens."

DIVISION OF LABOR—ITS ADVANTAGES AND DISADVANTAGES.

IT is only in a civilized, or enlightened, state of society, that regular employments are performed; and as society advances in wealth and power, the number of distinct employments increases. The principle is permeating every branch of art, industry, and science. In the homely yet useful trade of shoemaking, some employers will only cut out boots and shoes, some bind them, some close them, some put on the heels, &c. Among tailors, some work-people only cut goods, some make nothing but vests, some coats, and others pantaloons, while some confine themselves to the making of boys' clothes.

By division of labor, time is saved, skill and fitness increased, better tools and machinery contrived, and the cost reduced. It brings about perfectness, and increases strength of the particular muscles exercised. It simplifies occupations, and requires less exertion to obtain a knowledge of them. It suggests ways of saving time, labor, and money. It affords opportunities for social intercourse and intellectual pleasures. It gives to the better classes of workmen more wealth. By it greater speed is obtained also.

In art many advantages are gained — indeed, it is essential to success in any one. The more minute the divisions and subdivisions of occupations, the more probability is there of each one being carried to a state of perfection. Indeed, it requires a lifetime to attain to superiority in one branch only. In painting, who could expect to compass all the styles of landscape, portrait, and historical? In engravings, who could excel in the various branches of mezzotint, line, stipple, &c.?

In science a division is still more essential. "As society advances, chemistry becomes a distinct science from natural philosophy. The physical astronomer separates himself from the astronomical observer, the political economist from the politician, and the legislator from both. Each, confining himself to his peculiar branch of science or business, attains to a proficiency and expertness therein which would be hardly possible were his time consumed and his attention diverted by a greater variety of pursuits."

The General Post-office has been cited by Dr. Whately as an apt illustration of the division of labor. If each individual had his own letters to carry, the time lost and the expense incurred would be enormous.

In "London Labor and London Poor" we read, "Say furnishes a strong example of the effects of a division of labor, from a not very important branch of industry, certainly — the manufacture of playing-cards. It is said by those engaged in the business that each card — that is, a piece of pasteboard of the size of the hand — before being ready for sale, does not undergo fewer than seventy operations, every one of which might be the occupation of a distinct class of workmen. And if there are not seventy classes of work-people in each card manufactory, it is because the division of labor is not carried so far as it might be; because the same workman is charged with two, three, or four distinct operations. The influence of this distribution of employment is immense. I have seen a card manufactory where thirty men produced daily fifteen thousand five hundred cards, being above five hundred cards for each laborer; and it may be presumed if each of these workmen was obliged to perform all the operations himself, and supposing him a practiced hand, he would not, perhaps, complete two cards in a day; and the thirty workmen, instead of fifteen thousand five hundred cards, would make only sixty."

The greater the number of occupations, the wider the field for activity and enterprise, and the less likelihood is there of too great competition. Americans are said to excel in ingenuity and rapidity of execution, but the English in thoroughness, arising from the great subdivision of labor in England, and confining the instruction of an individual to one branch of a trade.

"In the domestic system of manufacture, the work is too often carried on in ill-ventilated rooms, and, until the last few years, there was no restriction to the age of the young employed, or to the number of work-hours per day."

Said Alexander Hamilton, "It is a just observation, that minds of the strongest and most active powers for their proper objects fall below mediocrity, and labor without effect, if confined to uncongenial pursuits; and it is thence to be inferred that the result of human exertion may be eminently increased by diversifying its objects. When all the different kinds of industry obtain in a community, each individual can find his proper element, and call into activity the whole vigor of his nature; and the community is benefited by the services of its respective members, in the manner in which each can serve it with most effect. To cherish and stimulate the activities of the human mind by multiplying the objects of enterprise is not among the least considerable of the expedients by which the wealth of a nation may be promoted. Even things in themselves not positively advantageous sometimes become so by their tendency to promote exertion. Every new scene which is opened to the busy nature of man to rouse and exert itself is the addition of a new energy to the general stock of effort. It is, therefore, to the interest of nations to diversify the industrious pursuits of the individuals who compose them."

But there are some disadvantages attending a minute division of labor. It limits the observation and dulls the faculties. Those in the lower departments of labor suffer most from the ill effects. Combe, in his Moral Philosophy, enters more particularly into the results, and I give his words: "It rears an immense number of industrious men, who are utterly ignorant, except of the minute details of their own small department of art, and who are altogether useless and helpless, except combined under an employer.

If not counteracted in its effects by an extensive education, it renders the workmen incapable of properly discharging their duties as parents or members of society, by leaving them ignorant of everything except their narrow department of trade. It leaves them also exposed, by ignorance, to become the dupes of political agitators and fanatics, and renders them dependent on the capitalist. Trained from infancy to a minute operation, their mental faculties neglected, and destitute of capital, their labor and their skill cannot be exercised for the promotion of their own advantages. They are, therefore, the mere implements of trade in the hands of men of more enlarged minds and more extensive property; and as these men also compete keenly, — talent against talent, and capital against capital, — each of them is compelled to throw back a part of the burden on the artisans, demanding more labor and giving less wages, to enable them to maintain their own position."

OPENING OF NEW EMPLOYMENTS FOR WOMEN.

SELFISHNESS and prejudice have closed, and kept closed, many of the employments in which women might have engaged. They have been monopolized by men, and men have been enabled to sustain their monopoly by public opinion. But they have suffered from the results of their injustice in the loss of health, strength, and manliness.

A wider scope is needed for the employment of active, intelligent females. Even some of the few branches of industry open to women have been done away, within the last few years, by the invention of machinery. The general use of sewing machines, and the introduction of stencil plates for maps, have thrown a large number of women out of employment. The mass of women, in moderate circumstances, seem to be hedged in more and more from year to year.

Mrs. Stephens writes, "Look at the employments vouchsafed to our women. How few they are; how scanty and how worthless! That which no man will touch is always good enough for a woman. Look at their pay when they labor diligently and faithfully all their lives long, poor creatures, in the hope of saving a little for the day of sorrow! And these employments are vouchsafed, and these prices are paid by *men*, and among men — men who would have the women of their country believe that they have a hearty desire to promote the welfare, and the comfort, and the goodness of woman. God forgive them."

Says the author of "Women and Work," "We hear cries that the world is going wrong for want of women; that Moral Progress cannot be made without their help;

that Science wants the light of their delicate perceptions; that Moral Philosophy wants the light of their peculiar points of view; Political Economy their directness of judgment and sympathy with the commonalty; Government the help of their power of organizing; and Philanthropy their delicate tact. Hospitals must have them, asserts one; Watches must be made by them, cries another; Workhouses, Prisons, Schools, Reformatories, Penitentiaries, Sanctoriums are going to rack and ruin for want of them; Medicine needs them; the Church calls for them; the Arts and Manufactures invite them."

One great corresponding cry rises from a suffering multitude of women, saying, "We want work." It is unjust to say, sneeringly, if women wish to work, why do they not?

Some exclaim, O, keep woman to woman's work! We say so too, as far as it is practicable. Is there not enough work in the United States to keep all employed that are willing to labor, and wish to? We dare not say there is not a man or woman that wants remunerative employment but what can obtain it. No; we know it is not so. In our large cities there is many a genteel young woman that would be glad to obtain employment for her board; and there are hundreds, yes, thousands, of women thrown upon their own resources by the war who were tenderly reared, and possessed all the comforts, and even luxuries, of life.

"Blind, indeed, must they be who cannot see that there is a pressing from the ranks of domestic service as wives and servants; that there is another current, large and strong, for which a way must be opened. If it is not done, it will force itself into various channels. That is, in fact, already taking place. The departments of wood-engraving, plaster statuary, watch-making, &c., are being entered. Teachers, shopkeepers, and factory operatives have, for a long time, received file after file of women to their ranks. And what woman would force them back when it is that work, starvation, or ruin?"

The opening of a new field of labor in one country to women makes easier the way for its introduction into other countries. There are some women of great genius and daring courage, who tread down all difficulties, and dash aside all opposition, to make their way into and through an occupation suitable, but hitherto closed, to woman. Agricultural, trading, and manufacturing interests have received an impetus from the quick and vigorous exercise of woman's talents.

A woman should be able to acquire a standing in society by honorable exertion. It would be well for a woman to feel that she has the whole world to work in. If she has health, and is properly trained for a pursuit, she can somewhere find work to do; for a large portion of the earth is nothing more than a moral chaos, a wilderness of business. But women ought not to expect to occupy important places without proper training. They should be willing to pass through a series of gradations, such as is common with men, and also to acquire business habits.

To enter and prosecute new branches of female employment will awaken latent energy and talent, and do away with much idleness that now exists. "They who are always so willing to assist others, to their own detriment, should now, in turn, — for their wants call loudly for it, — be assisted and encouraged to strike out a new path by which they could assist themselves. There must be a change for the better in the efforts of women. Many are degraded by their poverty; and their degradation is the cause of nearly all the crime that is committed."

It is difficult to decide what occupations are most suitable for women without further trial, so little attention has been given to the subject. Schools for teaching girls some of the mechanic arts should be established in every town and city. Is not the Government or State as justifiable in taxing the population for the establishment of schools, where the industrial arts shall be taught, as the branches of a book education? One is essential to the existence; the other, though desirable, can be dispensed with. The rising generation of females will probably have more advantages in the selection and prosecution of suitable employments than the present.

With us, in the United States, there is even a greater deficiency in the variety of employments than with the nations of Europe. It has probably arisen from the greater demand for women in domestic life, and the lower wages paid for men's labor in Europe.

We have been told that there are about four times as many occupations open to women in New York as in any other city of the country. In the United States, pride and prejudice are not able to raise as great barriers as in older countries, whose foundations were laid during the mediæval age. Here, rank is not so distinctly defined by the grades that accident makes. Here, the hearts of the higher classes are not kept so within the bounds of their own choice circles, but run through the ramifications of a far-reaching humanity.

If a woman has education, health, judgment, some knowledge of human nature, and a small capital, she might, in favorable times for business, earn a livelihood in almost any suitable branch she selects. She certainly can when there are not already enough engaged in it. But it will be necessary for success that she give her time and undivided attention to her business, and she will be better qualified, if prepared for it early in life.

Perhaps it would be difficult for women in large cities to commence in those branches of business hitherto unoccupied by their sex. It might require more capital than in smaller places. Yet so many changes are constantly taking place in business establishments, in some cities, that a woman might enter at some favorable juncture. In the western towns that are springing up and growing so rapidly, women with a small capital, and a knowledge of business, and the wants of the people, could, with success, enter into some paying business.

Mrs. Jameson mentions a reformatory prison she visited in Europe, "governed chiefly by women — and the women, as well as the men, who directed it, were responsible only to the government." "There are offices, either entire, or half-sinecures, connected with our government affairs, that are well suited for women."

NECESSITY, TO WOMEN, OF MORE EMPLOYMENTS.

WOMEN more frequently err from ignorance of their duties, and the way in which to perform them, than from any inherent evil. I believe there are very few women that would go astray if honest employments were provided for them at *living prices*. Much of the degradation, madness, and suicide, that we hear of among women, in the humbler walks of life, arises from a want of properly remunerated labor — from destitution — from a want of sympathy and guidance from those of their sex in the higher walks of life with whom they have to do. It is the utter loneliness, and uncertainty of a home, from day to day, that drives many to desperation.

A woman is apt to grow selfish with no one but herself to think of — to grow bitter in her feelings if conscious that she is unjustly debarred from her natural sphere of action.

A man's occupation furnishes him with a source of thought and activity; it exercises his talents, matures his judgment, cultivates foresight; it stimulates to the acquisition of knowledge; it prompts to an efficient use of his powers and property; it promotes health and enlivens his spirits. The same effect would be produced on women that would devote themselves to the prosecution of some *intelligent* pursuit.

Educated women doomed to menial labor, (aside from that attending every one's own household,) feel that society has driven them to a position they were not made to occupy. And so the moral nature suffers. A constant sense of injustice preys upon the mind; while if some congenial pursuit were offered them they would enter it with eagerness, and pursue it with enthusiasm. If a boy belonging to a good family loses his father, and with him his support, or is deprived by adverse circumstances of an expected fortune, much sympathy and interest are elicited. Friends unite and counsel with him, and aid him pecuniarily while he prepares for business. How different is it with girls! There is rarely any provision made for the future. They, perhaps, are forced into some trade, already filled, that must be hurriedly, and therefore indifferently, learned, or must subsist in a poor, shabby way, in an indifferent home, oppressed with care and anxiety for those of their family similarly situated.* Such facts are proof that new employments must be entered by women. The condition of affairs in all civilized countries demands it. It is a want of the times, and must be met. If not, hundreds, yea, thousands, of our sex sink into ruin. The condition of woman cannot be stationary. It must either advance or recede.

The precarious subsistence of dependent women cannot but excite the sympathy and interest of philanthropists. Some remedy should be devised to furnish them with more permanent and reliable sources of support. The *few* employments hitherto opened to women are crowded. Some cannot find employment, and many that can, eke out but a scanty subsistence. Why should not women have a variety of occupations as well as men? Why should they not exercise some choice in the selection of an occupation as well as men? The mind now vacant, or filled with idle fancies, might be profitably occupied in directing all its powers to the acquisition or prosecution of some useful employment. The industrial energies of women need to be turned into a proper channel — their talents profitably

* Many clergymen with good salaries, and having congregations in easy circumstances, are either ignorant of, or affect ignorance of, the condition of poor, hard-working, and of destitute educated women. And when they are convinced of existing errors in society, they talk and write as if such errors could not be remedied, or propose some visionary, impracticable, remedy. (See "Woman's Rights," by Rev. John Todd.)

directed. There would not be so many suicides among the poor women of France and England if sufficient employment, at living rates, was offered them. The opening of new employments will do much to prevent prostitution. The low wages paid females, the small number of occupations open to them, and the excess to which they are crowded, are filling our prisons, our penitentiaries, and almshonses. Who will not try to save one soul at least? It will be a bright star in the crown of one's rejoicing.

It is necessary for women to have some definite idea of what their resources may be — to what branches of business they may fly with hope of success. The occupations of men have formed a circle; those of women have not been even the segment of a circle.

We need a more systematic arrangement of labor for women. In every city and large town there should be a market for labor just as there is a market for anything else. There should be, in the different callings pursued by human beings, enough employment for women suited to their natures and capacities. There should also be employment enough for men; but some in which they now engage is beneath their dignity as men, and unworthy their strength. They are pursuits that should be in the hands of women. A strong, healthy man behind the counter of a fancy store, in a millinery establishment, on his knees fitting ladies' shoes, at hotels laying the plates and napkins of a dinner table, is as much out of place, as a woman chopping wood, carrying in coal, or sweeping the streets.

By women having a variety of employments open to them they could command better prices for their work; for if one occupation did not pay they could learn another — one that did pay. We think a state of affairs would be brought about different from that in France. There all occupations are open to women, yet their wages are not more than half as high as men's. That is the result of a custom already established. Affairs might be differently arranged in a democratic government of the present time.

Women, in their ignorance of the nature of different

occupations, and the fear of being ridiculed or rudely treated, often pass by those best suited to them, and engage in those altogether unfit, while the men are only too ready, and too willing, to seize the opportunity of entering into the duties of the lighter, and easier occupations. All the most intelligent and well-paid occupations, and some of the most enervating and ornamental, are engrossed by men, while the most poorly paid, laborious, and disagreeable work is done by women. Thousands of females sacrifice their tastes, and even their talents, every day of the world, for the purpose of earning an honest livelihood. But if more occupations were understood by women, there would be no need of such sacrifice. Any person who opens a new branch of industry to women confers one of the greatest blessings on the inhabitants of a large city. Let women step forward into new fields of labor as a matter of justice to themselves. American women should prepare themselves for the higher departments of labor, leaving the lower to foreigners, who have more bodily strength.

Gail Hamilton, in "Woman's Wrongs," says, "Why don't those women, who are starving over the needle, make fine dresses for twenty dollars, instead of coarse trousers for twenty cents?" (Rejoinder. Why don't those women live in clean, well-furnished houses, provide their tables with wholesome food, and dress comfortably?) She says, "Why don't they become milliners and mantua-makers, and earn a fortune, and an independent position, instead of remaining slop-workers, earning barely a living, and never rising above a servile and cringing dependence?" (Reply. Because there are hundreds of milliners and mantua-makers that scarcely earn wages enough to keep body and soul together, and as large a number that cannot get employment more than half the time.) She continues, "It seems to me that the great and simple cause of the low wages paid to women, is the low work they produce. They are equal only to the coarse common labor; they get only the coarse, common pay." (Remark. They do not get "coarse, common pay" equal to men doing "coarse, common labor.") She then suggests, "It is because they have not the requisite skill or money." (Remark. If they had skill, they would require money to rent respectable rooms, and in so doing, they would be no better off than those would who had capital to commence business in any other department.) Elsewhere she writes, "They cannot give up their sewing long enough to seek places. They have no capital to live on while in search of them." (Remark. Ah! there is the root of the matter.) Gail Hamilton proposes that thousands of underpaid sewing women maintain themselves by becoming servants. (Remark. Many of those women, who are seamstresses, have not the health and strength to go into the kitchen, and cook, and wash, and iron. There are already more women as domestics than places. What is to become of those who now do kitchen work if they lose their situations? No suggestion whatever is made to them, no provision by which they are to sustain themselves.)

Gail Hamilton writes of the indifference felt for the lowness of wages paid female teachers. So great is the struggle for self in this world that none but teachers are likely to feel an interest in the matter. She suggests that "women who have not the power, or the taste, to become trained and valued teachers, become trained housewives, or skillful seamstresses, or accomplished laundresses, or sweetmeat-makers, or strawberry fanciers, or counting-room clerks." I am sorry that Gail Hamilton offers nothing better to women teachers — nothing more in consonance with their education. Would it not be better for them to become physicians, librarians, proof-readers, engravers, modelers, carvers, photographers, telegraph operators, florists, fruit-growers, &c.? * Gail Hamilton would push educated, intelligent American women into menial service. She would call into play their material, at the expense of their spiritual, nature.

* See "Employments of Women," for sale by R. W. Carroll & Co., Cincinnati.

By being kept as domestic drudges, women are the servants of men intellectually, and morally, as well as physically. She runs into the very fault for which she sarcastically, and pointedly, criticises Dr. Todd's essays on "Woman's Rights." Are she and the doctor in partnership? Because teachers have not the spirit to yield to injustice in wages, and want of appreciation by the parents of their pupils, must they sink a proper ambition for positions suited to their tastes and acquirements? Like many others, Gail Hamilton sees the difficulties, but is unable to propose means for overcoming them. The number in the few densely crowded occupations engaged in by women for whom she proposes a remedy is comparatively small, and in adopting that remedy as many lose places as receive them. So that in point of numbers, none are benefited.

The only advantage accrues to housekeepers, who, for the same wages they now pay indifferent servants, are to supply themselves, and their friends, with those that are skillful and competent. But do not the present servants earn the full amount of their wages? If so, by paying more competent laborers the same rate of wages, it is asking more than an equivalent for the employer's money. It is reducing still lower the value of the labor of educated women. If the employer's interests are only to be considered, the motive is an extremely selfish one, and none the less dangerous that it shields itself under the cloak of philanthropy, and a professed interest in the welfare of women. What has been said is not intended as an excuse for the deficiencies of servants. Many of them are rude, disobliging, and incompetent. Let such mend their ways, try to learn how properly to perform their duties, and execute them with vigor and cheerfulness.

If men will continue to deprive women of the sources for gaining a livelihood, it is only just that they contribute to their support. This could be done by a tax levied on such work as women might do, but that is monopolized by men, and by requiring a percentage on the labor, or income, of unmarried men, beyond the age of twenty-five, or thirty. The marriage relation must remain one of selfishness, and materialism, until some such revolution is wrought.

When I learn how many women have, from want and ignorance of any worthy occupation by which to earn an honest livelihood, fallen victims to the wily snares of wicked men, how many have sunk into woe and wretchedness, degradation and ruin, I would urge all girls who have it in their power, as they prize their own salvation in this world and another, to learn some business, trade, or profession.

And here I would suggest to those women in the crowded thoroughfares of the eastern United States, who, by their hand labor, scarce earn a pittance, that they might do much better by going into the plenteous West, and engaging in the capacity of seamstresses in families, dairy-maids, and similar offices. If they take with them testimonials of ability and character from those with whom they have lived, they will probably fare better. There are few families in the Western States but would gladly give a young woman her board, and some pay for her work, or her board for part of her work, and the rest of her time permit her to take in, and have the proceeds of, work from others, as sewing and embroidery.

Many women find themselves a surplus in their own field of labor by the introduction of machinery, and consequent diminution of hands required. For such, new countries may present openings for employment of the kind they are fitted for, or if not in their own specific branch, in some other. And we would advise women in overstocked countries to emigrate, by all means, if they have health, pecuniary means sufficient, and friends to go with, or to go to.

"At present, language practically held by modern society to destitute women may be resolved into marry, stitch, die, or do worse." As a remedy, the author of "Woman and Work" says, "Apprentice ten thousand women to watchmakers; train ten thousand for teachers to the young; make ten thousand good accountants; put ten thousand more to be nurses under deaconesses trained by Florence

Nightingale; put some thousands in the electric telegraph offices over all the country; educate one thousand lecturers for mechanics' institutions; one thousand readers, to read the best books to the working people; train up ten thousand to manage washing machines, sewing machines, &c. Then the distressed needlewoman would vanish; the dedecayed gentlewoman and broken-down governesses would no longer exist." What could be a more practical and common-sense plan?

We met with this newspaper statement: "A woman, who was recently arrested in London for begging in male attire, confessed that at various times during the last seven years she had acted as stoker on a Cunard steamer, porter on the Great Western Railway, sailor, and bar-tender." But to come nearer home. A young woman of Minnesota was obliged, by the impossibility of getting remunerative work, to put on men's clothes, and go with men into the woods, to be employed at thirty dollars per month, as cook. She was discovered to be a woman by the work-warden, while chopping wood, and dismissed.

Many, perhaps, remember to have seen a notice, a few months back, of a tailoress in Cincinnati, who found it impossible to get enough sewing at such prices as would support her, and, in consequence, donned male attire, crossed the river, and sought work in Covington as a tailor; but her sex being discovered, she was apprehended and brought before the court.

Another instance, of a similar nature, was that of a girl who sold fruit among the soldiers. Thinking she would be safer from insult, and quite as likely to sell her fruit for a good price, she disguised herself as a boy.

Madame Pfeiffer mentions a young girl in the penitentiary on Blackwell's Island, sentenced for serving on board ship as a sailor; and several cases came to notice during the war, of women who were without means and work, that enlisted as soldiers.

The war caused many women to enter occupations beneath their education and manners, because they had not been trained for any skillful labor, while the scarcity of men opened advantages to many women who had the enterprise and energy to engage in business. As a proof of the latter statement, I subjoin a paragraph I clip from a newspaper: "A poor but well-educated New England girl a few years since opened a real estate office in St. Paul, and last year the profits of her business were five thousand dollars, and she now has an estate of one hundred and fifty thousand dollars."

In another paper I find this paragraph: "A Wall Street firm has a regular lady customer, who daily speculates through them to the amount of fifty or a hundred thousand dollars."

MACHINERY—ITS MERITS AND DEMERITS.

MACHINERY has served to furnish the great mass of mankind with the comforts of life. The diffusion of manufactured products is now almost universal. Formerly the favored few enjoyed the results of mechanical skill and artistic design; now the multitude receive them almost as the water they drink, and the air they breathe. Particularly is this the case in the United States, where wealth is more generally diffused than in the older countries, and where the man of health and industry is the architect of his own fortune.

The use of machinery, it is generally admitted, diminishes the demand for manual labor. It does so to a great extent. Yet the increased cheapness of some articles manufactured brings them more in demand, and consequently, after a time, as large a number, or nearly so, of workmen may be employed in the management of machinery as were before in making the same goods by hand. Such, we say, is the case with some machinery, but not with all. Political economists may talk as they please of the increased demand of articles manufactured by machinery, and their proportionate cheapness; but we do know that many have been thrown out of employment by the use of some kinds of machinery. Not that we object at all to machinery, or to its use; but the immediate result is often deplorable—the loss of bread to the poor, who, by it, have been deprived of employment, and cannot find other remunerative labor. It would be well if employers would interest themselves to secure labor for those so displaced.

An intelligent shoe-binder told me, in 1862, that she did work then for thirty-seven cents for which she had formerly received seventy-five; and a shirt-maker told a friend of mine she could get but two dollars a week at that time—1862—for which she had formerly received four. The fall in prices was attributed to sewing machines. One educated and refined woman, who had been reduced in fortune, and was striving to make a living, told me that if she could, without destroying property, and thereby wronging others, she would burn every sewing machine in New York. Yet, when sewing machines were brought into use, they enabled women to do much work previously performed by men only; but now nearly as many men as women use them. The manufacture, merely, of sewing machines, has given employment to a great many men.

The tendency of machinery is to enrich the few, and impoverish the many. On the introduction of a new machine, many operatives are liable to have their wages reduced; but this reduction rarely continues. Yet the compensation is still very low compared with the cost of living. "The whole secret of using machinery lies in this: that the workmen do not work for themselves. The workman sells his time, strength, skill, and labor, all his ingenuity, all his cleverness, all his industry, all his health, to his master. If he performed a thousand times as much work as he does, he would be no better off. His master would be the only person benefited. The greater the quantity of work done, the richer would the masters and upper classes become; but not a jot richer would the workman be."

In 1812 an insurrection of the working people occurred in England. They destroyed a great deal of machinery. They were tried and severely punished. Some were imprisoned, some transported, and a number executed. In Western Prussia, owing to the introduction of machinery, the wages of spinners and weavers fell, four years ago, to starvation prices. A cotton weaver, working all day and part of the night, obtained but seventy-two and a half cents for two weeks' labor. The linen weavers did rather better, getting seventy-two and a half cents for sixteen hours' work, while the spinners did not get quite two cents a day for their work. As Mrs. Collins says in the "Lace Runners," (by Charlotte Elizabeth,) "Ah, well may the manufacturers get iron, and wood, and leather straps, to carry on their business for them, for such things can't give out tears of hunger, and sorrow, and pain."

In some cases strikes in England have exercised inventive talent, and been the means of producing machinery that defeated the object of the workmen, thereby throwing many of them out of employment, and reducing the wages of many others.

Says Mr. Davis, "In a country where there is a redundancy of workmen, where the demand for the commodity decreases, or where the manufactory has been previously established, and carried on by manual labor, machinery is, and must be, highly injurious."

We greatly wish that some remedy could be devised by which the disadvantage arising from the loss of labor to many, on the introduction of new machinery, might be counterbalanced. We refer more particularly to the late inventions, not so much to the machinery used in the manufacture of cotton and woolen cloths; for these articles we know had, previous to the war, a greatly increased demand, owing to the reduction of prices occasioned by the comparative cheapness of the material, and the reduction in the cost of its manufacture.

Inventive talent is a distinguishing feature of Americans. The machinery produced by them is noted for its lightness, simplicity, and adaptability. The variety of labor-saving machinery in the United States surpasses that of all other countries.

Thousands of foreigners, that annually come to our country, are enabled by their economical living, and strong muscles, to underwork Americans in their prices.

"Great Britain, in 1850, was going through an amount of work with four millions of laborers, which, without machinery, could not have been accomplished except by a working population of six hundred and four millions." All this machine power has been produced within the last century.

In fact, during the last fifty years, more has been accomplished by industrial labor, guided by science, and aided by art, than during any one hundred and fifty years previous.

There will come times of great changes in the occupations of thousands, as improvements in manufactures, and machinery, are continued. The more machinery is used, the more universally intelligence is wanted in the workers. Physical force is no longer sufficient, as in by-gone days, for the success of the laborer. More skill, and less strength, is required in using machinery than in working by hand. Inventive talent, rightly used, is a great economizer.

"Without machinery there could be no human labor at all, for everything beyond our naked fingers is machinery; the needle, the spade, the distaff, the plow, are as strictly machines as the steam engine." The invention, and employment, of extensive and complicated machinery, is eventually of advantage to mankind, though, as we said, in its introduction it is generally the means of throwing many out of employment. It certainly diminishes hard labor, and if other occupations, involving less toil, can be opened to operatives, thus deprived of employment, it removes the ground for objection and prejudice, and proves a benefit to all concerned. But the great difficulty lies in the opening of more occupations than now exist. Inventive talents have already been taxed to their utmost in this way. The labor and toil of men are increased with the improvements of the race, but are counterbalanced by the increase of machinery. Notwithstanding the invention, and use, of machinery, constant and wearing toil is the lot of the larger portion of the race.

The question has often suggested itself to my mind, What is the proportion of those employed in hand labor compared with those that work on machinery? Is there not enough hand labor to furnish employment for all that cannot be employed on machinery?

By mechanical contrivances less bodily exertion is required, the work is done more expeditiously, and at less expense; so there is a saving of time, labor, and money. As a single proof of expedition, we would state that twenty-nine hundred envelopes are made in an hour by machinery.

The number of machines made, and the increased quantity of goods manufactured, *as a general thing*, employ, in the course of time, about as many, or more, work-people as were before employed in the fabrication of goods only. Though at the introduction it may throw some out of employment, it eventually brings employment to as many more. To such as doubt it, I would refer to a little work called "Results of Machinery," published in London, and republished in this country.

One of the most remarkable illustrations we can offer of the great increase in the value of material by the labor and skill expended, is the following: "Among the marvels of watch-making, we would mention, that a single pound of steel, costing fifty cents, when manufactured into one hundred thousand screws, is worth eleven hundred dollars, and when sold, ultimately brings at least fifteen thousand dollars; and when manufactured into watch-springs, it is worth eighteen hundred dollars, and these in turn bring eight thousand dollars."

WORK ASSOCIATIONS AND COÖPERATIVE SOCIETIES.

WORK associations are composed of people of some particular trade, who unite their money and labors and establish a business for themselves. They may borrow means, paying interest, or take into partnership some capitalists, who furnish means, and receive a proportion of the profits.

There are probably one hundred coöperative associations in England. There are work associations in France and Germany, of tailors, cabinet-makers, masons, &c. They have long had an existence in France. One dates back to 1694, and contains one hundred members. About one hundred and seventy mutual aid associations exist among workmen in Paris. Work associations may become motive powers of vast influence, and a source of mutual benefit to the higher and lower classes.

The guilds of European countries are very similar in their nature. They are organizations for furnishing aid to members of their own guilds when sick, or out of employment. They promote strength and unity in the different trades. According to Mr. Loudon, the guild companies of Germany exercise a prohibitive power over the marriages of their members, lest, I presume, by a surplus of workmen in any one branch, it should tend to reduce the wages of journeymen. Tailors, brush-makers, carpet manufacturers, and those in some other trades, have guilds in England. Each member contributes a small sum weekly. By it, too, some crafts are enabled to acquire high and uniform wages, by supporting for the time those who, being beaten down in price, refuse employment.

The origin of guilds and fraternities is quite ancient. It is supposed, from papers now in the British Museum, that they existed among the Saxons. Even among the Athenians and Romans they were known. We find, in the "Domestic Manners and Customs of Asia," by Dr. Edrehi, mention made of processions formed in Constantinople, at different times, of guilds of the city. He takes his descriptions from Evlia, a Turkish traveller and historian, and from Von Hommer. According to Von Hommer, guilds date back as far as the most flourishing epoch of the Bagdad caliphs. "The guilds or corporations of Constantinople consisted of forty-six, subdivided into five hundred and fifty-four minor crafts, at the period of the last grand muster, under Mustapha III., in 1769. These subdivisions comprised every calling gaining a livelihood by science, art, commerce, or handiwork, including the church and liberal professions."

In the United States the government is in the hands of the people, and though we would not, for a moment, encourage the slightest disregard for the laws of the country, yet we would say to the laboring classes, particularly of *women*, when your wages are such that you cannot, by constant labor, earn the necessaries of life, make a strike — call for higher wages — but to do so, you must be united in effort. No personal jealousies should be permitted to interfere with the public interest of your class. Wages are often raised by means of strikes; but it is only for a time, if a surplus of persons remain in the trade. The wages fall back to where they were. And the loss of time and money during the strike often amounts to quite as much as the gains — besides, it produces a temporary derangement of all business. Unless wages are very depressed, strikes are productive of evil. They disarrange society, giving play to bad passions, and producing distrust and confusion. They render business stagnant, not only in their own department, but every other. An immense amount of labor is lost to a community by strikes. An estimate can be found in this way: if six hundred men engage in a strike, for one day, it is equal to the loss of work of one hundred men for a week. The strikes of shoemakers in the New England States, about seven years ago, and the strikes of all classes of trades-people throughout the country, about five years ago, threw much light upon the condition of trades, the wages paid, &c. In many cases, the advantages derived from a strike, are only temporary, but not always, for the visible expression of opinion gives power and strength. The principal advantage to be derived is in calling public attention to the wrongs of the business, eliciting public interest and influence, and thereby redressing wrongs. It is the means, too, in many cases, of changing into other channels a surplus of labor from one that is overstocked.

It might be an advantage to women in the various trades to have protective unions, and a standard of prices. If the women, in any trade, would combine, and with determination refuse to work for less than certain wages, would they not obtain them as men do? There are protective unions among men in Boston and various New England towns. Also, some in New York, Philadelphia, and other cities. Some of the shoe operatives formed an association in Lynn, at the time of the excitement in 1862. It was a stock company, and the shares such as to put it in the power of any one to become a member.

We would recommend to the laboring classes the establishment of coöperative stores. Since 1843 they have been established quite extensively throughout Europe. A work entitled "Coöperative Stores," has been published by Leypoldt & Holt, New York, giving much interesting information on the subject.

The plans in operation for aiding and improving the working classes of England, are, Savings Banks, Friendly Societies, Annuities, Loan Societies, Life Assurance, Coöperative Stores, Temperance Institutes, Trade Societies, Industrial Partnerships, Land Societies, Mechanics' Institutes, Building Societies, Working Men's Colleges, Reading Rooms, and Mutual Improvement Societies. England is far ahead of the United States in the variety and number of such organizations, and of newspaper, periodical, and book literature pertaining to these matters. A description of some of these organizations can be found in a work containing a vast amount of valuable information, entitled "Progress of the Working Classes," 1832–1867; sold by Routledge & Son, New York City.

I rejoice when I see labor and industry clamoring for their rights. They can gain attention only by doing so. They have been too long overlooked and disregarded, both by those at the helm of state, (many of whom have risen there by the assiduously sought votes of laboring men,) and by the public in general, deeply engrossed in individual interests. More especially do I rejoice that women are making known the injustice they suffer from low wages, and from overwork in some cases, and a scarcity of remunerative work in others. Cold, starvation, and oppression have driven them to it.

Few employers have ever been known to raise the wages of their work-people without being asked, or required to do so. Most of them must be forced into it, and this is why work-people unite in associations for self-protection.

Looseness of principle has been charged against the working class, on the ground that they labor merely to obtain a livelihood, not to exalt or elevate their business. We would be happy to know the number in any department, even of art or science, that labor merely for the pleasure of it. The proportion would probably be one to ten thousand.

As demand and supply regulate even the price of labor, we think it will not be very easy to establish regular prices in large and changing cities like New York, except among superior workmen, who will be employed by those who are willing to pay fair wages for a good quality of work. But if there were a combination among the first class workmen of different trades, in cities of permanent population, that would not labor for less than stated prices, they might, in time, be able to bring employers into measures when they are disposed to act unreasonably. But they would need a home, and means to sustain them during the time, or depend upon pecuniary aid from societies in other places. The editor of the "Philadelphia Ledger," of January, 1852, said, "The remedy of laborers is combination, not competition, and combination to work in partnership instead of not to work at all."

The corporate bodies of a city, founded on capital and combination, are a great drawback to those who are not members of a corporation. They elicit prejudice, and suffer from a pecuniary competition with others situated like themselves.

There are some destitute people not fit subjects either for the work-house, or a charitable institution; but who should be furnished with work at a fair compensation. This is now being done in some cities.

CIRCUMSTANCES THAT INFLUENCE WAGES AND LABOR.

RATES of wages, in most cases, rise and fall according as the work requires more or less dexterity, or exertion, as the individual workman is more or less distinguished by skill, strength, or diligence, as the scarcity and the supply of workmen is greater or less, as the days are longer or shorter, as the cost of living is high or low, &c.

The circumstances which cause the recompense of employments to rise above, or fall below, the common level are stated by Adam Smith to be the five following: "1st. The agreeableness and the disagreeableness of the employments themselves. 2d. The easiness or cheapness, or the difficulty and expense of learning them. 3d. The constancy or inconstancy of the employments. 4th. The small or great trust which must be reposed in those who follow them. 5th. The probability or improbability of succeeding in them."

We have seen it stated that the value of an article produced, is the labor required for its production; but this statement does not always hold true.

The proportion of wages for labor, to taxation, varies in different countries. Some have proportioned wages to the population, some to the taxation, some to the various rates of profit, and some to the price of food. But the circumstances that influence wages and labor, and form a connection between the two, are complex. Any one cause will not form a sufficient foundation for a theory.

"Senior accounts for the anomaly that wages and taxation are not proportional, by saying that labor in some countries is not productive of exportable commodities."

It is said the best paid workmen in *some* classes of labor are the most thriftless. If so, the fault does not lie in good wages being paid, but in the want of correct principles and virtuous habits. Such workmen could not be benefited by a still greater advance in wages, but might become more wasteful and profligate. It would be well if such men received even less wages. But it would be sad if those dependent on them, as wives and children, were to suffer from the curtailment. The best remedies for the reform of work-people, are to deliver lectures on subjects of a nature calculated to improve, induce them to attend church service, and give a sound moral education to their children. Some of those who are paid very high wages for their services, or acquire a reputation in their business, or follow an unhealthy vocation, become, after a time, idle and negligent. Those in occupations poorly paid, are likely to become careless, and, in most cases, only indifferent workers can be obtained.

If an individual is not satisfied with his employer, he had better remedy his condition by seeking another, or working on his own responsibility, and if he has capital employ it in doing so. Or, perhaps, he may be invited by some other employer, who knows of his dissatisfaction, to accept a place with him. Any change made in an occupation usually has in view one of four advantages, greater wealth, honor, ease, or better health.

" There are three circumstances, each of which, other things remaining the same, would enable the working classes to increase their consumption of wealth: 1. A rise in the ratio of wages. 2. A greater demand for labor. 3. A reduction in the price of articles of general consumption."

Experience, skill, and judgment in an occupation can command the best wages. The age of the individual should also be taken into consideration. This is rarely done with women, but always with men and boys. Men with large families to support usually receive better wages than single men. The inquiry is rarely made of a middle aged, or elderly woman, whether she has a family to support, and most employers never care to know. Women's labor is not paid for in proportion to the time consumed, the trouble or danger attending it, nor the benefits to accrue from it. The conduct of girls in saloons, factories, workshops, &c., will depend very much on the character of employers. Wages will vary, in a measure, according to the character of the establishment. Competent, well-behaved girls will demand, and receive, in respectable establishments, a better price than others.

The value of the work, the skill of the worker, and the demand and supply of labor, should determine the rate of compensation. But there is another item that enters, materially, into the price to be paid for labor, or anything else. It is the ability of the purchaser to pay. The disposition to employ labor will depend much on its profitableness, and the security of capital so invested. Labor in large cities, like everything else, is reckoned according to its quality, and the time consumed. Indifferent work brings a poor price, while skillful labor commands a high price.

The smaller the number of work-people in any branch of mechanical labor, essential to the support or comfort of life, the higher the wages they can command. Wages are, to some extent, proportioned in various countries to the cost of living of the working classes. These classes, of course, differ very greatly in intelligence, invention, virtue, and skill, and the greater these qualities the higher the wages the workman demands, and the better, generally, his mode of living. The supply and demand for labor will also influence wages.

" For all material products there is both an actual and a speculative demand — for labor there is only an actual demand. Therefore, a general rise of prices must always operate against the laborer or person employed on salary or wages. But wages not only never rise so much as other commodities, but never rise as soon. They do not rise until speculation has engendered a spirit of extravagance and increased consumption, and then wages take an advance about half as great on an average as that of merchandise and other things. Wages fall sooner, because merchandise may be, and is, held for high prices, if need be. Its fall is broken by the disposition and ability of the owners to hold on, and, as far as possible, prevent loss; but the laborer cannot hold on — he must sell his commodity at once for the most it will bring."

The degree of perfection to which arts, manufactures, trade, and agriculture, are carried, determines the number of people a given tract of country is able to sustain, more than the natural resources of that country, for as a nation advances in civilization the wants of its people increase, and with the wants the invention of occupations by which to supply those wants. It is not often that both farmers and manufacturers thrive at the same time. When produce is low the farmer suffers, when manufactured goods are low the operative suffers.

"The workmen most affected by the aristocratic, popular, or general fashions, are, tailors, ladies' habit-makers, glovers, milliners, dress-makers, artificial flower-makers, plumissiers, stay-makers, silk and velvet weavers, saddlers, harness-makers, coach-builders, cabmen, job coachmen, furriers, livery stable keepers, poulterers, pastry cooks, confectioners, &c."

In reference to the prejudice existing against women receiving money for their work, Madame Bodichon says in her most excellent book, "Women and Work," "Money is only a representative of desirable things. It would be well if all should part with all they make, or what they do well for money; they will then know that some really want what they produce. What they produce will go to the right people, and they, the producers, will gain a power; for money is a power. Money may be a power to do good. If for your needlework you get money, you know that your work goes to some one who wants it. You are not always sure of that if you give it away; and you gain a power of sending a child to school, of buying a good book to lend to the ignorant, of sending a sick person to a good climate, &c. We may give this power up to another who, we consider, can use it better than we; but money is a power which we have not the right lightly to reject. It is a responsibility which we must accept. Of course we may give our labor, our work, our money when we think right; but it is as well to exchange them sometimes for money to be sure we are as valuable as we think. Some work is beyond all price, and many prices are far beyond the value of the works."

SKILLFUL LABOR.

SCIENCE has made earth give up her most-valuable treasures. It has taught the sailor to plow the waters of the deep blue sea, has caused it to yield up its richest gems, has explored nature's labyrinth, and penetrated into some of her most latent secrets. It has revealed many mysteries both in the sea and on the earth. Art may continue to invent, and science to produce her ample stores, but the intelligence of man is needed to make a judicious use of them. The tendency of the present age is more material than spiritual.

Adam Smith says in his "Wealth of Nations," "The property which every man has in his own labor, as it is the original foundation of all other property, so it is the most sacred and inviolable."

People may be divided into two classes — those who work and those who do not. Again, the first class may be divided into those who work for a living, and those who do not.

"If people are looked at in their different occupations, striking differences will be immediately perceived: 1st. In the *skill*, *talent*, or *intelligence* that is exercised. 2d. In the *tools*, *instruments*, *machinery*, and *structures* that are used. 3d. In the *materials* that are worked. 4th. In the *processes of making* or *manufacturing*. 5th. In the *products* that are created."

Mr. Wade states, "The wages of a skillful laborer are a compensation for the exertion of both strength and skill; the wages of an unskilled laborer, for the exertion of strength only. It is only those who have paid the price, either in money or money's worth, to obtain a knowledge of the business of the skilled laborer, that can compete against him for employment."

A person of intelligence may command higher wages than a dull, phlegmatic person engaged in the same occupation. And one that has taste, skill, and experience will command higher wages than one that has not. Workers that are skillful and intelligent earn good wages, while those that are stupid and ignorant obtain only low wages. The better educated a person is, the more skillful is the labor done by him or her, if the same degree of attention is given. The intelligence of the brain extends to the hands.

In the manufacture of almost every article of goods, there are different departments which command different prices according to the skill required, the danger of the work, &c. Even in these separate departments there are, in extensive manufactures, different grades of workmen whose prices vary according to the quality of their work.

Men's labor that is painful or destructive to health is generally well paid. I am sorry to say the same does not hold true of woman's work. But in woman's work, as well as man's, skilled labor is best paid. Those employments requiring talents and learning should, and generally do, command the best prices. The rich, who are most likely to need such services, are able to pay good prices. The money, talents, time, and application necessary, as an outfit for such employments, render the number occupying them comparatively small.

One cause of so much pauperism in the cities is the unwillingness of the poor to go to the country. Women, with sewing machines, could in many parts of the Western country obtain employment, by going from house to house and doing the family sewing.

The greatest kindness we can do women is to encourage, and aid them, in preparing themselves for some non-domestic industry. The girl raised without industrious habits, and not trained to some employment, will find it difficult to keep her head above water if she comes in competition with skilled workers. Some allowance should be made for any want of skill in the few occupations that have been opened to women, because of the great competition and low wages. A woman must be able to look forward to promotion in her occupation, and an increase of wages with it, to acquire skill and success. As women have less strength than men, they should, in those occupations requiring strength, skill, and speed, endeavor to acquire sufficient skill and speed to make up for a deficiency of strength. The great cry is that women do not make themselves superior workers — they do not qualify themselves thoroughly. It is said that for the same wages the majority of women are willing to do a larger quantity of work carelessly than a smaller quantity carefully. If women will learn to work thoroughly and skillfully, there cannot then be such injustice in the remuneration of their work, nor foundation for the assertion made by some that they are paid the worth of their work. We do not believe there is sufficient cause for the complaint so generally made of imperfect work by women. It is like the cry of bugaboo to frighten bad children. It is mostly done by employers to silence and crush workwomen, and as an excuse to the public for the wages they pay. The reason most women do not make more efforts to acquire proficiency in their occupations, arises from their being obliged to labor constantly to meet the necessities of the present, not because they are without the energy, enterprise, and ambition to do so, nor because, as is often charged against them, they look forward to marrying as an escape from labor.

Women would do well to train themselves thoroughly for their work. The most industrious and skillful workers not only receive best wages, but are most sure to obtain employment. Besides, one that is agreeable, intelligent, and conscientious, who can think for herself, and perform her work without oversight, is more likely to secure employment and good wages than one who is the reverse. Women suited to low places will have to take them, and those suited to high places will secure them, if they have health, self-reliance, and perseverance.

The war that has lately closed may cause some educated women of capital to engage in the higher occupations, and thereby make labor for women more honorable. It may also be the means of raising women now among the laboring classes to higher posts of responsibility and remuneration. So a general change in regard to woman's work may be wrought by it on the western continent.

When a number of men or women are employed to do the same kind of work, some accomplish more than others, yet are paid the same. Might it not be well to institute prizes as an incentive to slow or careless workers, and a reward for the diligent and skillful? In the higher branches of labor, a workman's wages are proportioned to his mental ability and moral force.

In the manufacture of ornamental articles, an inventive talent and superior taste are requisite. In a statistical report we read, "The manufacturers of Paris frequently direct, and suffer in their turn, the caprices of the world, and the fashion of the elegant world. The workmen, quick and intelligent, bend themselves with a marvelous address to all the changes of form, and a constant appropriateness of things, according to the taste of the buyer. It is thus that Parisian industry succeeds in obtaining easy sales, first by an important local consumption, and afterwards by numerous forwardings to various parts of France and foreign countries."

In London there are trade societies which make laws relative to how many apprentices may be taken by each employer, to preclude the possibility of an injury to their trade by a surplus of workers, and low wages arising from competition. And when a man has been long in business he has a sort of tacit permission that his son shall continue the business when he retires, or ceases to be.

4

OCCUPATIONS SUITED TO TASTES, HABITS, AND CAPACITIES.

CONDITIONS in life are various, yet in the life of each one are intermingled joy and sorrow, care and pleasure. There is a wonderful accommodation in nature — a beautiful adaptedness. What is lost in one way is gained in another. Nothing is wasted. All seems directed by a wise hand to fulfill some purpose. Your talents may accomplish great results in one occupation; mine may be valueless in that, but equally useful in another.

Among the Egyptians and Spartans every male member of a family followed the calling of his father.

Dante makes Charles Martel to say, "The want of observing their natural bent, in the distribution of men to their several offices in life, is the occasion of much disorder that prevails in the world."

Physical and mental abilities should do much in deciding the choice of an occupation. Some people are best suited to a sedentary employment, some to an active one, some are expert, some awkward, some strong, some weak, some are constitutionally sound, some are physically defective. Of course, individuals should engage in employments with which any infirmity, or defect, will not interfere. Some are mentally incapacitated. A merely mechanical occupation is best for them. When there is a tendency to any constitutional disease, of course such employments should be avoided as would tend to develop or hasten that disease. For instance, an individual with weak lungs should not engage in the manufacture of paint, or the business of a painter. One unable to stand long at a time should not act in the capacity of a salesman. Sedentary and monotonous employments are apt to produce morbid sensitiveness, and an extremely meditative state of mind. Therefore, it would not be well for those inclined to melancholy, and in poor health, to select such an employment. Those occupations requiring skill, taste, and patience, and not much strength, are best adapted to women.

Some people are gifted with a much keener exercise of one sense than another, and this sense is frequently cultivated to the neglect of the others. It is, therefore, most fully developed, and of course comes most readily and naturally into action, under circumstances where one of the senses could as well be operated on as another. One in whom the auditory nerve is particularly sensitive most enjoys a sweet enchanting voice, or a delightful strain of instrumental music. To another, a beautiful scene in nature, a charming picture, a piece of statuary, a delighted audience, or something of the kind that appeals to the sense of sight, gives a greater relish. To the blind, the sense of touch yields unfeigned pleasure. Blind people will place their hands on the clothes, and even the faces of their friends, and delight in holding their hands, and so manifest affection in a way that the conventionalities of society preclude the seeing. This more than ordinary development of any one sense, should be taken advantage of in the selection of a pursuit for the afflicted.

Some English writer on municipal government says, "Many years ago, during a residence in Warrington, at that period the seat of a number of branches of industry demanding artistic skill — as the manufacture of flint glass, of files, and of all kinds of tools — when sitting, one night, by the fire of a tool-maker, I was struck by the beauty of the small files, vises, and other tools, used in watch-making. Knowing that he employed apprentices, I asked if he found that they had all the steady patience, the clearness of sight, and delicacy of hand, required for such work, to which he replied that not half attained the skill to qualify them at the end of their term for journeymen; that some gave up the attempt to learn the branch, and went to another; that others, who completed their apprenticeship, if they remained, got employment only when trade was brisk;

when it was slack, they were the first to be discharged; whilst others, again, became laborers, that is, served the skillful hands. I next inquired of a glass manufacturer, himself originally a workman, what proportion, apprenticed to the flint-glass making, were worth the retaining as journeymen, when he replied, Out of ten apprenticed, not three prove good hands; the others mostly fall to the lower branches, as tending the furnaces and like; a certain number, too, are retained in the place of boys, that is, as the glass-blowers' assistants; but when fresh apprenticed lads are taken, or when trade is slack, these inferior hands are sure to be dismissed! In respect to glass-cutting, he said that probably not half the apprentices turn out expert; that they drop away out of the branch; but he was unable to say to what else they betook themselves. With the same object I continued, in subsequent years, to inquire of master shoemakers, tailors, letter-press printers, bookbinders, and of masters in other trades, demanding dexterity and skill, and have found a considerable proportion of those put to acquire such branches either fail to do so and drop lower, or they remain in them, and are known by the name of *botchers*. In this way the descent of numbers in every trade goes on continually, and shows an inequality in mankind as to talents that will ever baffle the hopes of those enthusiastic reformers who, in their schemes, or rather dreams of social improvement, overlook this natural diversity, and who would regard all the individuals composing the laboring class as entitled to share in the fruits of labor. I refer to the natural inequality — for which there is no help — as distinguished from culpable inequality, the effect of evil passions and tempers, which generate habits injurious, or even completely obstructive to success in life."

Mrs. Jameson says, "A wisely-organized system of work — intellectual and moral as well as mechanical work — provides for this natural inequality, and does not place human beings in positions which they are naturally unable to fill with advantage to themselves or others; and that would be a strange law which should oblige a master manufacturer to employ *botchers* in the place of skilled workmen, because they present themselves, and because they all have a right to live by their work."

Many things are to be taken into consideration by a careful parent in placing a daughter out to learn a trade. The character and standing of the master and mistress, their skill in business, their oversight of the morals of those in their care, should all be known. The reputation of the apprentice will depend much upon those with whom she learns a trade. The character and conduct of the apprentices already employed is an item to be considered. The same, and many more things, should be taken into consideration in the selection of a vocation for daughters. In a trade suited to a woman's taste and capacity she might acquire a position, and even wealth, that she never could in another.

The intellect, education, and intelligence of women engaged in each employment probably vary as much as among men, in the same, or similar occupations. A general impression can be formed, by almost any one, of the average grade of intellect, and amount of intelligence, in each department. But an estimate of the proportionate difference would require a careful investigation. For instance, the majority of store girls have more refinement and intelligence than factory girls. An exception should be made of those formerly at Lowell. Those engaged in teaching are superior to both. Among seamstresses there is a greater diversity, descending from the reduced but delicate, refined and cultivated woman, who has lost property and relations, to the most ignorant and stupid specimens of humanity.

A girl should ascertain as nearly as she can for what her powers and talents qualify her. Her health should also go far in deciding what she may undertake. It requires ingenuity and physical strength to succeed in some of the industrial branches. In the country, women spend more time in the open air than they do in town. They rarely suffer any bad effects from it — indeed they generally have better health.

The intelligence of most American women calls for some

employment more exalted than domestic service, or factory labor. Coarse indeed must those souls be that would doom women, who have been tenderly raised, and carefully educated, to the menial employments that become the hardy and ignorant. Tact, taste, and organization, physical and mental, adapt some to employments unfit for others; consequently some wisdom is needed in the selection of an occupation.

The poor have few facilities for obtaining information; but if the advice and assistance of a benevolent and judicious person can be obtained, it will greatly facilitate the advancement and interest of an apprentice, or even of a skilled worker.

I have heard some men object to certain occupations as being too fatiguing for women, when they knew that hundreds and thousands of women — white women — were performing labor that was ten times more laborious and detrimental to health. In such cases they were generally actuated by some selfish or interested motive.

A lady once remarked to me she did not see why daughters might not inherit any peculiar talent as well as sons; if so, why a woman might not be an architect, sculptor, &c., as well as her brother. The cases are numerous in which such talent has been manifested and creditably developed.

In many of the mechanical arts women could be advantageously employed. In some of these arts perhaps a part of the labor would require great physical strength, but the lighter parts could easily be done by them. In some the entire work could be performed by them.

The majority of men as well as women are forced into business habits by necessity. These habits become a part of the every-day existence of an individual. From this cause, and from the excitement attending business, a fondness for it is acquired by some people. An individual will succeed best in the business he likes.

The greater the number of occupations in a community the wider the field for talent, ingenuity, and exertion, and the less danger is there of too great competition in any one branch.

EFFECTS OF OCCUPATIONS ON HEALTH.

MEN, in most branches of labor are paid such prices, that when their health fails, they have something left of their wages, to keep them from starvation. Women receive barely enough to keep them alive while at work. They are constitutionally weaker, and liable to fall sooner as victims to their occupations. What are they to do when their health fails, or old age creeps on? Years of suffering, and inability to work, are embittered by the thought that they have labored as hard, and as long, as their health would permit, but their wages were so inadequate that they could not lay by for a time of need. How great the odium that should attach to employers who pay their women a niggardly pittance!

In making investigations on the matter of health, as influenced by occupations, some employers will not admit their occupation is unhealthy, although it is universally known outside of the occupation. Some are not sufficiently acquainted with the results on the health to give any definite intelligence, or make statements, the truth of which they have never tested. Many work-people have never thought of the subject, and would be reluctant to acknowledge their employment was unhealthy, even if they knew it to be so. Their statements are more likely to be what they feel than what they think.

Almost every occupation is more or less injurious to health. Says a writer in the "North American Review," (52-31,) "There is no trade, as Mr. Bain well suggests, which might not be injurious to persons subject to one kind of weakness or another. A physician might, if so disposed, get up a case against any employment of civilized life sufficient to excite public sympathy and abhorrence; but, so long as men cannot live without working, they must work in spite of inconveniences. The labor of a factory operative is much less arduous than that of the smith; less prejudicial to the lungs, the spine, and the limbs, than that of the shoemaker and the tailor. Yet most travelers are struck by the lowness of stature, the leanness and the paleness which present themselves so commonly to the eye at Manchester, England, and above all, among the factory operatives." The problem is partially solved by "Dr. Hawkins, who noticed with surprise and regret the total absence of public gardens, parks, and walks at Manchester."

Colliers, miners, forgemen, cutters, machine-makers, masons, bakers, corn-millers, painters, plumbers, letter-press printers, potters, and many other classes of artisans, and laborers, have employments which, in one way or another, are more inimical to health and longevity than the labor of cotton mills. Some classes of professional men, as teachers, lawyers, and clergymen; with students, clerks in counting-houses, shopkeepers, seamstresses, &c., are subject to as great, and, in many cases, to much greater confinement and exhaustion than the mill operatives.

Of the answers made to questions, by Factory Commissioners, to the medical men, appointed by the Parliament of Great Britain, to investigate the diseases and accidents to which factory children are particularly liable; "the majority state, that they are not subject to any particular disease, but are liable to accidents from machinery. Several were of opinion that children are subject to swelled ankles, from long standing, and in some cases, to distortion of the knee-joint; and that a scrofulous or consumptive tendency is increased by their occupation." Asthma is not an uncommon disease with factory operatives. The loss of color and vitality, in the children that work in factories, is a sad and striking feature. Four out of five of those employed in English factories in 1833 died before reaching the age of twenty. When an operative loses his health he generally changes his employment, and the morbid action produced in the first often terminates fatally in the second. For instance, "A young female leaves a dusty employment on account of the distress which she feels in respiration — the bronchitis, which this occupation has produced. She tries another, which is comparatively innoxious; still her cough continues, and she declines in flesh and strength. Unable at length to follow any regular employment, she is received in the house of some relative in the country, where finally she dies of consumption. Her death, of course, never enters the mill-book of her first employer. Cases of this kind are of frequent occurrence, and sufficiently explain the low ratio of mortality which appears to take place in baneful employments." The noisy and exciting labor of a manufactory, with the physical diseases apt to be engendered, more generally brings about dissipation than the quiet out-door life of agriculturists. The lack of education and self-control, with the fluctuations to which their business is subject, tends to make operatives impulsive, and in times of scarcity and discontent, their movements are often of a desperate and daring character. Added to this is the unnatural excitement induced by a residence among a great many people.

It is injurious for a woman to labor long in one position. If she stands a great deal it will bring on disease. A large number of shop girls of Philadelphia are suffering from disease so induced, together with the result of tight clothes, and their pressure about the hips. And here I would take occasion to say, credit is due the late Mr. Levy, of Philadelphia, for the change he wrought in the condition of shop girls. Previous to his introduction of the system, girls were never permitted to sit down while behind the counter. If a person sits too constantly it will prevent a free circulation of blood, and a healthy digestion. The stooping posture of seamstresses, and many engaged in mechanical pursuits, is apt to affect the digestive organs, impede the circulation of the blood, and bring about consumption. Persons engaged in occupations that require them to sit constantly should keep the body erect. If a stooping position is indulged, the spine cannot retain its strength. The lungs and the heart ought to have full play, for restricted respiration, we all know, is opposed to health. The whole body should be moved every few minutes, and the head thrown back that a full breath of air may be imbibed. The work-rooms should be well ventilated, and as much exercise as possible taken in the open air. "In the case of milliners and dress-makers in the London Metropolitan Unions during the year 1839, as shown by the mortuary register, out of fifty-two deceased, forty-one only had attained the age of twenty-five; and the average age, of thirty-three who had died of disease of the lungs, was twenty-eight."

Large numbers of tailoresses and dress-makers in the United States die from consumption — victims to badly ventilated rooms, cramped position, straining of the eyes, excess of gas-light while at work in the evening, and the severe exercise attending a protracted running of sewing machines.

Attending most sedentary occupations, there is a depression and exhaustion of spirits, produced by the want of pure air, of out-door exercise, and lack of variety in scenes, objects, and faces. The mind takes a peculiar and morbid turn. Long and continued sitting renders the body unhealthy, and soon the mind follows suit. The most unhealthy and exhausting of manual occupations engaged in by men are best paid, but the same does not hold true of woman's occupations.

Says Wendell Phillips, "To-day, if you will go with me to the city of Brussels, I will show you a thousand girls making lace, and losing their eyes in four years of the labor; and I will show you the rest of those lives passed in the hospitals, in starvation, or in prostitution."

The gas and vapors generated in the manufacture of some chemicals are very deleterious, and consequently the health of the workman suffers. The diseases of painters, and workers in lead, are severe. Paper-hangers, from inhaling the aceto-arsenite of copper, used to give some kinds of wall-paper a brilliant color, are frequently suddenly seized with mercurial paralysis, which causes them to lose control over their muscles. The silverer of looking-glasses suffers as greatly, and in the same way. The phosphoric acid used in making lucifer matches seriously affects the bones of the jaw, and in some cases the jaw has been eaten away. Scavengers are liable to inflammation of the eyes. Stone-cutters, sculptors, and mill-stone dressers often have their eyes injured by chips of the materials; and glass-blowers, smelters, &c., from bright light. Many other occupations produce disease from over-taxing the eyesight. I have been told that china-painting is hurtful to the eyes, but I think it cannot be seriously injurious, as I have never observed diseased or inflamed eyes among china-painters. Burnishing, I think it most likely, is trying to the eyesight, and the pressure of the working tool on the chest may be injurious to people with weak lungs. Engravers, sewing machine operatives, and those who read or write a great deal, are liable to inflammation of the eye, or palsy of the optic nerve. Shoemakers and cobblers suffer from the continual pressure of the last upon the stomach. The extensor muscles of the wrists of file-makers often become paralyzed. Dippers in potteries, from inhaling the poison, sometimes become raving maniacs. In one class of occupations the skin is affected. The miller is subject to an eruption produced by the attacks of the meal mite, and some bakers suffer from the baker's itch, and the grocer, by handling sugar much, is infected with animalcule. The dry-grinders of cutlery are short-lived, arising from the unhealthiness of the occupation. The average limit of life with them is twenty-nine years. Miners are liable to diseases of the chest. They suffer from rheumatism, and distortion of the body, and often their lungs after death are found to resemble lumps of coal in color and hardness.

Dealers in old clothes, and rag-gatherers, are reported not to be more unhealthy than people in other occupations. It is said that persons living at or near gas-works are remarkable for their good health. "Tradition reports that during the plague in London, the dustmen were the persons who carted away the dead, and it remains a fact among this class to the present day that not one of the men died of the plague, even during its greatest ravages. In Paris, too, it is well known that, during the cholera of 1849, the quarter of Belleville, where the night soil and refuse of the city is deposited, escaped the freest from the pestilence; and in London the dustmen boast that, during both the recent visitations of the cholera, they were altogether exempt from the disease."

It will be found, on inquiry, that the majority of patients in hygienic institutes, and hospitals, are there from over taxation of body or mind in business, from pursuing an unhealthy occupation, or from following one the proceeds of which did not furnish the necessaries of life.

The causes of difference in the longevity of a class of people, aside from extrinsic causes, cannot be positively determined, but are mostly dependent on their physical constitutions, the nature of their soil and climate, the degree in which they possess the comforts of life, their diet and exercise, freedom from anxiety of mind, their knowledge of medicine, and their occupations.

The ages of the workmen in any branch of trade are a general indication of the healthy, or prejudicial nature of it. When the circumstances are favorable, the average duration of life will be high; when otherwise, low. Health seems to be a matter that is rarely taken into consideration, and made to influence the selection of an occupation.

Dr. W. thinks a man has best health in that occupation he likes most. He finds farming does not agree with him, although raised on a farm; but his present calling, as editor, does, though one man in three could not stand it. It is because he likes it.

The principal circumstances unfavorable to health and longevity, as given by Mr. Thackrah, of Leeds, are; excess or deficiency of food, bent sitting posture, long standing, great muscular effort in lifting weights, steam, artificial heat, impure air, dust, and gaseous impurity of the atmosphere, anxiety and mental application, long sitting and delay of micturition, compression of the chest, bending of the head for long periods, close application to minute objects, as in watch makers, engravers, tambour workers, and dress-makers; poisonous substances acting through the skin, as lead, printer's type, and mercury, or on the eyes or ears, as scarlet color, lime, dust, and the noise of machinery. Either extreme of temperature is also unfavorable to health.

"Among the inconveniences of some employments, which are not prejudicial to health, are, rapid changes of temperature, moisture, local atmospheric humidity, and many of the odors arising from the manufacture of vegetable substances, and animal effluvia."

Pure air, sufficient recreation, out-door exercise, refreshing sleep, with nutritious and well-prepared food, taken at regular intervals, will, if observed by those engaged in sedentary pursuits, prove the best conducers to health. Freedom from anxiety is also an important promoter of health and happiness. The increased comfort of dwellings is a blessing to the mass of people. A more general knowledge of the laws of health, and the progress of medical science, are doing much to promote longevity.

Cutter states, in his "Physiology," that a certain manufacturer in England found that when his factories were well ventilated, the laborers ate more heartily. He remarked to some person he could not afford to let his workmen breathe pure air.

It is not uncommon in some trades for the work-people to take holiday on Monday, and some that attend do their work indifferently. But this is not an argument against their having a day of rest now and then. It only proves that they have not received such moral instruction and example as to make them prize their privileges.

Many suggestions for the prevention of disease might be offered. Two of the most general and important are cleanliness and ventilation. In certain branches of labor, a retention of the beard and whiskers by men is found advantageous. By the use of voltaic batteries the metal can now be deposited by the water-gilder without the use of quicksilver, and by the use of flues for carrying off floating particles of metal. Persons working in chemicals, unwholesome effluvia, &c., are recommended to wear over the mouth a respirator enclosing a layer of charcoal. An amorphous phosphorus, that does not yield phosphoric acid, has been invented, and is used by some manufacturers of lucifer matches. Oil of turpentine, exposed in saucers in factories, will also serve as a safeguard. Those liable to cutaneous diseases are advised to smear their hands with raw mutton, or beef suet, and then rub them with a cloth to fill the pores, and wipe off any excess, just before working in the articles that cause the disease. "Artisans, whose eyes are endangered by superabundance of light, are instructed to use glass shades, or chimneys tinted with a very faint blue. Those whose eyes are exposed to injury from chips, or particles of dust and grit, are advised to wear goggles or wire gauze, and needlewomen are solicited to be careful to have the light thrown on the work, not on the eye, to change the color of the material as often as possible, and to adopt the North China fashion of working in rooms hung with green, and having green blinds and curtains to the windows. Mr. Abraham has tendered to the dry grinders of cutlery a magnetized wire gauze, and others have constructed for him a fan on the principle of winnowing-machines, which blows the dust clean away through a flue in connection with the chimney. M. Bernot, a Frenchman, has recently invented a file-cutting machine, which, it is said, will execute work more even than hand-work, and thus relieve the file-cutter from the danger of losing his hand by paralysis. A light frame of copper wire, covered with wire gauze of large mesh, and a ply of thin silk, worn as a mask, fitting closely around the chin, but standing off from the mouth and nostrils, will enable flax-dressers, and workers in stone, to defy the dust, and at the same time enable any one to go through the dense smoke of a conflagration, breathing freely. Shoemakers, if they choose to adopt them, can no doubt procure contrivances by the aid of which they can pursue their occupation standing, and without pressure on the stomach; and tailors, by the exercise of a little ingenuity, can protect themselves from the dangers which attend their present cramped and stooping posture."

THE EFFECTS OF OCCUPATIONS ON THE BODY, MIND, AND MORALS.

A HABIT of submission and constraint, united with solitude, strengthens our passions and increases our evil propensities.

The desire of possession is natural, and, when properly regulated and modified, profitable.

The value of knowledge depends on the uses to which it is appropriated. I have seen people in some vocations whose vanity led them to feel the vocation was beneath them, and consequently they performed their duties carelessly, and without zeal.

An absorbing interest in business, and a great effort to acquire riches, will retard the cultivation of virtuous habits and benevolent feelings.

Both physically and morally, there is a marked distinction in the workmen of unlike occupations. The miners of Great Britain differ materially from the agricultural population, and the cotton operatives from the workers in metals.

"As an example of the mental culture of the collier children in the neighborhood of Halifax, the sub-commissioner states, that in an examination of two hundred and nineteen children and young persons at the bottom of one of the coal pits, he found only thirty-one that could read an easy book, not more than fifteen that could write their names, — these latter having received instruction at some day school before they commenced colliery labor, — and that the whole of the remaining number were incapable of connecting two syllables together."

There is more crime in manufacturing than in agricultural communities. We attribute it to their fierceness and recklessness, and to disease engendered by the occupation, and the irritability produced thereby. In Sheffield, according to Dr. G. C. Holland, there were, in 1834, 711 beer and public houses; in 1841 there were 908, of which some were supported solely by young lads and girls, who thronged them nightly. These youths were employed mostly in the cutlery manufactures. Of these girls Mr. Home writes, "Their appearance, manners, habits, and moral natures (so far as the word *moral* can be applied to them) are in accordance with their half-civilized condition. Constantly associating with ignorant and depraved adults, and young persons of the opposite sex, they naturally fall into all their ways; and drink, smoke, swear, throw off all restraint in word and act, and become as bad as a man."

Work-people in whose occupations employment is most uncertain are most restless and reckless. They will be more energetic and productive, but less reliable.

"The artisans in the well-paid branches," says Dr. Holland, "are invariably the best educated, and exhibit in their conduct a higher tone of morality." He thinks "that an exaggerated degree of civilization, or intellectual progress, is inferred from the ability to read and write. It is viewed more as an evidence of education than as a means toward it."

Some people think women are unfitted for the discharge of home duties by staying in stores and factories a few years. I do not. I think if the moral associations are good, they are improved in some ways. The mind is undoubtedly strengthened, the wits sharpened, the perceptions quickened. I have heard the complaint that girls acquire a fondness for fine dress by staying in stores. I think such a propensity may be developed, but the cases are rare in which it is created. To this some add the complaint that store girls spend everything for board and dress — never lay by a cent. I think the majority get, in ordinary times, from three to five dollars a week. If they pay for board and clothes out of that, I should be happy to know how much it would be possible to lay by?

A certain lady said to me, "It is women's duty to labor for heaven, men's for earth. No lady should ever have to labor for a living. It is a reflection on men. It is a disgrace to the father, husband, brother, and son of such a lady. I would not like to see women labor in America as they do in France. It would make men lazy — they are naturally fond of physical ease. I would not see men driven out of their employments." To this I make the rejoinder: I would like to see men driven out of those employments that are not suited to their physical strength — such as women should occupy. The lady referred to above, thought "men should be the providers, women the distributors." This is a very pretty system, and might do very well if you could convince men that it is right, and induce them to perform their part in carrying it out; that is, provide the means for distribution.

INFLUENCE OF OCCUPATIONS ON THE DOMESTIC, SOCIAL, AND RELIGIOUS NATURE.

TO render ourselves and others happier, or more useful, seems to be the end and object of every pursuit. Morally, what does not profit will hurt. Our tastes and wishes grow refined, or coarse, according to nature and cultivation. We are mentally as well as physically dependent. Indifference and egotism are two great enemies of every improvement. Our occupations, and the circumstances and associations attending them, go far toward forming the character. In the possession of health, and our faculties, we have a good capital. The difficulty usually lies in not knowing how to make a profitable use of it.

There is a constant test of moral character in the struggles of business life. Many sad and disheartening circumstances are connected with the experience of us all, who try to faithfully and fully perform our duties. It is difficult, in the hurry and competition of business, to be perfectly correct, and study the interest of those with whom we have to do as much as our own. It requires well-grounded principles of right and honor, and considerable force of character. On the other hand, a struggle in business life has its good effects. It curbs the would-be presumptive, and encourages the timid; it makes us live out of ourselves; it makes us more practical, and more industrious, and gives us moral stamina. Employment gives a better insight into the thoughts and feelings of others. We are at once brought into a knowledge of that which most interests them — that on which their very existence depends, and often the existence of others. We enter into closer connection with their hopes and fears, joys and sorrows, their plans and aims.

It would be interesting to study the effects of occupations on the *disposition* — to learn whether a person is rendered by his occupation amiable or peevish, gay or grave, obliging or disobliging, confiding or suspicious, harsh or gentle, brave or cowardly, manly or effeminate.

Closely connected with this is an inquiry into the effects on the *moral nature* — if one is rendered honest or dishonest, idle or industrious, sober or drunken, profane or reverent, just or unjust, cruel or humane, generous or penurious, truthful or false; what desires are created or increased — whether for wealth, fame, position, and power, or a state of quiet, unobtrusive retirement.

Also on the *social nature* — whether a man, by intercourse in his business with ladies superior to his wife, loves and appreciates her as well, or *vice versa;* or whether, by daily seeing a large number of ladies, he ceases to feel an interest in all, or whether, by the rarity of having business intercourse with any, he ceases to feel an interest in any and all; whether, by intercourse with both sexes, as in a store, he feels a greater or less interest in his race, or more in one sex and less in the other; whether it inclines one to seek society or to shun it, to love it or to hate it, to be communicative or silent, to be agreeable or disagreeable, to be affectionate or misanthropic, charitable or uncharitable, modest or immodest; whether a firm friend or a fickle one, false or true, forbearing or vindictive, kind or censorious.

It runs also into the *home life.* The inquiry arises whether a man, as the result of his occupation, likes his family more or less; whether he desires a quiet life in a home of his own, or the more exciting one of a boarding-house or hotel; whether he endeavors to render his home agreeable or disagreeable — in short, whether a man is made a better husband, father, and master by his occupation, or a worse one.

Manners are another modification. The occupation may tend to render an individual rude or courteous, coarse or refined. Even a man's *language* is not merely interspersed with technicalities among his craft, but rendered by his occupation crude or polished, pointed or blunt, rough or smooth, negligent or choice, vulgar or chaste, prudish or loose, appropriate or inappropriate.

Not less interesting would it be to learn the effect of occupations on the *intellect* — whether it is strengthened or weakened; whether the faculties are sharpened or blunted; also, which faculty is most exercised, whether imagination, memory, reason, &c.; also the character of mind required for each — whether is most desirable, a clear, logical, or a quick, impulsive style of mind; whether a concentrated and consecutive train of thought, or merely a good memory; whether a high idea of intellect is required, or whether a medium one, or even if a very ordinary mind would answer; whether much cultivation of mind is required; if so, the nature of that cultivation — whether it be a particular or a general cultivation; whether it promotes thought or checks it; whether it gives a right direction or perverts it; whether the train of thought induced is important or trivial, exalted or groveling; whether encouraging hope, or producing depression of spirits, running into despair, and even madness; also, whether a feeling of trust or terror is induced, of caution or recklessness. The aims and aspirations are to a great extent formed and directed by the occupations.

The effect on the *religious nature* might also be considered — whether a person is made credulous or skeptical, reverent or irreverent, exalted or debased, with high hopes of a better world, or despair of reaching such a world; whether more or less fond of religious duties; whether inclining to be speculative or practical, to consider God all merciful or all just, as a God of love or a God of anger, or blending the qualities in his all-glorious majesty.

We find human character is very much the result of education, disposition, and circumstances. Added to these, as we have mentioned, are the effects of occupations, the subject embracing in its range not merely mental, moral, and social, but to some extent political science. It would be a theme sufficiently fruitful for a large volume.

PECULIARITIES OF EMPLOYMENTS.

THE manners, language, characters, and dispositions of people, are very much influenced by their business pursuits. Their tastes, habits, and appearance are also influenced in the same way. A close observer knows that a tailor is usually bow-legged, a farmer pigeon-toed, a scholar stoops, a sailor reels, a blacksmith has large, brawny arms, and a weaver small legs, while an orator, and an auctioneer, are each noted for large mouths.

The character of mind is as distinct in most men as the features. So the particular work in which one kind of mind might excel would not be at all adapted to one of a different style. Much of the success, attending all kinds of labor, arises from the application of mind to that labor.

The comparative morality and intelligence of those engaged in different occupations is a study of much interest. It is said that every body has a mania, and that, *with most people*, I am confident, *is their occupation.* On meeting with a milliner, if you could read her thoughts you would probably find they are a comment on your bonnet; if a dress-maker, that her thoughts are running on the fit of your dress; if a great reader, you will find books the natural topic; if a teacher, the training of the rising generation will be an absorbing theme. If you are much in the society of a wood-engraver, outline, expression, lights and shades, will run as naturally into the conversation as dawn into daylight. The low, quiet tone of voice usual to a nurse for the sick, is noticeable to a close observer. Most policemen are noted for their silent vigilance, and clergymen for their sociability. Coarse work has its influence on the speech, actions, and manners of an individual. Yet the measure of one's inward nature, by the occupation, is not altogether a true gauge. Women's pursuits are more unvaried than men's. For instance, very few women, except those who make wearing apparel, ever undertake the entire fabrication of an article. However, the same may be said of most men.

"We will say a few words on occupations characterized by fluctuation, competition, and pushing. Although these are the least eligible for women, it is a strange fact, for the most part, that occupations at present open to them fall under the category. Millinery and other branches of trade conducted by women, are subject to the same, if not keener competition than branches of trade conducted by the other sex; the letting of lodgings is precarious and fluctuating; and what position involves more anxiety and turmoil than that of a mistress of a boarding-school? What less security than that of an artist, or a contributor to the press? The competition and pushing of a certain class of tradesmen, mercantile traveling, and the incessant puffing of quack shops, have so filled the public eye that it is forgotten that the mass of business is conducted quietly and unobtrusively; is such as might be undertaken by woman with ease to herself, and without offense to others."

The suspicion required to be a good lawyer — to detect the motives of the accused — and to trace crime from its cause to its effect, must be morally injurious to the possessor. I know no class of educated men whose brains to me seem so full of cobwebs as those of lawyers. Their ideas are misty and undefined, and they express themselves in a vague, indefinite way. They rarely talk to the point, or answer a question plainly.

"The fact that the practice of medicine draws its support from the miseries and sufferings of the world is no objection to its respectability. What profession is there that does not draw its support from some suffering, necessity, or disability, unless it be that of the mountebank?"

Mrs. Gaskell mentions that an acuteness and intelligence of countenance has often been noticed in a manufacturing population. A restless and migratory spirit is said to be one of their peculiar characteristics. The brightness and freshness of complexion in the middle and higher classes of the English is lost to the factory operatives, owing to their early and close confinement to labor.

Most map-colorers are gay and cheerful in their disposition. They are fond of dress, and frequently exhibit much taste in the selection of colors. In lithography the draughtsman is almost invariably sober, the pressmen too often given to drink.

I think the selling of eatables, and the preparation of them, have a tendency to render people, so engaged, very material. "From what I could learn," says Mayhew, "it seems to me that an inordinate or extravagant indulgence of the palate, under any circumstances, is far less common among the female than the male sellers in London."

I believe it will be found that nearly all persons engaged in driving horses, such as cabmen, stage-coach drivers, &c., are peculiarly partial to intoxicating drinks. The carriers of London, who buy at slaughter-houses the meat of dead horses, and sell it for cats and dogs, are mostly drinking men. They walk from forty to fifty miles a day.

The minds of the bone-grubbers and mud-larks exhibit a vacancy that does not arise from any natural or inherited defect.

Most men engaged in manual labor have broad shoulders, thick bodies, and strong arms. Irish women engaged in the drudgery of housework, or agricultural labor, are usually very hard workers.

"The effect of early and severe labor in coal mines is to cause a peculiar and extraordinary degree of muscular development in collier children; it also stunts their growth, and produces a proportionate diminution of stature. Labor in coal mines is also stated, by a great number of most respectable witnesses, to produce a crippled gait, and a curvature of the spinal column, as well as a variety of disorders — among which may be enumerated affections of the head, rupture, asthma, rheumatism, and loss of appetite;

and this not merely in a few cases, but as an habitual and almost inevitable result of their occupation."

Out-door employments are conducive to long life. Two bird-catchers over seventy years of age died in 1852, in England, who had been at the business since six years of age.

In the classification of occupations, in an abstract of the British census, the tenth class is devoted to persons engaged about animals. "This tenth class," says the compiler, "is altogether a peculiar race of men; silent, circumspective, prompt, agile, dexterous, enduring, danger-defying men generally, but modified variously by the classes of animals which occupy them." Mayhew treats of the subject more fully as follows: "The fondness of a whole body of artificers for any particular bird, animal, or flower, is remarkable. No better instance need be cited than that of the Spitalfield weavers. In the days of their prosperity they were the cultivators of choice tulips; afterward, though not in so full a degree, of dahlias; and their pigeons were the best flyers in England. It is curious to remark the refining qualities of particular trades. I do not remember seeing a bull-dog in the possession of any of the Spitalfield silk weavers; with them all was flowers and birds. The same I observed with tailors and other kindred occupations. With slaughterers, however, and drovers and Billingsgate-men and coachmen and cabmen, whose callings naturally tend to blunt the sympathy with suffering, the gentler tastes are comparatively unknown. The dogs are almost all of the 'varmint' kind, kept either for rat-killing, fighting, or else for their ugliness. For pet or fancy dogs they have no feeling, and in singing birds they find little or no delight. The bird-catchers have quietness of speech and manner, which might surprise those who do not know that any pursuit which entails frequent silence, watchfulness, and solitude forms such manners." In London most barbers rear canary birds.

"In comparing, indeed, the different branches of the same trade, as the several divisions of grinding, we observe the strictest correspondence between intelligence and the duration of life; and the higher and more steady the remuneration, the more independent, moral, and respectable are the individuals. It is a singular fact, but it is, nevertheless, indisputable, that the more destructive any of the various departments of grinding, *the lower the morals and the remuneration* of the workmen. The wet grinders, as a body, are greatly superior to the dry in education and pecuniary circumstances."

"Let any one enumerate the various modes in which men obtain their subsistence, and he will immediately perceive that, with one or two exceptions, they are chiefly mechanical processes, or such as easily become so. In the case of the whole laboring population, there can be little doubt of the matter; but in many cases the work of a mechanic requires far more ingenuity than the business of what are termed the better classes. That of a clerk, for example, tasks the mind less than that of almost any mechanic. And a merchant's operations are, in the vast majority of cases, matters of mere routine. The greater number of persons act usually in the capacity of subordinates, and the superiors themselves, for their part, act by rule. Law, medicine, and the business of government require, it is true, intellects of the most commanding order."

No doubt the same occupation, followed one generation after another by a family, serves to keep up the distinction of rank that exists in old countries.

The poor sell most in small shops with open fronts, or out of doors, as is evident to those who have had occasion to pass through the poorer portions of a city.

It is a singular fact, that in most large cities, streets of any importance have each their distinctive features. In New York city, Wall is the street for bankers, Beekman for stationery and envelopes, Maiden Lane for jewelry, the lower part of Broadway for fur merchants and cap manufacturers, and Nassau for second-hand books and engravings.

SELECTION OF AN OCCUPATION.

WHAT a mingling of good and evil, light and darkness, there is in this world! The events of our lives seem a confused medley, and we scarcely begin to realize any particular aim in our being, until, by physical disabilities, we are partially unfitted for its accomplishment. And so it is in the business world. When we look around and consider in what a chaotic mass its elements are, we are tempted to ask what will be the end of all this? Is there to be no more definite organization? no more harmony?

Some one has said, "Our trades, professions, and serious pursuits are not always matter of choice; nay, they are often prosecuted from duty or necessity, against one's own inclinations; and afford, therefore, no certain test of individual predilection." This, in many cases, is true. Circumstances do much to decide the choice of a pursuit, or draw us into one without a choice. Want of means, state of health, influence of friends, or other circumstances, may proscribe that pursuit to which our inclinations tend, and in which we might acquire renown. It is our duty (if circumstances will permit), to select that employment in which we shall be most happy and useful — that which is best suited to our disposition and temper of mind. For what is pleasant to one is disagreeable to another — what is rest to one is labor to another.

We know that *some women* are engaged in employments to which they are not at all adapted. But a comparatively small number of women engage in any regular employment, and therefore a great many cannot, of course, mistake their profession. We know also that *many men* are engaged in employments to which they are not at all adapted.

If women pursue the higher branches of industry, it will elevate their position socially, morally, mentally, and physically. They will have a greater incentive to cultivate their minds. They will be more respected, and will acquire something like the independence and influence of men.

The kind of study, the nature of the arts and sciences to which women turn with most pleasure, and have the greatest desire to excel in, depend entirely on their temperaments, and the early direction given to their minds and tastes.

Some of the discoveries in the arts may be traced back to those who were not immediately connected in business with those arts, but whose leisure moments were devoted to the study of them.

As girls come to take an active part in practical pursuits, it is well for them to consider their finances, their abilities, and the natural bent of their inclinations, and all the circumstances to be considered in such an undertaking. Or if they enter a business that does not please them, they may perhaps make an advantageous change. One may have a strong aversion to a pursuit to which another is strongly attached. The solitude of the country may in some be conducive to the growth of every virtue, and all the better feelings of our natures, while in others it may be unfavorable to the growth of mind, manners, and morals.

Females, as well as males, should early examine with care, and pursue with ardor, that course which nature and inclination mark out for their peculiar exertions. If some pursuit is determined on, it should always be kept in view and all the energies devoted to it, for as we cannot excel in many, — I might say in more than one, — it is better to be proficient in one than have a superficial knowledge of several. The selection of a pursuit is a matter of much importance, and should not be made without proper consideration. Much of the future happiness and welfare of the individual will depend on it. Women should have a larger number of regular and permanent occupations opened to them.

As the views of the populace become matured and refined, the crude and unformed state of the mass better organized, the capabilities and tastes of children will be more studied in the selection of pursuits for them. A knowledge of any one that is honest and virtuous, for which a child has a preference, should be cultivated. The professions will not then be so crowded, and mechanical genius will be more encouraged and cultivated. The industrial arts will be in repute, and the intelligent direction of talent be more respected. The discipline of mind, and systematic course of action, that result from a thorough and well-directed education, will assist in this matter. A general knowledge of what business pursuits are prosecuted must be acquired to consider one's own adaptedness, and make a selection, or to be able to make another choice in case of failure. A deeper interest is felt in business pursuits as a knowledge of them is increased.

By general inquiry of the number that could probably be sustained in any one business, and learning the number already in it, one can judge whether it is advisable to enter. To learn the average number of women employed in any branch of business, it would be well to ascertain the maximum in a certain number of the largest establishments, and the maximum in as many of the smallest, and then find the average of the two.

Most manual employments are subject to fluctuations. They are generally most flourishing in spring and autumn. It is well there is not an equal amount of work at all seasons, for many would sink under it. As it is, they are enabled to recruit some during slack times for after labor. Yet the wages of women are so low that they can scarcely afford to lose a day's time.

"Some employments do not promote either health or virtue, but merely afford the means of subsistence. It is a well-ascertained fact that those occupations which are the most *useful*, are the safest, and those commodities which can least be dispensed with, pay, in the aggregate, the largest profits. The demand for them is stimulated by actual want, and grows with every increase of the means of production."

To insure success a profitable direction should be given to labor. Capital and labor must be united to render either most productive.

Common sense, health, and determination to learn, are the great requisites to insure success in any undertaking. Some think women never succeed in those employments requiring concentration of thought, and refer to type-setters and tailoresses; but the inferiority, I think, arises from the want of discipline in girls, compared with that of boys, who are trained from their early years to a pursuit. It is thought by many that women succeed better than men in those occupations requiring rapidity of execution, and mere mechanical labor that does not exact much physical strength.

BUSINESS QUALIFICATIONS.

"EVERY occupation has some leading essential quality which its follower must have, or success is impossible. The great cardinal powers of business, as they may be called, are *strength* — *ingenuity* — *good address* — and *strong nerve or enterprise.* Some occupations require only one of these essentials with other qualities, to carry them on with honor and success."

A knowledge of business, promptness, the strictest integrity, close application, agreeable manners, an obliging disposition, and strength of character, with a steady, vigorous course of action, founded on right principles, will usually bring success. A well-balanced intellect is, of course, essential.

The vicissitudes that frequently occur in trade, debar many from risking their all in undertaking business on their own responsibility. Of course an engagement in business should not be attempted without proper qualifications, and some experience. Rent, clerk's hire (if necessary), stock of goods, with personal expenses, must be taken into consideration. Hope and caution, prudence and forethought, are needed by those who carry on business for themselves. It is well to secure, as friends, people of morality, education, intelligence, refinement, influence and wealth. The misfortune is, the worthy poor rarely have the time, opportunity, and means of making friends.

Every kind of business has its vexations. Those who would succeed must remain steady in their pursuits. A person that is often changing from one enterprise to another seldom becomes an adept in any.

Women need to give their minds wholly to their work.

That is one of the secrets of success, and one in which men generally greatly exceed women. The reason of men being better able to concentrate their minds on business is, their health is more robust, their minds more free from care, and they more certain of being well paid for their labor.

Of course the grades of intellect, and degrees of intelligence, vary greatly in the different employments. If work is of a meditative kind, the mind should be given entirely to it. But relaxation should not be neglected. Every care, and every thought of business should then be thrown aside. Much will be gained — nothing lost.

The most active women are usually the most truly and judiciously kind. Woman's intelligence is increased, her faculties developed, and her energies brought out by industrial labor that causes her to mingle with others. It will be found that in those countries where women are most engaged in industrial affairs they are more intelligent than the same class in other countries.

One of the largest merchants in New York, who employs several women in his store, complains that he cannot find intelligent girls, or he would employ them still more extensively. If he advertises, he has perhaps fifty applications in the course of the morning, but not more than one or two of that number are competent. If he paid better prices he could probably obtain a better class of store girls, those more intelligent and reliable.

Says Dr. Elizabeth Blackwell, "Women are the first in charities in all nations. They are sometimes in works of charity considered troublesome and uncertain allies, but it is because they want business qualifications."

Some writer has said, "The natural gifts of mind are bestowed on none so abundantly as to supersede the necessity of continued mental exertion." The general principles of business may be acquired, but common sense, and judgment, are necessary for carrying out the details.

In many cases two or three women might form a partnership and advantageously engage in business for themselves. A lady said to me, "When matters are righted, and women hold the position they should, men of capital will be ready to take women of business qualifications in partnership, even though they are without capital, for educated, shrewd business women would draw them custom. A woman must have nerve and intellect," added she, "to transact business successfully."

A very intelligent workwoman said to me, "Women will find it necessary to hold their footing with men in business transactions, for the *majority* will impose on women if they can." It is true. And what is meaner, some men will impose on women, that would not venture to try to impose on men, for fear of losing their reputation as correct men. And to add to such meanness, some men, when they find they cannot impose on women, for fear that those women may expose their attempted imposition, immediately say hard things of them.

Many American women fail in business from the want of self-possession and self-reliance. They are brought up too delicately, and to think work is a disgrace. With the industry, enterprise, and intelligence, of a majority of those in Northern States much may be accomplished. Yet even there, a large number of men are becoming effeminate in their manners, feelings, and habits, arising from their self-indulgence, and feminine occupations, while the health of the women, so far as our observation and inquiry extend, is no better than that of women that have been reared in Slave States.

In thinking over some of the most enterprising and philanthropic works executed by women during the last fifty years, I find the majority of women who have been successful in those works are English. It led me to think of the superiority of the constitutions of the English to Americans. It enables them to labor more constantly and more continuously. Some of the women referred to above are of English birth, but now reside in the United States. I think emigration does much to develop business habits.

In no country do women of all classes enter as much into the business occupations of men as in France.

Says a writer in the "Monthly Review," "Among the Slavonians the two sexes almost exchange their peculiar natures. The Slavonian man is generally weaker in his power of conception, in will, and in determining the will by his conceptions. The man fully receives the impulse, in all his actions, from the woman; as the man of the Germanic race desires to give it to the actions of the woman. The Slavonian women possess and manage their own property, as soon as they are of age, in all respects independently of the men. I have seen women who were the most faithful wives, the fondest and tenderest mothers, manage alone a property which required the activity and circumspection of men; nay, more, bring that property into complete order; and I have heard the testimony of perfectly impartial men, whose situation qualified them to deliver an opinion on the subject, declare that they had managed and regulated it with astonishing firmness, penetration, and circumspection."

Women must be educated to industrious, systematic, business habits, from childhood, as men are, if they expect to stand on a footing with men in business relations.

A trustworthy, competent business woman, if she can obtain good wages, and invest her savings so as to yield some profit, may lay by for times of slackness, of bad health, and old age.

Industry, economy, and business judgment, are essential to the increase of our own capital, or that of others with which we are intrusted.

When educated women enter business pursuits, labor will be respected more highly. It will serve to bring about a closer connection between the sexes, to establish a warmer interest, and greater congeniality. It will strengthen family ties. It will stimulate to the acquisition of fame, or fortune. Speculation creates a stimulus in business that may enrich others besides the speculator.

6

WOMEN'S LABOR NOT JUSTLY COMPENSATED —AND WHY.

THE value of labor is too apt to be estimated, not by its usefulness, and the good it may bring, but by the rate at which it may be obtained — by the necessities of the laborers. Labor should be estimated by the amount of good it does in supplying the necessities, and promoting the welfare of mankind, individually and collectively, and wages should be proportioned thereto.

As business is now done, women's self-respect and ambition are not called forth. Consequently women employed to work are more idle and less to be depended on — they are more likely to take advantage of an employer's time than men. But if they had the same number of hours to work that men have, and were paid according to their industry and activity, a better discipline would be established. There would be more honor, and principle, and justice, on both sides.

There is no union or society among women to keep up the regular standard of prices — so the majority work for what they can get. The low wages of female labor tend to increase the feeling of dependence in a woman, and tempt her to marry merely for a home.

Many events are tending to draw attention to these matters. How many hundreds, even thousands, of virtuous and worthy girls have been thrown out of employment by the late terrible war! After the great financial revulsion of 1857, many were rendered homeless and helpless. The "New York Tribune," referring to them, says, "It is estimated there are not less than seven thousand ready to go West, because society here has withdrawn its succor from them. At best they can but earn a pittance. A woman may be defined to be a creature that receives half price for all she does, and pays full price for all she needs. No hotel or boarding-house here (nor elsewhere, we will add) takes a woman at a discount of fifty per cent. Butcher, baker, grocer, mercer, haberdasher, all ask her the utmost penny. No omnibus carries her for half price. She earns as a child — she pays as a man. Besides, her sex, if not barbarous custom, cuts her off from the best rewarded colleges. Her hands, feet, and brain are clogged." We ask our readers to pause and inquire if this is not true.

Men have not reflected enough on the poor compensation for woman's labor, or have not seen exactly how to remedy it. It is a relic of barbarous ages and barbarous nations. I do not wish to reflect on my countrymen. I know that many of them possess kind and noble hearts, and, some of them, would like to see justice done to women.

It requires just as much to support a woman as a man. Her dress requires more. Often infirm, sick, or aged parents are relying on her for a support, or, it may be, orphan brothers and sisters. Or, even if it were not so, a woman needs to lay up something for times of sickness, old age, and want of employment, as well as a man. It is far more difficult for women to gain a living than for men. They are less certain of finding work, and when they do, are worse paid. They dearly earn what they get.

Men are better able by nature to take care of themselves. Their physical constitution, the tendencies of their education, their preparation for some definite calling, better enable them to do so. Yet to men is intrusted the making of laws to regulate labor. And well they use that power to their own advantage, if we may judge by the comparative compensation of man's and woman's labor. Might is right, seems to be their governing principle. Why cannot just and correct men, in our State legislatures, take the matter in hand and pass laws granting woman an equal compensation with man for her labor? Which of our legislatures will be the pioneer in this cause of humanity? There are many *kind* and *honorable*, and, we hope, *just* men in our legislatures. May they take action on this subject because it is right, and may they receive the good opinion they deserve from their fair countrywomen.

A German gentleman told me he had observed, in all countries that he had visited, that one day's labor of a man will pay for two days' living. Would that I could say the same of woman's labor.

The proportion of women's wages to men's in the industrial branches is from one third to one half. The difference is somewhat influenced by the kind of work. What a man would receive one dollar for, a woman would get only from sixteen and two thirds to fifty cents. The *average* proportion is from one third to one half.

The principal causes of the difference in prices paid, are, the large number of women dependent on their labor for a livelihood, and the small number of employments pursued by women, arising from prejudice, opposition, and the want of training; also the nature of the non-domestic occupations engaged in by them, they being mostly of a kind that can be dispensed with.

In *cotton* manufactories women are better rewarded as *weavers*, than in most branches of industrial labor. Yet in them the wages are very seldom more than half that of men. In *woolen* manufactories the wages of females are still better, though the weaving is more laborious. In *metal* manufactories the wages of women run from one sixth to one third those of men.

In no country is woman justly remunerated for her labor. One employer told me the principal reason for women not being better compensated is, they do not become so proficient in their business as men—not so thorough to the same extent. But he well knew they were not rewarded in proportion to their qualifications. Another employer said, "We pay men better because they can regulate the machinery, if it gets out of order, while the hands are at work." Women could do it, too, if they were taught how; and I would advise them to learn. Yet I doubt if regulating the machinery would make their wages equal those of men. Said one proprietor, "It is not we employers that make money. It is the middle-men. You will accomplish a good deal if you regulate the rate of wages." I thought so too, with as little justice, and humanity, as there are in the business world.

When men and women are employed in the same establishments, women have not the lightest, most healthy, and most pleasant parts of the labor. We would refer you to the *cotton*, *woolen*, and *silk manufactures*, and to the *coal*, and *metal mines*, for proofs of the assertion; but they have the *hardest*, *worst paid*, and *most unhealthy work*. In civilized countries it is a remnant of the former degradation of the sex. *Over-work* and *under-pay* are the curse of work-women. While they last, the poverty, and suffering, of women, will continue.

The reason women do not have strikes in the United States, like men, and demand higher wages, is, that many are ignorant; many cannot afford the time and money; some are so despairing they think it useless; some have a false pride about the matter; they think it would look unwomanly; but the principal reason is, they have no one to lead them, on whom they can rely. Female operatives in England have made strikes, at different times, for higher wages.

We have often felt disposed to give men credit for employing women in preference to persons of their own sex, but often the preference is given because they can be had for less wages. Any person of correct views and principles, respects employers that give their women as good wages as their men, for the same amount of labor, as well done, or payment in the same proportion, for less work, not so skillfully performed.

If women were in possession of some of the employments now monopolized by men, and as well compensated for their work, wicked men would have less money and power. They would not be so well able to gratify evil desires, and animal appetites.

With scarcely an exception, in the industrial avocations

of women, three fourths of what they earn goes toward defraying the expenses of board and washing. If they were better paid, they would have more self-respect, and, in having more self-respect, would be more desirous to secure, and more successful in securing, the respect of others.

Men learn a trade early in life; most women go to one when necessity compels them, and they have not time to qualify themselves as they should. Women rarely devote more than six months to learning any pursuit. We are aware that some may say, women are rewarded in proportion to their skill; and to some extent it is true, but not fully. A woman who spends but a few weeks learning her business, at a small cost, should not expect the same remuneration as one who had given years to it, at great expense. Women that sew as well as men, are, I am told, nearly as well paid in a few branches. Not to receive an equivalent for labor is certainly discouraging, particularly to a mother, whose young children look to her for bread.

Women want moral and mental courage. They receive such wages as men offer, without considering whether it is a fair compensation. They feel that to demand higher wages is a barrier they cannot surmount. And perhaps they cannot, in individual cases, as matters now stand; but if they would unite, and work *earnestly*, *unselfishly*, and *persistently*, they could level the mountains, and fill the valleys, that impede their progress.

If they would qualify themselves more thoroughly for their business, they would not feel the necessity of getting married for a home, for they would then be more likely to find employment, and be able to command better wages. Let women prepare themselves thoroughly for the higher departments of labor, and demand proper compensation, and persevere in doing so until they receive it.

A certain manufacturer of patent medicines in Philadelphia, who employs some women, said, "My women once insisted on having as high wages as men. It would not do. They were cutting off their own heads." I ventured to inquire why they might not have as good wages, if they did as much work, and did it as well. He said, "*Women could not be ordered about like men*, and it is not right that men should be supplanted."

In New York the Jews have done much to cut down prices. They are said to be extortionists, and a lazy people that prefer to live off the profits of their seamstresses, and other work-people, to laboring with their own hands.

Most employers, I am informed, prefer having their work done by the piece. I should think the plan preferable also to work-people. The work of slop-shops is very low, but it is given out, and paid for by the piece.

I would recommend to my readers a French book, by J. Boucher de Perthes, entitled "Woman in her Social State — Her Work and her Remuneration." It makes important statements, and throws out valuable suggestions. The author says, "Errors and abuses have been accumulating for years — yes, centuries — in trade, manufactures, and every department of labor. So that what is now custom is looked upon as right, or rather without any inquiry whether it is wrong, and capable of being remedied. So great is the competition of manufacturers that some will say, 'We cannot pay our work-people more; others sell at a certain price, and unless we can make a better quality of goods for the same price, we may not sell at all, or unless we can make goods of the same quality at lower rates. Any way, we cannot sell goods of the same quality for more than our neighbors, and therefore cannot without a loss of profit, and probably final ruin to ourselves, pay more to our work-people.' This is plausible; and in such cases, at such times, we justify the interference and regulations of government. And in case it is not done, a combination of work-people should take the matter in hand, and demand adequate wages." We would suggest what to us appears even a better plan — the establishment of coöperative associations.

The result of insufficient wages is a problem that time and circumstances are fast solving. Already have some of the European countries furnished a sad and terrible solution. Under-paid labor has very truly been called robbery.

Is that term mild enough? What patience, what self-control, what a power of endurance, are required to live under oppression and injustice! Some, so situated, hesitate between want and vice. Comparatively few people know what it is to need the necessaries of life, and therefore few know the temptations arising from want.

If more occupations are entered by women it will give them more independence pecuniarily. It will do much to overcome misery, and oppose intemperance. It will check the still more fearful scourge that is working ruin and death.

To pay women better prices for labor will give it a dignity in public estimation. The effect will prove beneficial not only to workers, pecuniarily and socially, but its influence will extend to those indirectly affected.

The great demand, in England, for female labor in factories, and the low prices paid, have given rise to the cruel system of child-murder. In order to make the infant sleep, during the mother's absence, the young child that acts as nurse, or the old woman that takes charge of it for a few farthings, gives it Godfrey's cordial. A long, slow poisoning is the result, and the child falls a victim, or lingers on, a weak, diseased creature, murdered by one who has given it life, and loves it better than her own soul. Another abominable practice, becoming common in England, is that of the mother fastening a sponge, saturated with a narcotic, in the mouth of her infant, when leaving it in the morning, to be gone all day at her work. The principal cause of the loss of infants at birth, by Irish women, is attributed to the contraction of the pelvis, induced by tying them when children in chairs, while the mothers are at work.

What prompts to this neglect of children? Why is all this misery and cruelty committed? Why this inhuman child-murder? Because there is a demand for female labor. And why this demand? Because it is cheaper. And why cheaper? Is it because women are better able to labor than men — that they have more strength? No; it is a result of the injustice women have suffered from the most remote ages. Most women in lunatic asylums are there from domestic trouble, from over-work, from inability to earn a living, or from the terrible fear that they may not be able to do so in the future.

In the "New York Herald," mention was made, during the strikes by the shoemakers in Massachusetts, "of a lady whose necessities compelled her to work on binding boots, for which she only received the miserable pittance of two cents per pair. She could only by hard work get through two pairs with her own hands in two whole days — thus netting four cents for two whole days' toil. Some women received but eight cents per pair for fitting and binding women's congress gaiters." One of the speakers at a mass meeting in Botanic Hall, New York, (1862) remarked, "Hundreds of journeymen shoemakers of Massachusetts support their families, while making shoes at ten, eight, and sometimes five cents a pair, and then have to take orders upon the grocer, tailor, and even upon the doctor; and all this, sir, within the pale of New England civilization."

In the "Monthly Record" of the Five Points House of Industry, August, 1859, is an account of a visit by the superintendent to a poor widow. It reads as follows: "I found her hard at work making boys' cloth caps, trimmed with braid, and bow, and buttons, lined with glazed muslin and wash-leather, and with patent leather front; for the making and pressing of which she received two shillings per dozen, or two cents a piece. We could not believe it, and asked to see her pass-book. It was true. 'In good times,' she said, 'I used to get three shillings and sixpence per dozen, but now the price is reduced.'"

In London fifty thousand females are working under sixpence per day, and above one hundred thousand under one shilling per day. "Shirt-makers in London make a dozen shirts for two shillings. Waistcoat-makers earn only from three to four shillings a week; workers for the army clothiers receive eight cents apiece for jackets and trousers, earning thereby two shillings a week. Shoe-binders work eighteen hours a day, and earn one shilling and sixpence a week. The mantilla-maker sits from nine in the morning till eleven at night, and makes about four shillings and eightpence a week in busy seasons; the upholsterer seldom earns four shillings a week; the worker in furs the same way. The embroiderer gets from one shilling to one shilling and threepence the dress; the garter-maker works from eight in the morning till nine at night, to earn about four shillings a week clear; the brace-maker earns only from one shilling to one shilling and three and a half pence every week, working twelve hours out of the twenty-four, finding cotton and candles, and besides has three months slack in the year, during which she gets about fourpence halfpenny a week." See "Frazer's Magazine," vol. xli., to which we are indebted for the substance of part of what we give on wages in London. "Two women engaged there in drawn bonnet-making received each, for from eighteen to twenty hours' work every day, Sundays included, through the year 1842, fourpence one farthing; in 1847, threepence halfpenny; through 1848 and 1849, twopence halfpenny. From thirteen thousand to fourteen thousand females in London are engaged in slop-work, earning, on an average, twopence halfpenny a day, of whom one fourth, having no husband, or parent to support them, have no chance between starvation and prostitution."

At a singular meeting held a few years since at the British school-room, Shodwell, one thousand female slop-workers were present, by far the greater part in clothing to which the word *rags* was literally applicable in its fullest meaning. "None of that number had earned more than five shillings a week. Ninety-nine had earned only one shilling, ninety-two had earned under one shilling, and two hundred and thirty-three had had no work at all during the whole of the week."

Says a writer in the "North American Review," vol. xli. p. 348, "The wages of cotton manufacturers on the continent of Europe may be considered as varying from fifty cents to one dollar and twenty-five cents weekly. The population of France may be stated at thirty-two millions. Of these seven and a half millions receive less than twenty dollars a year for their support; and nearly twenty-three millions of the inhabitants are compelled to procure the necessaries of life with from five to eight sous daily."

Colman, in his "European Agriculture," says, "There is a constant struggle for the agricultural population of England and Ireland to sustain themselves, but any surplus is beyond their reach. Women rise at five o'clock in the morning, working for four shillings (one dollar) per week. Children of the ages of four, five, and six years work in the gangs at threepence a day, their hands blistered."

"In Paris," says the author of "Parisian Sights," "the average wages of the men are seventy-five cents a day, of the women thirty-three cents. There are eighty thousand domestics, who average less than twenty cents. The worst paid workmen are the cotton spinners, who receive only from twenty to forty cents a day, women often not over fifteen cents."

The crowded state of the labor market of women, and the high price of living in cities, render their condition lamentable. How insufficient are the wages of many to support them comfortably, and enable them to lay by something for sickness and old age! Think of their low-roofed attics, and damp cellars, where they are huddled together like so many cattle. Tell me, Christian men and women, are these your sisters? Have they, too, come from the stock of Adam?

A surplus of labor always produces depreciation of wages. Wages should depend on ability and application. The competition of women's labor with boys', in the non-domestic departments, is one cause of their low wages. Thousands of women never marry, that must and do earn a living, but work for less wages than men, even doing as hard work, and doing it as well. When more employments are opened to women, they will be able to command higher wages; for if one occupation does not pay, they can enter another.

Both employers and laborers are interested in the rate of wages. The vast amount of work required in this country, owing to its newness, its government, its institutions, and the amount of capital invested by those in foreign countries,* aside from that employed by our own people, with the wide extent and cheapness of land, tend to fix a comparatively fair price on men's labor, and on women's a better one than in most countries. Yet an improvement might be made in paying a higher price for female labor. Indeed, the scanty compensation paid woman's labor is a reproach to the country. Some people have attached much blame to the ladies of the United States for wearing fine goods brought from Europe, where pale, half-clad girls, for a mere pittance, are wearing out their lives to make them. They blame the pride and vanity Americans also indulge, in the purchase of elegant furniture, of foreign manufacture. They insist that American goods should be used, though less beautiful, and a good price paid, that industrious Americans may be encouraged in their labor. If ladies will imitate Parisian styles in making up articles of dress, let them, at least, buy American goods. And let them buy at establishments where the work-people are properly compensated. Humanity prompts assistance to those who need it, and in what way can that be rendered to the healthy poor more efficiently than by furnishing such employment as they are capable of at reasonable rates?

It is the duty of governments, so far as they can, to assist in this matter. They should make their contracts with just and honest men — men that pay operatives a fair price, and do not overwork them. They should give their work to such contractors only, as pay their workwomen a specified price, allowing a reasonable profit to the contractors. Let such men supply the army and navy with clothes. All the clothes, even shoes, for the army and navy, could be made by women. The difference in the price paid by government to honorable contractors will be a comparative trifle, while it will not only do good in itself, but be an example to individuals and societies. If government contractors give good wages to women for their work, storemen and

* See "Resources and Prospects of America," for sale by Routledge & Son, New York.

shopmen will be induced to increase their wages, and so a general change be gradually wrought. "A nation can buy nothing cheap which slackens the arm of its industry." Good prices for work, abundance of food, and reasonable charges for clothing and shelter, will give material comfort to work-people, and serve to render them prosperous and happy. The right distribution of labor is a matter of vast importance to a nation. The money and facilities required to furnish all its members with labor and compensation, are beyond the control and command of hundreds, or even thousands, of individuals; consequently it should be made to some extent a legislative and national affair. "The progression or emancipation of any class usually, if not always, takes place through the efforts of individuals of that class — and so it must be here. All women should inform themselves of the condition of their sex, and of their own position."

Cooper, in his "Condition of the Working Classes," writes, "A general rise of five per cent. in the rate of wages, if considered in the abstract, would appear a matter of little consequence; but in fact, it would confer a great benefit upon the poor. The additional sum paid to the workman would add to the means of the members of the middle classes, who are dependent upon such workmen, and enable them, as well as the laborers, to become greater consumers. This increase in the consumption of the different descriptions of goods, would cause a corresponding increase in their production, and create an additional demand for labor. The wages paid for this labor, by adding something more to the means of the poor, and their dependents, would still further increase the consumption of goods, and consequently their production, and so create employment for more labor."

An Englishman told me that labor is just as well paid in England as in the United States, for there house rent is not so dear, the credit system is more common, and the interest on money is much less.

A French woman remarked to me, that in France ladies of wealth do not work, and so the laboring classes of women are better paid for their labor; but in this country everybody works. This country is better, however, in one way than France for the poor. There an enormous price must be paid for a license to go into business, but here it is not so.

People should endeavor to ascertain how an employer pays his work-people before they patronize him, and be willing to pay a fair price for what they purchase, that the employer may be able to pay a just equivalent for work.

A lady who prides herself on her literary reputation, being asked by me why men should receive better wages than women, replied, "Because the cares of government devolve on them." Are not women of property taxed to support the government? The compensation of that lady was not as poor, in comparison with male authors, as that of women in most other pursuits. And here, I would make an exception in the comparative compensation of men and women for mere brain work. More justice is done such women, because they can better demand and secure what is due them. From the exorbitant price a few educated ladies ask for their productions, they doubtless suppose their influence and importance are enhanced thereby. Yet it is only those that have acquired a reputation as writers, that can command a high compensation. I have it from excellent authority, that if an article is sent to a newspaper, and it is known to come from a woman, it is less likely to be published, and if any compensation is allowed, it will be smaller than to a man.

Meyrick says, "Overwork is the result of low wages. To what are we to trace the evil of low wages? There seem to be three chief causes: First, an over-large supply of laborers; secondly, a determination on the part of shopkeepers to provide their customers with goods at the cheapest rate possible; and thirdly, what lies at the bottom of the two others, the unchecked working of the principle of competition."

The rates of wages, and the price of living, are pretty much the same in all the cities of the United States. In towns and villages both are less, and in the country there is a still greater difference. The further south you go, the better are the prices paid — yet living is somewhat higher. In some places wages are lower in winter than in summer, because the hours for work are shorter. Yet the worker is at the additional expense of fuel, and of more clothing, and that, too, of a more expensive kind. In addition, the prices for food are higher.

When I consider the injustice done workwomen by lowness of wages, scarcity of remunerative employment, trickery of trade, and the limited number of occupations opened to them, my blood boils with indignation. Read "London Labor," and ask the result of the impression on your mind. If women were paid in proportion to the quality and quantity of their work, at the same rate that men are paid, there could be no reasonable objection to women entering any occupation they desire to. It is unmanly and unjust to cut short a woman's wages merely because she is a woman. Instead of strong, healthy men receiving higher wages than delicate women, we think the plan should be reversed. Men are able to do more, and work longer, than women. A tax should be levied on the property of unmarried men for the support of single women without property, or else a better price paid for their labor, and more employments opened to them. Many people think women's wages will never be raised until they have equal political rights with men. It is quite probable that such is the case.

A New England farmer writes me, "In small districts there is *sometimes* a scarcity of labor in domestic service. The reason is, Yankee girls will not go out in that capacity. All such work is done by Irish girls. That is one reason woman's labor in the industrial branches does not pay better. So many women are seeking for such work that there is great competition, and they underbid each other."

We read, that "in Iowa the labor of women is estimated about as high as that of men; and as they are generally industrious and frugal, they are quite independent of the other sex."

Reasonable prices for all kinds of work are paid women in California. Lady teachers in the public schools of San Francisco receive the same salaries as men.

BAD RESULTS OF INSUFFICIENT WAGES.

"THE physicians of England say that in the female side of lunatic asylums, the largest class, but one, of the insane, are maids-of-all-work, (the other being governesses). The causes are obvious enough: want of sufficient sleep from late and early hours, unremitting fatigue and hurry; and even more than these, anxiety about the future from the smallness of their wages."

"It will be ever memorable that during the transition period, in which Ireland passed over from destitution and despair, to comfort and progress, the nation was mainly supported by the industry of the women. In the succeeding period, and after the famine, the desire for the lowest-priced labor led to the employment of women and children, and the strange spectacle was then common of women toiling on the farms, or in pastures, while the strong men were nursing the babies and the grannies at home."

In some pursuits women are quite as capable of bodily and mental superiority as men, but have not become so, because not educated to do their work so *thoroughly* and *skillfully* as men. Particularly is it so in the sewing department. The majority of women who sew for a living are not capable of doing so by hand as neatly and skillfully as men, and that accounts, in some cases, for lower wages.

Many persons complain of a great laxity of principle among work-people. If so, may it not arise, to some extent, from scanty remuneration, and from living with no other aim but that of contributing to the physical wants, without leisure and money for refining and elevating recreations? All evil does not originate in poverty and desolation, but some does.

We read in "Time and Tide," by John Ruskin, "The value of any piece of labor — that is to say, the quantity of food and air which will enable a man to perform it, without losing actually any of his flesh, or his nervous energy — is as absolutely fixed a quantity, as the weight of powder necessary to carry a given ball a given distance. Let any half dozen of recognized London physicians state in precise terms the quantity and kind of food, and space of lodging, they consider approximately necessary for the healthy life of a laborer, in any given manufacture, and the number of hours he may, without shortening his life, work at such business daily, if so sustained. And let all masters be bound to give their men a choice between an order for that quantity of food and lodging, or such wages as the market may offer for that number of hours' work."

The rules of labor adapted to men are applicable to women. If there are just enough food, fuel, shelter, and other essential comforts of life, to supply the entire population of the civilized race, then it is evident that all waste and improvident use of such things subtract so much from the comfort of others.

Occasionally we hear the remark, that if people do right, and are industrious when young, they will not want for a home when old. This would be true if everybody in the world did right. But the condition of people is often the result of the sins or extravagance of those to whom they are bound by the ties of marriage or consanguinity. And again: poverty may, and often does, arise from failure of health, from reverses in business, and unfortunate investments of money, and not unfrequently from becoming security for the debts of others.

It is a blessed thing that a few homes are provided for the old age of those that have none. Would to Heaven more were established.

We believe if the way in which a large portion of female workers are obliged to live in *this*, and, we suppose, *other civilized countries*, on account of low wages, were made known, it would make all Christendom tremble. The women are not to be blamed, but pitied. They might have been happy and useful citizens, if their labors had been properly rewarded. A reasonable means of subsistence is necessary to preserve from temptation to evil. If a woman cannot, by severe drudgery, earn enough to save herself and young children from cold and hunger, wretchedness and degradation, woe, woe be to that community of which she is a member.

Madame Romieu gives, in her "Woman of the Nineteenth Century," as a cause of prostitution in France, the insufficiency of the wages of many of the working women to support life. Rev. John Barlow says, "It has been observed to me by a distinguished friend, who formerly filled the office of Secretary of State in the Home Department, that the increase of crime has generally been in the ratio of the want of employment for the people, and that it is probable that the same cause may operate toward increasing insanity."

"Parent Duchâtelet attests that of three thousand lost women in Paris, only thirty-five had an occupation that could support them, and that fourteen had been precipitated into this horrible life by destitution. One of these, when she resolved on this course, had eaten nothing for three days."

To bestow charity on a woman able and willing to work is lowering her dignity, and wounding her self-respect. To be obliged to accept charity causes intense pain to one of a refined and sensitive nature. Yet, if a woman's resources will not maintain her, what better can she do? Nothing. But she may console herself with the consciousness, if she works all her time, to the best of her abilities and knowledge, that society and her country entitle her to a support; that it is due her from them; and that any wise, humane, and judicious government would make adequate provision for the support of its worthy, industrious women.

Of a company of needlewomen and slop-workers Mr. Mayhew convened in Paris, he says, "They were unanimous in declaring that a large number in the trade — probably one fourth of the whole, or one half of those who had no husband or parent to support them — resorted to the streets to eke out a living. Not unfrequently has prostitution arisen from unselfishness, in trying to provide for the necessities of fatherless children, or an infirm mother, when no other way offered, when virtuous employment could not be obtained, and charity withheld its hand."

Poor fallen ones! that found neither place nor people to turn to for succor. Who will be the first to cast a stone? Their sad hearts are pained by a consciousness of having done wrong, to which is added the bitter reproach that by a majority of their sex they are censured and scorned. Calumny and slander, with their tongues of fire and heart-piercing swords, may, to the well disposed, be rending asunder the very fibres of their hearts. Sadly to be lamented is the fact that with some the choice lay between starvation and ruin.

A correspondent of the "Christian Inquirer" says of the statement in a work by Dr. Sanger, "The average duration of a prostitute's life in New York is just four years. Ill treatment, by parents and husbands, sends one tenth of this army of vice into their wretched calling. But the saddest fact of all, and one most disgraceful to our Christian civilization, is, that full one fourth of the lost women of London and New York were driven to the streets and the brothels by destitution. The terrible alternative has been starvation or hell. *Employment at fair remuneration* will do more to rescue in season those for whom the vortex of the brothel is yawning, than all the Magdalen societies in existence; for while those societies afford occasional recovery to the few, the other method will secure *prevention* and *safety* to the many."

"The vices of the poor," says Mrs. Gaskell, "sometimes astound us here; but when the secrets of all hearts shall be made known, their virtues will astound us in a far greater degree."

There seems a deficiency in tracing the causes of crime and poverty, and a want of common sense in providing practical means for preventing, checking, and curing these cancers of society. The great effort seems to be to relieve, not to cure; to extend charity, ignoring the higher virtue, justice. Those able to work want remunerative labor, not charity. Charity to those able to work, and willing to do it, is a loss to the giver and the recipient — to the giver in money, and the recipient in execution. It is surprising what a vast amount of time, labor, and money is spent in attempts at charitable and philanthropic works, that amount to nothing at all, for the *want of judicious, common sense, systematic arrangement, and execution.*

IT REQUIRES AS MUCH TO SUPPORT A WOMAN AS A MAN.

IN commencing this subject, we would state for our premises, that sufficiency for one individual would be considered starvation by another. The requirements of different classes of society vary as greatly as the classes themselves. The standard for the price of labor, in all countries, is an ability to obtain, with its proceeds, the necessaries of life. But a variety of circumstances, that increases with the civilization of a nation, tends to influence and pervert this standard.

Universally there is more waste of time and money among men than women. Men make their money easily, and spend it freely, at least a majority do, where their own comfort or pleasure is to be the return. No mechanic will work in ordinary times for less than from two to four dollars a day. How many women, of equal intelligence, can obtain as good wages for mechanical employment, even when skill is the only qualification, and women are as competent? The patience and perseverance of women counterbalance the strength of men.

A shop-girl once remarked to me, "Workwomen have too much *pride*. They will starve to dress well." By *well* I suppose she meant decently, for the majority I have seen, were dressed as cheaply as they could be to look decent. Rather should we commend women that they have the *laudable pride* to make a respectable appearance on so small a sum. Pray what has a woman to spend for dress who receives from two to five dollars a week, and who cannot possibly board for less than two thirds of her earnings? Boarding, some employers inform us, is rather cheaper for women than men.

But I find it to be the case, that they usually pay quite as high for the same quality of board, and find it more difficult to obtain. From fifty cents, to two dollars and fifty cents, a week, is as much as the majority of shop-girls can spare for clothes, medicines, doctor's bills, &c. Their clothing costs as much as men's, or more, and they must pay as dearly for every comfort and privilege. Yet they are paid only from one sixth to one half as much for their labor. And most workwomen are at times out of employment; besides, they fail in health earlier in life. In payment of wages women should certainly be on a footing with men.

When we consider that most people eat one thousand meals in the course of a year, require clothing to suit the seasons, must have shelter for three hundred and sixty-five nights every year, if not for as many days, and in some latitudes fuel nearly half the year, we know that as the hand labor of women is compensated, there can be but little, if anything, laid aside for sickness and old age. Some people complain that women work as a means, not an end. *How many men are exceptions to the statement?*

Nothing is more important to an individual, or a family, than pecuniary matters. Debt causes unhappiness, and, if increased, and continued, will, in many cases, lead to suicide or crime.

Economy is a virtue necessary for accumulation and success in business. In the middle classes, economy does nearly as much to enrich as industry. The working classes need to practice it for their own good, and to exercise judgment in their expenditures. A close estimate should be made of what portion of the income may go to the separate expenses of dress, fuel, rent, and the table. It is well to save, if possible, for future needs, or to purchase implements with which to render one's labor more productive.

When a woman becomes competent to transact business on a large scale, if she has capital, and is not afraid to risk it, she will be likely to succeed, if she can keep clear of a swindling partner. But women must prepare themselves *thoroughly* for business, if they expect to come in competition with men, whose business education has commenced in boyhood, and has been prosecuted continuously, with intense application.

Of what use to some women are talents and education? They do not turn them to account. They are no better off than the poor sewing girl; indeed, do not accomplish as much for the good of the world. The defect arises from the useless education given women, the false shame attending labor, a tardiness in discovering what they should do, and, when discovered, the want of a prompt and systematic course of action.

The majority of women, living in ease, are unable to sympathize with those struggling to gain a subsistence. They are unconscious of the depressing influence they exert.

We must suffer, to learn to benefit those that have suffered. To endure privations ourselves, is the only sure way, in which to know the wants of others, and how best to meet those wants.

WOMEN REQUIRED TO LABOR TOO LONG.

WHY should women labor fourteen, fifteen, and even sixteen hours, every day, when men work but ten? Is their physical strength greater, that they can endure it? Why do they not combine, and strike for the ten-hour system, and higher wages? It has been done in England; why not in this country? Or why not demand the *eight-hour* system, as men are now doing? It is true, there are some men that require of their workwomen but ten hours' labor, and we know of a few that never require but nine and a half, and of a still smaller number that require but nine.

We know that many of the women engaged to sew for slop-shops spend fifteen or sixteen hours, out of the twenty-four, at their needle. Shirts, coats, vests, and pantaloons for men, and cloaks and mantillas for women, are the chief articles for which the lowest wages are paid, in proportion to the time required to make them.

In some of the most fashionable dress-making establishments of London, during the busy season, which occupies about one third of the year, the usual number of hours for work is fifteen. But in times of pressure, which often occur, this number runs to eighteen. In some establishments, in London, the young women do not get more than six, sometimes four, sometimes three, and now and then not more than two hours for sleeping, and some even work all night. The proprietors of some houses there, that would like the credit of being humane, begin at four A.M. and close at eleven P.M.

In London, in 1853, about fifty millinery and dress-making establishments entered into an agreement, that they would not require the services of their work hands for more than twelve hours, during seven months of the year, and thirteen and a half during the remaining five months, including an hour and a half for meals. It was found, during the next year, that quite a number had broken the contract.

"The workwomen for good slop-shops," says Mayhew, "that give fair, or tolerably fair wages, and expect good work, can make *six* averaged sized mantles in a week, working from ten to twelve hours a day; but the slop-workers, by toiling from thirteen to sixteen hours a day, will make *nine* such sized mantles in a week. In the season of twelve weeks, one thousand workers for the slop-shops, and warehouses, would, at this rate, make one hundred and eight thousand mantles, or thirty-six thousand more than for the fair trade. Or, to put it in another light, these slop-women, by being compelled, in order to live, to work such over-hours, as inflict lasting injury on the health, supplant, by their overwork and over-hours, the labor of five hundred hands, working the regular hours."

"Can this be true in a Christian land? Are the delicate frames of mere girls ground down, exhausted, withered, by this inhuman trade, by labor that runs over the ten hours of man's day of labor? Are all the show, and glitter, and gayety, and fine apparel, and fashionable attire of the women of higher rank bought at the price of such suffering of mind, and body, as is involved in labors of such length? Is it true that the female drudges of the lower female world are oppressed with something that approaches the reality of Egyptian bondage? What under-currents of misery there are, which do not meet the eye as it glances along the glittering shops of our large towns! The world has a gay frontispiece, but there are hideous pages in the book."

Bulwer, in his "Monarchy of the Middle Classes" says, "Prolonged and exhausting labor, continued from day to day, and from year to year, is not calculated to develop the intellectual, or moral faculties of man. The dull routine of ceaseless drudgery, in which the same mechanical process is incessantly repeated, resembles the torment of Sisyphus, — *toil, like the rock, recoils perpetually on the wearied operative.*

The mind gathers neither stores nor strength from the constant extension of the muscles. The intellect slumbers in supine inertness, but the grosser parts of our nature attain a rank development. To condemn man to such severity of toil, is, in some measure, *to cultivate in him the habits of an animal.* He becomes restless. He disregards the distinguishing appetite and habits of his species. He lives in squalid wretchedness, on meagre food, and expends his superfluous gains in debauchery."

It is related by the commissioners, appointed by Parliament to investigate the factory system of England, that some cases were found, among the women, of the plantar arch of the foot having given way. One deformity was known by the name of the factory leg, and curvature of the spine was common. Some women stated to the commissioners that they often had to do without their breakfast for want of time to eat it. Pains in the limbs, back, loins, and sides, were often so great from standing that the children could not sleep, and they were sometimes known to faint from fatigue, and often the overseer would have to scold and whip them to keep them awake. At night, after labor was over, children were often found hid in the store, among the wool, rather than go home. A witness stated he had often seen them dragged out of the store, and beaten out of the mill. An old man that had charge of a poorhouse, where injured operatives were brought, remarked to one of the commissioners, "I've gotten no head for numbers, but this I know, that by far the greater part of the accidents as comed in, happened in the last two hours, when folk gettin' tired, and careless."

Many operatives require stimulants, to keep up their strength, so that they may fill their hours of labor. It is said that there is much opium-eating among the work-girls of Philadelphia. Most of them return from their work with their physical strength exhausted, their vitality gone, and the desire to eat something, and drop to sleep, is paramount to every other. What time have they for moral and mental culture? A few of those who are not required to labor so long, feel that after the exertions of the day they should go to some place of amusement. There they are apt to fall in bad company, for such places, as would be likely to entertain them profitably, they cannot pay to attend.

Women and children under the old factory system of England worked twelve hours, sometimes fourteen, and sometimes even sixteen hours a day. Now the operatives in all the principal branches of textile manufacture in England work ten and a half hours a day, and have holiday on Saturday after two P. M.

That women endure as long, and as much, as men, is a rule, and not an exception, though physically less able to do so. Men do not work as hard as women, and therefore are able to keep in harness longer. In thousands of cases the strain upon woman's nervous system, and brain, is beyond endurance, as the grave, and the lunatic asylum, can testify.

In the lower classes of the United States women have to work too long, and too severely. In the middle and higher classes, the majority of young women scarcely work at all. It would be well if the work could be more evenly adjusted.

There should be regular hours for women to work, just as there are for men. Everything should be done in moderation. Even devotional exercises need to be regulated by reason. It is sinful for a man to spend all his time attending church service, praying, and reading the Bible, while his wife and young children suffer for food and clothes. A really devout spirit, guided by judgment, would lead him to labor as well as pray.

The hours for work are very irregular in metal manufactures, running from ten to thirteen a day, but in some places extend to fifteen or sixteen a day, for weeks together. The shops are dark, and those used for stamping are several feet below ground, and consequently cool and damp. Women are more employed in metal manufactures in Europe than in this country.

OCCUPATIONS OF MEN AND WOMEN.

THERE is not the same disproportion between the means of subsistence, and employment, in the United States, that exists in the overstocked cities of older countries. In the old settlements of Europe, where the working class is larger than the demand for its services, low wages, and want of employment, are the common cry.

Twenty years ago about one fifth of the work-people in the cotton manufactories of England, were men, one third women, and the remainder children; but the proportion is different of late years.

The average number of men and women the world over is the same. In new countries there is a majority of men, in the old countries there is a majority of women. More are there dependent on their own resources, and of course a larger number are likely to fit themselves for occupations.

In the Northern United States there is a majority over the Southern States of unmarried women. Of course the comparative number varies in different places; but where there is a majority of women, we find there is a larger number of employments pursued by women.

The more a nation advances in civilization, the greater will be the increase of employments. Wants will increase with the means to gratify them. The imagination will be taxed to produce artificial wants, when natural ones cease to occupy all that live by labor.

INCREASED NUMBER OF SINGLE WOMEN.

"IT appears that there is a natural excess of four or five per cent. of females, over the males, in English population. There is, however, an actual ratio of thirty per cent. of women now in England who never marry, leaving one fourth of both sexes in a state of celibacy. This difference further appears to be constantly on the increase." "Two women in five of the whole number of English women are unmarried." According to the "National Review," of April, 1862, the actual proportion of women in Great Britain, *above twenty years of age, who must and ought to be single, being six per cent.*, the actual proportion *who are single, is thirty per cent.*; but of every one hundred females, of twenty years of age, and upward, *fifty-seven are wives, thirteen are widows, and thirty are spinsters.* Aside from the want of opportunity of single women to marry, are the want of health, cold hearts, independent tempers, or indulgent selfishness. One million and a half are unmarried females. Of this number half a million are wanted in the colonies, half a million in domestic service, and half a million are to be disposed of in some other way." "In Great Britain there is so much poverty, that marriage in the lower classes is discouraged by political economists, parish overseers, tax-payers, and government." "Of women at the age of twenty, and upward, forty-three out of every one hundred in England and Wales are unmarried."

If there is any discrepancy in the statements made, as to the exact proportions of the sexes who marry, it will be considered that the quotations are from different authorities.

The average number of marriages, in the United States, is seventy-five to one hundred marriageable women. Therefore twenty-five out of every one hundred are not engaged in the duties of matrimonial life. According to the census of 1860, there were, before the war, in Massachusetts, thirty-seven thousand more women than men; in Connecticut, eight thousand; in New Hampshire, seven thousand; in New York, eleven thousand. There are, at the *present time*, over seventy thousand more women in Massachusetts than men. It is said that one third of them are either unmarried or childless. Many single men of the Northern States emigrate to, and settle in, new countries, or engage in some roving occupation, while many married men seek employment away from home, in mills, factories, and workshops, spending years trying to accumulate property that they may send for their families, or render them more comfortable on their return.

In California, a few years back, there was a loud call for wives for the miners. Mrs. Farnham saw the necessity for women in California, and offered to take a large number out; but she was ridiculed, and her motives maligned. There is still a need of respectable women there. A man remarked to me that there are too many women in the world, and suggested that some be transferred to California. He thought by sending them to agricultural countries, where there are manufactories, they could get work as operatives, and at the same time have good opportunities of marrying farmers. As a general thing, there are most men in the country — most women in the city. According to the calculation of one who gave some attention to the subject, there is in New York city a proportion of women to men as three to two. His remedy was, that one third of the women be sent to where there is the same surplus of men; that is, where men are in the proportion to women of three to two. Such places offer in the new States and Territories of the Great West.

In an article styled "Woman in Society," the statement is made, that "in California there are three men to every woman; in Washington, four men to every woman; in Nevada, eight men to every woman; and in Colorado there are to every woman twenty men."

The number of single women increases with the advance of civilization and refinement. As nations advance in wealth, the people are apt to acquire luxurious and effeminate habits, that unfit them for exertion. The women become delicate, and the men idle and self-indulgent. The ancient marriage custom of paying for a wife in flocks, or land, or money, or labor, is reversed. The bride is now expected, if belonging to a wealthy family, to receive a marriage portion. The fact does not arise so much from a greater inability to appreciate women, as from the more expensive habits of people, the greater wealth needed to supply those habits, and the less profitable nature, pecuniarily, of women.

"Increased habits of luxury must lessen the chance of estimable offers; women, therefore, ought to accustom themselves to those pursuits, which will render them less dependent on the other sex, or enliven those lonely hours of retirement which frequently fall to the lot of poorly portioned celibacy. It is not only necessary that they should be economical, but that they should have a general knowledge of business and money transactions, at least sufficient to escape imposition. To this should be added activity of mind, that they may avoid the *ennui* inseparable from idleness, and the diseases incident to a sedentary life. Improving study of all kinds, is here a most valuable acquisition; and elegant accomplishments cannot be pursued with too much avidity, provided they do not injure the health."

Now that marriages are becoming more rare, rich women must have something else to occupy their thoughts, and poor ones some means for gaining a livelihood. In addition to the causes we have mentioned, the decrease of men by the war in this country, will make the number of marriages still less. More than a million of women have been deprived of their property, or of those on whom they depend for a support. The houses of numbers in the Southern States, have been destroyed; they have been deprived of their servants; their families have been broken up; some have had all the prejudice and animosity of political difference brought to bear against them, and so thousands of women are deprived of their all. But in the Southern States there is a unity of feeling, and unselfishness, that will supply women with the necessaries of life while they are to be had; and the women have acted nobly toward each other, have cheerfully undergone privations, and performed work of which their fair hands had no experience previous to the war. In the Northern States, many thousands have been deprived of the comforts of life by the death, or wounds, or unknown fate of husbands, fathers, brothers, and other relatives. Large numbers of these women are working, or seeking work, to earn the bread of life. Many others are incapable of work, or ignorant where to obtain it and how to perform it.

The number of single women in this country, possessing property, is small compared with those that are dependent. If their property and energies would open new fields of employment for the dependent, how noble would their lives be! How warmly would their memories be embalmed in the hearts of their countrywomen!

During the reign of Augustus Cæsar, the greatest encouragement was given to matrimony in the Romish Empire. When the people were numbered, any man who had not a wife, was subject to a fine, and those who were without, were not allowed to give their oath in the tribunals.

"Let us bear in mind," says Mrs. Jameson, "that for every man who does not provide a home, there must exist a woman who must make, or find, a home for herself, somehow and somewhere." The virtue of a man may be suspected who sneers at marriage.

"Out of six millions of women, *above twenty years of age*, in England, Scotland, and Wales, more than two millions are independent in their industry — are self-supporting, like men," while *in England* alone, three million of women, or *half its female population, are engaged in paid labor.* Fifteen thousand of that number are governesses.

"In a community where a larger proportion of women remain unmarried than at any known period; where a greater number of women depend on their own industry for subsistence; where every pair of hands, moved by an intelligent head, is in request; and where improved machinery demands more and more of the skilled labor which women can supply, how can there be a doubt that the women will work more and more, and in aggregate ways, as combination becomes better understood and practiced?"

John Robertson, in a paper entitled "Thoughts on the Excess of Adult Females in the Population of Great Britain," with reference to its causes and consequences, says, "I endeavored to show that the female sex, in Christian countries, are probably designed for duties more in number, and in importance, than have yet been assigned them. The reasons were, that above the twentieth year, in all fully peopled states, whether in Europe or in North America, women considerably outnumber the other sex; and that, as this excess is produced by causes which remain in steady operation, we detect therein a natural law, and may allowably infer that it exists for beneficent social ends, — ends, amongst others, such as those I am attempting to explain and recommend. In carrying out these and various other objects of importance, I am persuaded that the agency of the female sex is necessary, and that without the well-organized aid of benevolent and educated women, municipal government will ever remain limited and imperfect."

MORE POOR WOMEN THAN MEN.

THERE are almost twice as many poor women, in different countries, as poor men — the proportions being forty-six to twenty-seven. Probably one third of the American adult population is dependent on another third. It is right — a duty for men to support their wives always, and their daughters, and sisters, until they are thoroughly educated, and prepared to support themselves. And then, a man should be ready to assist daughters and sisters, and direct them how best to succeed.

The number of poor in this country, both men and women, is becoming fearfully large. Besides, the number of paupers (i. e., those dependent on public charity) is increasing, though it is mostly confined to immigrants. Is there no vagrant act, or is it not carried into execution? We should think not, in some of our large cities, from the number of able-bodied foreigners that throng the streets, thrusting into the face, or hands, of every passer by, a paper, or book, descriptive of real or pretended affliction. The most heart-sickening feature, however, is the idleness and degradation in which most paupers, and some of the poor that are not paupers, rear their children.

In order to make the wicked, who are destitute, virtuous, first feed and clothe them. They can better listen to instruction and counsel when comfortable. Much crime undoubtedly arises from inability to supply physical wants honestly. Give the poor well-rewarded labor, not alms. The poor are often charged with being improvident. They spend lavishly while they have anything, and then suffer want. They seem unable to regulate their expenditures judiciously. It arises from not being trained to habits of prudence, system, and economy. They are usually generous to those of their own class that are in want, and in that respect they might shame many that rank higher in the social scale. To have a place of safe deposit for their surplus funds, however trivial in amount, is calculated to encourage a provident feeling. It will render them industrious and economical.

The excess of females in cities arises, in part, from a greater number of employments being open to them. Another cause is the great variety and excitement, and the superior social and religious advantages, afforded by a city life. In many parts of the country there is need for female help, but principally in the branches of domestic labor.

Women who have been reared in the country, and come to town to live, and there meet with reverse of fortune, are even more helpless than those who have grown up in the city. For the last mentioned have learned more of the resources open to women for gaining a livelihood, and they are more likely to have friends that can direct them. Besides, they are not so apt to be distracted by the noise, confusion, and excitements of the city.

A virtuous woman, on the score of her sex, has claims on society when she is destitute or desolate. The old, and diseased, and young children, should always, on account of their helplessness, be provided for — indeed, all unable to work should certainly be sustained. It is an awful thing that a woman may starve or freeze because she cannot obtain remunerative work. It is a disgrace to any community. A fund should be set apart by every state and city to furnish employment to such at reasonable prices. Many workwomen fare worse than brutes. Their subsistence is more uncertain. They have not wherewithal to obtain, while brutes can obtain subsistence, if at liberty to seek it. Some destitute, yet virtuous women, are not treated as well as the horses and servants of the rich. *They* are always provided with food, and made comfortable; but in many cases in our large cities, educated mothers of men that are to be are not made comfortable. They suffer from cold, and hunger, and the want of attention in sickness. Hard times, the season of the year, or an existing epidemic, is often made an excuse by so-called benevolent societies and government officers; but in many cases there is no foundation for such an excuse; and if there were, it is not justifiable. There would not be so many infanticides, nor so many idiotic, insane, deformed, feeble, nervous children, if more attention was paid by city and state authorities to making comfortable and wholesome provision for the poor women of their various communities. Vienna sets an example to the rest of the world in the provision it makes for mothers.

"At one time in Peru, all industry was controlled and managed by the state, the inhabitants being laid out into castes or professions, and the very hours of work regulated by the authority of the Incas."

When government or society provides remunerative labor to those capable of performing it, and sees that such labor is actually paid for, no further obligation exists. They are not under obligation to furnish food, fuel, and clothing to the idle.

What woman in a city is there engaged in non-domestic manual labor for a support that can lay by one dollar, two dollars, or three a week? Many of these women would be glad to hire themselves by the year for their food and clothing. What destiny awaits the children of such women? What time has the mother to form and establish the character of her children, even if she be competent? Will a continual groveling in the dust to obtain enough to keep life in the body, will the wretchedness and misery that arise from such extreme poverty, be likely to produce creditable citizens — moral and intellectual beings?

Compare the number of old women seeking work, or asking charity, in the streets of a city, with men occupied in the same way, and which is the larger? Compare their condition. Which has the more haggard, careworn, overworked appearance?

It would startle persons in better circumstances to learn the large number of worthless and dissipated, or indolent men, who do nothing to support their families. The number of married women, in New York city, that earn a living for themselves and their children, and, in numerous cases, for their husbands also, would amaze any but a New Yorker, or a stranger in the city who has learned the fact from observation. *Nor is the fact*, I am sorry to say, *confined to New York*, that a large number of children among the poor, and men also, are supported by the hard work of the women. O, the crying sin, the shame, *the disgrace, of a strong, healthy man*, not only neglecting to provide for his family, but even *spending the earnings of his wife!* But a day of retribution is coming, and terrible will it be! Many a struggle, that God only knows, is made, even in the middle walks of life, by some wives and mothers, to provide for their families, and keep up an air of respectability.

Women in nearly every country, except France and Great Britain, occupy subordinate positions in business. They should, unless they are properly qualified to occupy higher ones. Every woman should be so fitted to meet life that she can earn a support by her industry.

ADVANTAGE OF AN OCCUPATION.

SOME people say no woman should ever have to labor for a living; that it is a reflection on men. It may be; yet *that many thousands of women*, in the United States and other countries, *do have to labor for a living, is an indisputable fact.* Some women fly to matrimony as a refuge from poverty, or a reverse of fortune; but this is not always a security. If a woman marries advantageously it is well; but it is a misfortune for her to marry because she is unqualified to earn a livelihood.

To me nothing seems so essential for a human being, whether man or woman, as knowing how justly and honorably to provide for the physical wants. Every woman should be able to turn her labor, either mental or manual, into money. If she is poor, she can use her knowledge of business to advantage; if rich, she will have it as a dead capital, that may any day require to be brought into use.

The struggle made in early life to acquire a knowledge of a profession or trade, is a discipline, both physical and mental, the good effects of which never cease. Both mind and body gather strength by the effort. Knowledge is the groundwork for obtaining a livelihood, and the greater an individual's knowledge, *if of a practical kind*, the greater such a one's facilities for obtaining wealth and power.

The majority of women have not been expected to earn a livelihood, and that may be one reason that women have not been more thoroughly and extensively educated. But as the refinements, and corruption, of society increase, a less number of people marry. And as no woman knows but she may be the bread finder for herself, or even a family, does it not behoove her to acquire a knowledge of some means by which to do so?

In all densely settled communities it is not less important that institutions be established for imparting a practical knowledge of trades, arts, and professions, than institutions for giving instruction in book knowledge. Especially is it needed for women. Prejudice and vanity may oppose it, but common sense and humanity require it.

Without some kind of employment we cannot enjoy good health. See those whose circumstances in life are such that they have no occasion to take exercise, or spend any time in the open air.

If women were furnished with a practical knowledge of employments it would promote morality. Brought up to feel and think, as many are, that it is the duty of men to support them, they care not to prepare themselves for doing so; consequently many are tempted to commit errors, for which they are doomed to eternal beggary and degradation. Have not women as great need of force of character as men? Truly their temptations to err, though of a different kind, are quite as great.

But looking at the subject with regard to happiness, is not a woman's happiness as greatly promoted by learning of a useful, every-day kind, as a man's? Is she not more cheerful, when she has active, regular employment? And as to the influence of her learning, may she not make an impress, on a young and plastic mind, as powerful in its results as can be made on the mind of an adult? May not the result of cultivation in her, stamp on the youthful mind a force, a discipline, and ability to think, that may work wonders equal to those of a Newton, a Bacon, or Locke?

By the law of Solon, children were acquitted from maintaining those parents, in old age, who had neglected to instruct them in some profitable trade. It was customary among the Hebrews for all the sons to learn a trade, however highly they might be educated, or however wealthy the family might be.

To give a young lady a profession does not cost more

than is usually expended for the accomplishments; and O, how much more profitable it may prove! The development and discipline of her faculties, aside from the information gained, would be invaluable.

Women in the middle class should enter the industrial world — that world engrossing the time and attention of men of their own class — in order to gain a proper position, a sure foothold. If such a one marries, her husband will value her more highly, and her experience, and training, prove useful in raising her children. Woman's character is strengthened, her mind enlarged, and her feelings rendered more independent, by the activities of a business life.

When the Cossack men are absent from home, their wives take their places, and perform their labor in addition to their own. Almost every Cossack woman has a knowledge of some trade, as tanning leather, dyeing cloth, &c.

In houses of industry, girls should be prepared for some regular pursuit, and should be well qualified for it, if it be but nursing a child. In most cases a few months only are given to learning the millinery or dress-making business. Perhaps a girl's time and attention are confined to one part of the trade; for instance, she may have the shopping for materials to do, and learn nothing of putting them together; or in dress-making she may be taught to sew the goods, but is not taught to fit and baste. This last is not at all unusual.

If men will give their daughters a practical knowledge of business, they need not be so anxious to get them married, that they may relieve themselves of the expense they incur, nor need they dread to die, and leave them alone; for if they have good health, and industry, their own business attainments may secure them a livelihood. The acquisition of any valuable knowledge is never lost. A trade, or a profession, is a capital.

A severe struggle, in poor health, for several years, to obtain a livelihood among strangers, alone and unaided, taught me the bitter experience of a woman thrown upon her own resources without practical training. A thorough

English education enabled me to teach school, and so maintain myself.

Not a great while since, two cases illustrating the advantage of an efficient knowledge of some pursuit came under my observation. A highly respectable foreign family that had been suddenly reduced in fortune came to Pittsburg. The trip was very long and tedious. Crossing the ocean, the son, a most promising young man, died, and his father was so paralyzed by grief, that for a time he was rendered unfit for the common duties of life, much less business transactions. On arriving at Pittsburg, their place of destination, the family, without friends, and with a slender purse, rented a small cottage in the suburbs of the city. The mother, an energetic, warm-hearted lady, and her oldest daughter, determined to make profitable their knowledge of music, which had been extensively and thoroughly pursued, but only as an accomplishment. When I met this lady, her musical talents, affable manners, and agreeable conversation, soon won for her my interest and kind regard. Becoming acquainted with her, and knowing that I was partially aware of the circumstances under which she labored, she gave me an interesting account of herself and family, and at the conclusion remarked, "Blessed be God for having given me the means of now assisting in the honest support of my family. Were it not for my knowledge of music, I see not how, without some miraculous interposition of Providence, my little ones could be fed and clothed."

A few years ago a similar case came to my knowledge. A gentleman, talented, but unsuccessful in business, died shortly after his wife, leaving two daughters unprovided for. Their relatives were far distant, and knew nothing of the circumstances. One of these young ladies married; the other, on ascertaining the state of her father's affairs, learned a trade. She never married, but is now in independent circumstances, always contributing to benevolent objects, and has entirely educated a nephew, who is actively engaged as a minister of the gospel. She was remarkably economical, and self-denying, in the expenditures she made for herself.

WORDS TO THOSE ENGAGED IN PURSUITS.

IT is well to live with such a systematic arrangement of time that every day will bring its plain and positive duties to perform. Let the busy hours of work be interspersed with enough pleasures to impart spirit and brightness. Cultivate a youth and freshness of heart that will remain an evergreen when the winter of old age creeps on. Cultivate easy and natural manners, and the love of simple and delicate beauty.

Truth and integrity are the base-work of every virtue. Purity of thought, feeling, and discourse should be the glory of a woman. Kindness and consideration are desirable traits, particularly in social and domestic life.

Perseverance in business will accomplish much. A man in New York is reported to have made sixty thousand dollars by selling lead pencils at a penny apiece, and safely investing his profits. Another, we have heard, owns two elegant buildings on Broadway, who was once a rag-gatherer; and one an elegant dwelling on Fifth Avenue, who made his money in the capacity of milk-dealer.

With a proper knowledge of an employment, and suitable qualifications, a woman may employ capital successfully in carrying on her business. It will greatly aid her, whether it is inherited, or bequeathed, or earned, or borrowed, for it is a wonderful propeller in business. Besides the profit accruing to the possessor, it furnishes labor and wages to others. Most women engaged in mechanical avocations work for employers — for men with capital sufficient to support a division of labor.

The great elements for success in business are industry and perseverance. Never become discouraged and give up, unless you find yourselves unqualified, by education, habits, and health, for the vocations engaged in. Then seek others more suitable and congenial. Remember, it sometimes requires greater effort to bear small trials patiently than to perform great works. If you can struggle along, in a plain way, for a few years, you will be likely to do better than to borrow, and pay a high interest. But *never trust others to attend to your business*, if you can possibly avoid it. *See to it yourselves;* otherwise you may be drawn into a whirlpool, and swallowed up by hungry creditors.

"My heart's sympathies," says Mary Howitt, "go with the woman who labors for herself. Through all the difficulties, the prejudices, and disadvantages of pushing on her course through life, who yet does it bravely, and in sincerity, — such a woman is a heroine."

The springing footstep and buoyant heart lessen the labors and trials of life. Therefore, lighten each other's burdens. Look upon each other as fellow-travelers. Let no jealousy in regard to your employment exist. It is illiberal. Be perfectly candid and honest in your intercourse with those that have any sincere intention of entering into the same field of labor. If they have the qualifications, and there is an opening in the business, *tell them so*, and, as nearly as you can, the prospect of success. If there is none, do not hesitate to say so — that no false hopes be excited, to meet disappointment, chagrin, and perhaps the loss of limited means on which the individual is wholly dependent. Your attainments and experience should be at the disposal of others, so far as no serious sacrifice to yourselves is required.

If employed by others, your time is not your own in working-hours. Use it honorably. Be punctual at work, and regular in attendance. Be thorough in what you do. So act and live that your employers may appreciate your worth — may be able to confide in you. Be faithful to the interests of your employers, and show that you can appreciate kindness from them. Treat them with respect, and you will be more likely to receive their protection. If not satisfactory to your employer, and you cannot convince him of your usefulness, seek one who will pay you more, and better appreciate your labor. Controversy and struggle with your employer, without associates similarly situated, will sour your temper, and do no good. To exhibit a spirit of dissatisfaction and hatred will only embarrass you. If all your time cannot be profitably occupied in one establishment, endeavor to make up the deficiency in another; and if you cannot find work in one locality seek it in another.

Treat your associates in labor with kindness and sympathy, and you will be likely to receive a return of the same. Let your friendships be virtuous and honorable; let sincerity and mutual confidence characterize the connection; let obliging manners and respectful intercourse be maintained — then will the charms of friendship that poets have sung, and philosophers admired, *be realized;* then will the histories of such as Damon and Pythias, Orestes and Pylades, Horace and Mæcenas, be known among your sex as every-day realities. Life and spirit are infused by the expression of thought and feeling — by sympathy and blending of soul. "Love one another, bear with one another, forgive one another, and help one another on the road to heaven — then will your hearts be filled with peace and joy, and your mouths with praise." So live that you will be missed when you are gone. Endeavor to live well while you do live — leave the results with God. A bright, glowing gem, a little humming-bird, a floating flower, a fire-fly in the night, a rainbow through the storm — *these* are all beautiful, but they bear no comparison with the kind words from a loving heart. Remember this, dear ladies, when you see some fellow-pilgrim, weary and worn.

Be neat in dress, and economical. Board in well-conducted, clean, respectable houses, in a good portion of the city. Be careful about the company you keep. You will be judged of, to some extent, in that way. Try and avoid unfavorable comparison of your own condition with that of others. The early part of your life may be sad and gloomy, poor and obscure, but the latter part may be bright and prosperous. Almost every heart is oppressed with sorrow known but to few, and, in many cases, to none save God. Do not imagine you have more trouble than any one else. Until the secrets of all hearts and lives are made known, you cannot judge correctly, or make a proper estimate and comparison.

Seize every opportunity of learning all you can. You will rarely meet with any one but what can impart some information of which you were ignorant before — particularly in traveling will you find it the case. Of course a proper reserve and decorum are requisite. Sir Walter Scott made it a point to converse with strangers even when traveling in a stage-coach. Never be ashamed to ask for information. Every one can talk on that line of business, at least, in which he or she is engaged. It is said that Hugh Miller gained a portion of his fame by observations and remarks on subjects connected with his work, as a stonemason and quarryman.

Now and then you may reach chasms in the road of life, but let me beseech you to bridge them with faith and hope. When you reach the verge of such a chasm, particularly in pecuniary matters, gaze not into its depths, but gird up your loins, start anew in your race, and trust to Him who ruleth in the heavens. Terrible are such hours of suffering, and, without a living faith, are apt to be followed by a restless, uneasy state of discontent. A feverish anxiety, and unsettled state of mind, will unfit you for concentrated thought and effort.

Let your aims be pure and exalted. Act with prudence and principle, under all circumstances and discouragements. Cultivate those qualities that will make you noble, dignified women, whose influence is for good. Think for yourselves, advance with the age, the progress, the spirit of the times.

Steer your little barques on as smooth water as you can, for storms will rise on the sea of life; that sea will present shoals and quicksands, therefore prepare to sail it securely.

The position that you occupy depends, to some extent, on circumstances, to some extent on yourselves. If you do not uphold and speak favorably of your sex, how can you expect men to do so? If you do not cultivate your minds, how can you expect educated and intelligent men to respect you for anything else than your virtues? You cannot do too much to elevate your sex. Women have not enough respect for each other, and too much for the other sex. That is one reason they do not succeed better. They do not speak a good word for, and sustain each other in what they do; so their faults, as a class, are exaggerated. You rarely hear men slander each other. If there is nothing good to say, they are silent. It gives them force, and inspires confidence. It may be from fear, or a matter of policy, for I will not admit that the mass of men are, in any respect, better than the mass of women. If women would act in the same way, they could labor more effectually, and more for their good as individuals and as a class.

In marriage, woman must become socially raised by her husband, or depress her husband. She cannot elevate him in society. A moral influence, either elevating or depressing, almost invariably takes place on both members of a conjugal union.

All of women's mental and moral powers are seldom, if ever, brought into action. Women need a more thorough cultivation of their faculties, and a more complete preparation for their vocations.

It is not well to direct the thoughts wholly and exclusively to any one subject, lest the mind thereby become shallow, as the body would become spare and thin, if fed entirely on one article of food. But give a dominant influence to some one pursuit, making it the superior and controlling power.

No profession or trade is exempt from some difficulties. But such difficulties can usually be surmounted. What we accomplish by our own exertions is most prized.

By honesty, industry, and enterprise, for a few years, some men and women, in the most common occupations, acquire character, wealth, and influence, and engage in occupations greatly superior to the first. Perseverance, for a few years, in almost any occupation for which there is an opening, will insure success.

If a woman possesses a knowledge of some employment,

as hat-making, straw-braiding, &c., let her, on going to a strange city for employment, if she has no friends or acquaintances in the place, get a city Directory, and look over the names and places of business of those engaged in that craft, and then make application for work, if she has no one to do it for her. And I would add, do not rely too much upon what others promise they will do for you, but *make an effort for yourself.* If possible, take letters of introduction when you go to the city, for there are so many impositions, in a place of much size, that your claims will not be recognized without some tangible proof.

The selfishness of a city is so general and so thorough, that a stranger in it, without fame, money, or friends, may suffer neglect and indifference. A lone woman, under such circumstances, is likely to lose her kindliness, patience, and forbearance; to become suspicious and gloomy, and, in time, callous. On this account, I would advise a working woman to secure employment, if possible, in a village, town, or the country, in preference to a city. She will be more likely to make friends, and secure a permanent home. The poverty, misery, and degradation of thousands of women in our great cities, have arisen partly from the heartlessness and selfishness of the people, and partly from their ignorance of the real condition of those about them.

Let a woman strive to reflect honor on her pursuit, not her pursuit on her. The grade of a profession or trade is not estimated by its usefulness, but more by the class of persons already pursuing the vocation. A trade does not rank as high as a profession, in public opinion, because most tradesmen are uneducated. Study to learn if your undertakings are feasible, before commenced. There must be confidence, and firmness of will, to succeed. Hesitation and indecision will never carry you through. Determination of purpose, in a good cause, will carry one a great distance, and the *cause* too.

NOTE. I would recommend to my readers a little work by W. G. Blaikie, D. D., entitled "Better Days for Working People." For sale by Routledge & Son, New York.

CONDITION OF THE WORKING CLASSES.

BY the working classes we mean those that are engaged in manual labor, a few of whom are well educated, some partially so; but the majority are very limited in book learning, or have none.

The education of the laboring classes is the great work of this age — of this country, as it is in fact the noblest work of every age; for just in proportion as they are elevated, are intelligence, abundance, and virtue rendered more universal; vice, crime, and degradation dissipated, and security and the respect of all rights established.

The majority of working people are dependent on their wages for food, clothing, and shelter. Therefore when wages stop the necessaries of life stop. Most work-people, in the lower walks of life, are so engrossed in their efforts to provide for themselves and families, that they have but little time for social, moral, and mental culture. And in the time they have, their thoughts are so distracted by care, that they have not the composure necessary for real improvement.

In the Protestant church a more systematic organization is needed of its charities and reformatory labors. By it the Roman Catholic church is enabled to accomplish an untold amount of work.

The vices of civilization are too often adopted by the lower classes of work-people, without their virtues and refinement. Liquor and tobacco, in excessive use, are the evils that are working most misery and wretchedness among the laboring classes. Drunkenness is a curse by which some workmen ruin their souls and bodies, keep their families in poverty, and eventually destroy them.

The coarsest men work women as if they were beasts of

burden made for naught else, and have no respect for their opinions. This is degradation in the extreme. Where woman is merely a slave in her domestic, or industrial life, or regarded as an inferior being, there cannot exist men of virtuous and correct principles. When a woman's powers are overtasked, not only must she suffer physically, morally, and mentally, but the bad effects fall on the husband and children. The effect is ruinous to their moral culture. The sad, melancholy, fault-finding disposition produced thereby in the children, is a bane for ever to their happiness. Immoralities in parents are usually followed by physical weakness in the children.

Poverty is nothing to boast of, and when we meet with it, we may know the virtuous, if industrious, and sound in mind, are either suffering from the faults or crimes of others, or their own ill health, or mismanagement. Preventing indigence, (resulting from culpable causes), is best done by giving moral instruction to the young.

The readiness of the working classes to assist each other when hard run for money, is an admirable trait. How many a poor emigrant has been taken in, and kept, and cared for, by some countryman of his own, who had, by hard toil, earned a home in this favored land!

In all ages, and in all nations, some of the producing classes have been ill paid for their labor. The erroneous construction and undue power of money, have made the tens rich, and plunged thousands into poverty. They have sent hundreds to premature graves, starved the widow and the orphan, and given untold wealth to the miser. We cannot alter the evils of the past. We must act for the present and the future.

Active measures are being taken in England for improving the condition of the working classes. In the United States the home comforts of the mass of people are superior to those of any other country. The houses are better built, better lighted, better aired, and better supplied with wholesome water. Yet in all crowded parts of large cities, the impure air of the tall, dark, closely-packed houses, breeds miasma and disease. Clean, airy, well-constructed dwellings, should be provided for the poor, and rented at reasonable rates. Companies could be formed, and shares taken, by capitalists. Landlords should be compelled, by law, to build their tenement houses in such a way as to afford more than one mode of egress in case of fire, and they should be required to furnish a space of ground proportionate to the size of the house they erect, as breathing-room for the inmates. Laboring people much enjoy, and much need, plots of ground attached to their houses as garden spots. Nothing more securely fastens a family to a place, than the possession and cultivation of a garden. The restless and shifting life some work-people lead, is a great barrier to their moral and intellectual advancement. On that account there is not the same temptation to evil among the poor of the country, as among those of towns and cities.

The social organization of work-people is probably of a higher grade in the United States, than in any other country. Our working people are not so oppressed and overtasked, as those of older countries. It is seldom that labor performed by our working classes, is so great as to make a resort to stimulants a temptation. Any man, with good health and habits, can command the necessaries of life. Economy, industry, prudence, and sobriety, will furnish him and his family with a healthy, comfortable home. The anxiety and restlessness induced by a frequent change of dwelling-place, is detrimental to both body and mind. When the day's labors are finished, the repose and quiet of a home are essential to peace of mind.

During the last twenty years the men of the working classes, owing to the great advantages they have had in cities for improvement, by lectures, access to libraries, churches, and so forth, have greatly advanced in intelligence and refinement. Public schools inspire, in the middle and lower classes, a feeling of personal freedom and independence in business matters.

Compare the creature comforts of the working classes of our country with the peasantry of Europe. In Russia, Poland, and Denmark, they never use meat or butter, and in Norway and Sweden rarely enjoy meat. In France seven and a half millions are without meat or wheaten bread. In those countries, except France, Norway, and Sweden, all legislative and executive power is in the hands of the sovereigns and nobles. "According to M. Dupin, two thirds of the population of France, or twenty millions, are deprived of the nourishment of animal food, and live wholly on chestnuts, maize, and potatoes." "In France, the peasant girl dies of labor, the female operative of hunger. The poverty of the male operative would be wealth, abundance, luxury, to the female. In France, among the peasants, a woman is preferred for a wife who has a small appetite, a lithe and slender figure — from an idea that she will eat less."

In some portions of Europe there are but two marked divisions in society, the aristocratic and the working classes. The working classes can never rise. Their wages are so low that they barely furnish them with the necessaries of life. They have no time for self-improvement. In some of those countries, even if possible for working men to acquire wealth and learning, they cannot maintain a creditable position in society. In the United States it is very different. The working classes have every facility for acquiring education, and advancement in business, and social standing.

The health and comfort of the factory operatives of Lowell, a few years ago, excited the admiration, not only of Americans, but Europeans. No class of New England workpeople surpassed, or, perhaps, equaled them, in intelligence, morality, and education.

"The condition of the laboring poor seems the happiest in the progressive state; it is hard in the stationary, and miserable in the declining."

Education and common sense do not always give wisdom in the selection of a husband or wife. There is an incompatibility in the selection of partners among the laboring classes, that accounts for much domestic misery. Some men marry before they are able to support a wife comfortably, and some men, or their wives, spend all they earn. In either case no provision is made for the future, and, as a consequence, want and trouble follow. But it is otherwise when judicious, industrious, kind, prudent people marry.

The family where there is a virtuous, sensible, judicious woman, who is respected, and has the management of affairs, and control of the purse, is known by its comfort and neatness. Money is more likely to be wisely appropriated — less selfishly — more for the general good. Superiority of education in a wife, leads her husband to respect her more highly, consult her, look up to her, and be influenced by her in his affairs. This is one inducement to girls to use their opportunities for acquiring an education. Still greater is the influence when a woman's trade, or profession, aids her in contributing to the wants of the family, as her husband's interests are a guarantee for his affections. Married women, that work to support their children, work as hard to do so as men, and generally more so, for they have not only the labor attending the rearing of them, but the man's part also, that of providing for them.

The misfortune, with many of the poor, is, that they do not know how to work to advantage. The time and labor they expend to gain a bare subsistence, would, in some occupations, if properly applied, yield them a handsome maintenance. The statement would hold good, if the work performed was spent in places where it was most needed. But many of the poor have not the time, opportunity, or money required, to gain this information.

In no other country, as the United States, have the children of the poor such means of acquiring an education, while freedom of thought and speech is conducive to the forming of a correct estimate of matters and things in general. Yet there is much room for improvement in the condition of our working people. The influx of ignorant foreigners opens a work to the philanthropist, and political economist. Some coarse, ignorant foreigners have abused their privileges by their rudeness and insolence. We would recommend education for the darkened and disordered minds of the ignorant portion of the working classes; and clothing, food, and shelter for the bodies of educated, but destitute, working people, the means for acquiring which to be put in their power by legislative measures, if no others offer. The want of innocent amusements for the laboring classes in the United States, is greater than in most European countries. Museums, libraries, and public gronnds, are sadly deficient in many of the towns, and some of the cities. Bath-houses, too, are needed; cleanliness will do something to advance the interests of the poor, and surely, in this land of mighty rivers, there need be no lack of water.

A more even distribution of work and wages is desirable in all parts of the world. It would be well if the callings were supplied more according to the demand. There would not then be a surplus in one occupation, and a deficiency in another. And those occupations most essential to comfort and happiness, would be pursued more efficiently, while those that merely contribute to the artificial enjoyment of a few, would be partially dispensed with. A more just appropriation to women of suitable employments, and fair wages, is also needed. Both sexes will then be more likely to share in the possession of property. There certainly should be remunerative labor enough in the United States to supply all that wish it — both men and women.

In many parts of Europe the men go from province to province, and even to other kingdoms, seeking employment. Their families are left alone for months at a time. The low cunning, and sensual existence, that mark the state of the costermongers in London, show plainly the degradation that must follow to the poor from a want of employment, or inadequate compensation. The poor in Europe need rest for both soul and body. The mind is so constituted that it requires occasional refreshment and repose. The dull eye of the overtasked tells of too constant labor. The heavy, stupid face indicates animal preponderance, and spiritual starvation. Women and youths in England have got to frequenting ale-houses, and wasting their money and evenings in low orgies. There, drunkenness, smoking, and swearing, are not uncommon among the women that work in factories.

What a wretched life some workwomen must lead with their scanty wages, their insufficiency for comfortable living and clothing, and the utter inability to save from them anything for sickness and old age! The small, low-roofed rooms, and the numbers that sleep in them, would astonish those that have never seen them, or heard of them from a reliable source. Nor do we refer merely to those of European countries. Here is a description of some in New York, as given by a contributor to a newspaper of that city, in a series of articles on the condition of the workwomen there: "These women generally keep house — that is, they rent a single room, or perhaps two small rooms in the upper story of some poor, ill-constructed, unventilated house, in a filthy street, constantly kept so by the absence of back yards, and the neglect of the street inspectors — where a sickly and deadly miasm pervades the atmosphere, and in summer renders it totally unfit to be inhabited by human beings, depositing the seeds of debility, and disease, with every inspiration. In these rooms all the processes of cooking, eating, sleeping, washing, working, and living, are indiscriminately performed. For these rooms the tenant never pays less than from three dollars to four dollars and a half per month; and pay they must, and do. Some of the very worst single garrets, destitute of closet, or convenience of any kind, and perhaps lighted up by a hole cut in the roof, rent as high as two dollars a month. Of course every cent of the inmates' earnings is exhausted every week, and in many cases is not sufficient to buy any other food than a scanty supply of potatoes, and Indian meal, and molasses for the family. When winter comes, therefore, they are destitute not only of the means of adding comfortable clothing to their wretched wardrobes, but of procuring an ounce of fuel. Their work, too, at this season, is frequently cut off, and they are left no resource but the almshouse, or a pauper ticket for bread and coal. Here, too, they are often balked. The almshouse is full and overrunning." Since this was written, a more systematic arrangement has been made in New York city for distributing charity to foreign paupers by "The Society for improving the Condition of the Poor;" but the half-paid, hard-working laborer is not assisted or guided into more profitable avenues of employment by the society, and it totally *ignores educated, destitute American women.*

As the laboring classes are educated, and think for themselves what is their due, labor will be better rewarded. Some will rise to influence and power, and, remembering the state from which they sprang, will turn with sympathizing heart to the burdened wayfarers, and bring about the establishment of such laws as will ameliorate the condition of the working classes, and require for them more generous remuneration for their labor.

In this country nature has furnished men with sufficient capital for earning a subsistence, that are possessed of reason, health, and a knowledge of some employment. It is true there may be hard work to do; but that should be expected. If such people abstain from the use of liquor and cards, they will not be likely to suffer from a want of the necessaries of life; at any rate, they will be better able to procure them. In squandering his earnings for drink, a man not merely loses his money, but his ability to earn more, by the loss of health and strength. As intemperance continues to decrease among the higher classes, it will, we trust, gradually disappear among the laboring classes. Then men will have a desire to make their homes comfortable, and supply their families with what they need.

Many persons by being furnished with assistance or employment, for a short time, may gain ground they have lost, and march with a heart as bold, and a step as active, as the most fortunate. The difference in the condition and institutions of our people, the freedom of their laws, their roaming natures, the vast extent of our unimproved country, and its great resources, the construction of public works, and other numberless means for earning a subsistence, render us, to a greater extent, free from the indigence and pauperism that burden older countries.

The quantity of labor in any particular branch is regulated by the demand. If there is a surplus of hands in any employment, so that the wages are greatly reduced, or some are thrown out of employment, they should remove to where their species of labor is wanted, or seek some other kind of employment. Self-interest prompts to such a step. This is easily done in the United States. In England the poor laws, and laws of settlement, interfere with this freedom. Many of the Irish that settle in this country are shiftless. If they used prudence and foresight in their expenditures, they might less frequently be penniless. Among many of the lower classes of foreigners, that flock to our shores, there exist poverty, sickness, and affliction. The vast influx of those who neither know nor care anything about our institutions, but have the privileges of freemen and native born, have done much to bring about the lamentable war lately ended. The heavy taxation, produced by it, will probably curtail the privileges the children of these people would have had for acquiring an education. It has, by the disordered state of affairs in the South, done away with schools there nearly altogether. Of the vast body of uneducated female emigrants that arrive in this country, none are so fortunate as those who secure places as domestics in respectable and worthy families. They are sure of protection, and of as fair wages as they could obtain at anything else.

With a portion of the female working class there exists a bitterness of feeling in regard to their lot, an assumed independence of, and indifference to, those more favored; a proud sensitiveness, and often an imaginary sense of depression and injustice. There may be a foundation for the first of these feelings, and cause for the last, but to what extent it is impossible to estimate. So different are people, so various the circumstances that influence them, that such data are out of the question.

The great failure in trying to ameliorate the condition of the working classes, particularly of women, has been in applying a remedy to the disease without removing the cause. The worm-eaten tree has been bound up, instead of removing its defective parts. Charity has been substituted for justice, alms for employment. Poverty and misery have been relieved, but no pains taken to prevent their repetition.

In France, women's wages are much less than in this country; yet it requires less to live there. There one thousand francs, (one hundred and ninety dollars), per annum, are considered a good salary, while here most women receive at least twenty-five hundred, (four hundred and seventy-five dollars). There the aspirations of workwomen are more humble. They do not expect to live in the same style that working women require in this country. They have not the same fondness for personal adornment. We think the dress of the working classes everywhere should be plain and simple, becoming their labor and condition.

"The difference of the food of a rich man, and his poor neighbor, consists usually in the quality, not in the quantity. But the difference between their clothing, lodging, and furniture, is as great in quantity, as it is in quality."

The early employment of girls in factories has been objected to on the ground that it renders them unfit, when they are grown and have families, to perform rightly their duties as wives and mothers. It induces a want of thriftiness, and does not give them time to learn the art of cutting out garments, and making them. Neither is the still more indispensable art of cooking learned. And we know well a very important item, in rendering life agreeable to the working classes, is a knowledge of cooking, and sewing, and economical housekeeping. Some complain that if girls are employed in factories as they grow up, habits of cleanliness, order, and neatness are neglected, or never formed. It is thought to be one of the chief causes of crime and poverty among the poor of England. The health and education of children in such families are neglected, and home comforts are unknown. We think these objections, however plausible they may seem, do not fully exist. If women have received a proper home training, and have common sense, they will, in receiving good wages, lay aside what they can spare for sickness, and old age. This was exemplified in the factory operatives at Lowell, a few years back.

The depression in the social, moral, and political scale of

the working classes in the United States, we can safely say, is much less than in any other country. The work-people of the United States are increasing in intelligence, particularly the foreign population. Yet the wretched poverty, and terrible vice, of our large cities is an omen of fearful import, and may prove a weapon of awful destruction. Should it equal that of monarchical countries, our military must be increased, and taxes levied for its support.

Channing says, " The elevation of man consists in the elevation of soul, first through force of thought excited for the acquisition of truth; secondly, force of pure and generous feeling; thirdly, through force of moral purpose. The only elevation of a human being consists in the exercise, growth, energy, of the higher principles and powers of his soul." Again he says, " So far is manual labor from meriting contempt or slight, that it will probably be found, when united with true means of spiritual culture, to foster a sound judgment, a keener observation, a more creative imagination, and a purer taste, than any other vocation."

Women belonging to the working classes are more directly interested in public affairs than women of a higher station. On the prosperity of business depends their support. The levying of a tax, the introduction of a tariff bill, the blockading of ports, the suspension of banks, the closing of manufactories, the rates of wages, the number of working hours, are all matters in which they are more or less immediately involved. The members of families in the working classes are thrown more intimately together, and converse more freely than those in the higher circles of life.

The anxiety and responsibility attending business matters are felt by men alone in the middle classes; in the working classes they are shared by the women. More sympathy and assistance are given by the working classes to each other, than by those less dependent. The members of well-bred families in the working classes are more firmly united, more closely attached, than those of any other. They are more willing to make sacrifices, and more ambitious in aiding each other to rise in the world.

DRESS OF WORK-PEOPLE.

I DO not know of any reform more requisite for comfort, and the promotion of health, among the workwomen of America, than a style of dress different from that now worn. A more sensible plan might be adopted. The skirts should be shorter, and the weight made to fall more on the shoulders, and less on the hips. They should be sufficiently warm, but of light materials. The short dresses of the Germans are much more reasonable. They are not only more comfortable, but better adapted to their vocations. They do not impede the progress. The movement of the walker is lighter and more free. Neither do they collect the mud and snow, as longer ones do. Women should not wear hoops in their work-rooms, as they check the progress of all whom they meet, in narrow passes, and between the machinery.

In the large bookbindery of M. Maitre, near Dijon, in France, the women wear a uniform, supplied by the proprietor, that I think must be a useful and sensible one. It is loose and graceful, somewhat like the Turkish costume, but the skirt is united with the trousers. The Turkish costume is best for women at most kinds of work, whether agricultural, manufacturing, or of a domestic nature. It is safer and more convenient. The long skirts that have been worn have rendered many a woman an invalid for life.

I have heard some people object to the fondness of dress evinced by the workwomen of the United States, but never the same objection urged against the workmen. For my part, I think nearly as much effort to dress well is made by the male, as the female, part of the working population. If a female domestic betrays a weakness for fine clothes, a workman will be afraid to select her for a wife, and a man of higher station will not be likely to make her his wife, let him say what he will. "Drink, Dress, Debt, are three D's which the devil is very fond of," says the author of letters addressed to working women in the "People's Magazine."

In older countries, work-people do not aspire to live in the same style as those superior in wealth and rank. But the democratic nature of our government is calculated to foster a spirit of pride, and self-importance, more among the lowly and ignorant, than any other class of people.

A lady remarked to me that she thought working women are more excusable for trying to dress well than idle ones, who do nothing — that it is more excusable in uncultivated girls than in the highly educated, who should be able to rise above a feeling of the kind. The motive is to please those of the opposite sex, that usually prompts a woman to adorn herself with rich, rare, or handsome attire. Frequently, the moving cause is a spirit of rivalry with others of her own sex. A too great fondness for dress, we know, is the bane of many working girls. They spend all for dress — so have nothing when out of employment. It is undoubtedly, in some cases, the cause of prostitution. Simplicity of dress and manners bespeaks the well-trained mind. Women of high birth in England, when at their homes in the country, wear short dresses, and in winter, warm stockings and double-soled shoes.

If women would wear a plainer style of dress to church than most of them do, it would be a great blessing to the working class of women, who would be more willing to attend church, as they would not feel so acutely the marked difference in the quality of their apparel.

CHILDREN OF THE WORKING CLASSES.

CHILDREN in good health are naturally buoyant. They love to indulge in active, joyous freedom. Their little limbs require bodily exercise. And fresh air is wanted to harden their bones, to render their muscles firm, and nerves strong.

No doubt most of our readers know that institutions exist in France and England, and one, or more, in this country, where the infants of working women are, gratuitously, or for a small sum, kept and provided for during the day.

Most parents engaged in hard labor for the support of their children are apt to neglect that moral training so essential to their welfare, and the good of society. They are so much engrossed in providing for the animal wants of their children that they neglect the necessities of their higher natures.

Some parents are ignorant and bigoted, and in that way neglect the improvement of their children. Some are trifling, and should have their children removed from under their influence. A number are so anxious to see their children rise in the world, and be exempt to some extent from the physical labor they have performed, that they raise them with false views of life and its aims. The boy, instead of being a mechanic, would prefer to be a lily-hand clerk, or a third-rate professional man. The daughter, instead of assisting in household duties, will spend all her time reading novels, practicing her music, shopping, or flying from one to another of her butterfly acquaintances.

It should be early impressed upon the minds of children that facts should be stored in the mind as if they were to be used. If the brain is made a storehouse, and filled with important facts, of what value are they unless wisely and practically used?

Encourage in your children any indication of talent. It is a fact that almost every one who has arrived at any distinction in life has been encouraged in childhood in the prosecution of what was attempted. John Gibson, the sculptor, attributes his success to the encouragement given by his parents for his fondness for drawing when a child. Benjamin West traced his success to the same cause.

An American writes us, "French women are what we call very smart. Very few of them, unless they are quite rich, set themselves up as great women, and make their husbands work for them, but expect to do at least half the work in the restaurant, store, shop, &c. This is the fashion, and no person thinks hard of it. What becomes of the children I do not know. I suppose they are smart enough to take care of themselves."

To be taught to gain a livelihood is a matter of vital importance, both morally and physically, with the children of the poor. All parents should be required to send their children to school for a given time, as in most countries of Europe, and they should also be required to give them a knowledge of an honest vocation. The government should demand it. Parents should be required to support them comfortably while attending school, or if not fully able to do so, the expenses should be made up from the public treasury.

Girls are not brought up as they should be, with a view to making their information lucrative. Even the daughters of hard-working parents, are not trained with the object in view, of making what they learn, a matter of dollars and cents.

A proper home-training is much needed in all ranks of life. People in all classes and conditions of society should, above all things, give their children industrious habits. It is my opinion that parents who desire their children to learn a trade should place their sons and daughters at school about the same age, and keep them there until they are sixteen or seventeen years old, or even longer, if they can afford it.

They should, if intelligent people, select the studies of their children, having them pursue those most likely to be of *greatest practical use.* By the time they have arrived at the age mentioned they can have become thoroughly grounded in the English branches, conversant with French, or German, and have learned to either draw, sing, play, or dance enough to enjoy with zest their leisure moments.

Parents should be careful about the kind of people with whom they place their children to learn trades. It would probably be well to have both sons and daughters commence learning a trade about the same age, and, if possible, place them where they may enjoy each other's society. If the trade learned by the daughter is one requiring skill and practice, do not hesitate, if it is her wish, to give her an apprenticeship of the same length as your son. Then, if your resources will admit of it, let her live at home, assisting her mother in the house duties, or carrying on her trade, or instructing her young brothers and sisters. But if you furnish your son with capital to do business, do the same for your daughter. Let her have advantages equal, in every respect, with your son.

Parents that intend to fit their children for professions should furnish them with every advantage possible. It is difficult to say at what age they should finish a classical and professional course, the abilities of individuals vary so greatly. But if they are not through until they are twenty-five years old, they may effect more, if they live until fifty years of age, — that is, during the remaining twenty-five years of their lives, — than people of ordinary attainments who live to one hundred. The concentration of thought, the maturity of judgment, the logical force acquired, will give them the ability to accomplish much in a short time, and their influence will be of a kind to make its impress.

We frequently hear the complaint that American youth are not rightly trained — not disciplined. Intelligence and virtue are more necessary than anything else for the existence of a self-governing people, as in the republic of the United States.

One of the saddest features in the history of the majority of working girls is, that they have no one to improve their morals and manners, to form good habits, and cultivate a pure taste and conversation — in short, no one to set them a good example, and exert a good influence. Particularly is it so with girls from the country, separated from their families. All that they can earn is spent for shelter, clothing, and food. They have nothing to spend for books, recreation, or in sickness, and many are unable to purchase comfortable clothing. Their health is ruined by want of sufficient rest and out-door exercise; their moral nature degraded, embittered, and brutalized, and their minds stunted and darkened. The want of an education, and of a good home influence, tends to destroy their self-respect and ambition.

We think that few girls or women that have worked for a living expect to lead an idle life if they marry. We cannot think them so silly. Their responsibilities and obligations are increased by the act, and they should summon every energy for their enlarged field of duty and service.

It is estimated that nine out of every ten women that marry are the wives of poor men.

Neither marriage nor maternity do, with the French women, interfere with their competition in business with men.

We have never been able satisfactorily to solve the problem why parents should more object to their daughters acquiring and prosecuting a pursuit than their sons. It is most likely to be so with ignorant, conceited, or purse-proud parents. The opposition that some daughters encounter, when they urge the matter, is a terrible trial to the temper. Parents may fear it will reflect on them as improvident. We can see no reasonable objection, particularly if the parents are not rich, and the girls have not a pleasant home, where they are welcome. But educated as girls are, few of them wish to know any other than domestic labor. Parents do not object when their daughters marry and go away. In this case they know there can be no reflection. Some fathers may be equally gratified to be relieved of the expense in the one case as the other, though delicacy may prohibit the expression of their feelings on the subject. If a girl has a profession or trade, she can marry or live single; if she has none, she is expected to marry, unless she has a reliable income, or parents to support her.

Labor being remunerative in this country, and easily obtained, has prevented parents from placing their children at work-places at a very early age. Consequently the number of children in factories, in proportion to the number of adults, is very much smaller than in Great Britain.

"In 1837 a law was passed in Massachusetts which requires that no person, under fifteen years of age, shall be suffered to work more than nine months, in any year, in a factory, the remaining three to be passed at school."

In Paris there are several schools of design where young women are instructed in the arts and manual professions. There are thirty workshops containing sixteen hundred young girls, to whom work is furnished. There are several schools for adults in Paris, where gratuitous instruction is given every evening from eight to ten o'clock.

"A Mr. Ackloyd, a manufacturer of Dublin, has between three thousand and four thousand persons in his employment. He had one thousand children in schools in connection with his works; those from eight to thirteen years of age only worked half time, and attended the schools, thus receiving industrial and scholastic teaching. The change from school to work was very much liked by the children. Evening classes were established for the young women he employed. Needlework was taught, cooking classes established, and music was not forgotten."

NATURAL TO BE EMPLOYED.

WE see the desire exhibited, in every order of animal creation, to be in motion, in their waking hours. It is the most natural state of existence. Activity, either of mind or body, is the best element of happiness. The listless ennui of those that have nothing to do — nothing to interest — is opposed to a sound mind and healthy body. Every human being has an appointed mission — a destiny to fulfill. A person, usefully and honorably occupied, has not time to heed the siren voice of temptation. The only reliable pleasure is in being employed. Particularly is it so with the nervous, restless organization of Americans. Their natures crave active employment, as a hungry man craves food.

Says a practical English writer, "I believe that more than one half the women who go into the Catholic church join her because she gives work to her children. Happier far is a Sister of Charity, or Mercy, than a young lady at home, without work or a lover. We do not mean to say work will take the place of love in life; that is impossible. Does it with men? But we ardently desire that women should not make *love their profession*. Love is not the end of life. It is nothing to be sought for; it should come. If we work, love may meet us in life; if not, we have something still beyond all price. If women were in active life, mixing much with men, the common attraction of sex merely would not be so much felt, but rather the attractions of natures specially adapted to each other."

Did no sin exist in the world, neither man nor woman could be doomed to the performance of uncongenial labor; indeed it might be that none would be necessary. As it is, most people are so constituted, and circumstances are such, that they must labor. But labor is rendered much lighter if we love it. If one's tastes, temperament, and inclinations are satisfied, employment becomes more a pleasant pastime than a performance of duty.

Industry is a virtue, and without it, the other virtues are not likely to flourish. Some think people are by nature inclined to be indolent and slothful. Those that would oppose the doctrine refer to the activity of children. They never, in a state of health, prefer inactivity. What greater punishment to a child, than have to sit with folded hands and motionless feet?

Col. Higginson says, "A pupil in a school of design once told me, that, in her opinion, the majority of the scholars sought the occupation, not as a means of support, nor to gratify an artistic taste, but solely for the sake of interesting employment."

Lieber, in his "Political Ethics," says very truly, "When any faculty for energy and activity has been given, there exists likewise an intense desire to exercise, practice, apply it. It is its very nature, and without it the world would be at a stand. Whatever we may undertake originally by way of interest, the love of action, the desire to leave some memorial of one's self, to produce and effect something, soon supersedes it. The nobler the mind, the more endowed the soul, the more intense is also the thirst, the more pressing the anxiety to act, to produce, to exert our powers — to imprint our minds on the world without."

How necessary, then, that a right direction be given to the natural propensities of our nature — that they be happily and usefully exercised. Heaven itself, we believe, is a place of activity. Were it not, what would become of the restless spirits of this world that find their chief enjoyment in activity? We cannot believe the first, great, and leading principle of our nature will be eradicated, but rather receive a wider scope for action.

WORK HONORABLE.

OUR Father in heaven works. He creates worlds, and supports, and governs, and directs them. His management and care extend to the minutest of his creatures. Christ worked. (John xvii. 4; ix. 14; xiii. 14; 1 John iii. 8.) All the animal kingdom labors. Why should man and woman, the most highly favored of all, be exempt?

Employment is sowing seed that will spring up, and bring forth fruit. Idleness is casting those seed in the ground, and letting them decay. Contempt should not be cast on any honest employment. Christ was a carpenter, Paul a tent-maker. Even Adam worked in the garden of Eden. (Gen. ii. 15.) The world is a workhouse, and all in it, of sufficient health and strength, are expected by the owner to labor. Consequently, no individual, possessed of his faculties, is exempt.

"There is a voice in the sun, who, day by day, cometh forth as a bridegroom from his chamber, and rejoiceth as a strong man to run a race, forbidding to be idle. There is a voice in the stars as they revolve in their everlasting march, forbidding to be idle. The billows of the sea, in their ceaseless rise and fall, have lifted up their yesty heads to preach against idleness. From the high angels of heaven, who rest not day or night, to the tiny insect whose world is a leaf or a water-drop, everything declares against the evils of idleness."

Without labor there could be none of the comforts or refinements of life; without the labor of the working classes the wealth of the rich would not save even them from personal exertion. "In proportion as man is relieved from the necessity of labor, he is debased in the scale of existence."

Society is like a piece of machinery. If the shortest lever, or the smallest wheel in complicated machinery, is defective, it will affect the operation of the whole. So, if some members of society are idle, or vicious, they will, by their influence and example, affect those connected with them. Each individual member must perform his or her part to render the movement of the whole harmonious.

Some people hold the opinion that to labor is not honorable or dignified. It is one cause of so many young people wasting their time, money, and energies. They are not aware that *to be, and do something, is far more creditable.*

Nothing is a better test of an individual's abilities than poverty. It leads him to try what he can do, and he is likely to persevere until he finds he is capable of accomplishing something. Some may say that toiling for material wants will diminish the beauty and strength of our spiritual nature. The fine gold may lose its lustre, but it will ever be gold, and when tried, will not be found wanting. "A person diligent in business shall stand before kings, not before mean men."

REFORM.

ONLY those who have undertaken any great social, moral, or civil reform can be convinced of the time and effort required to bring it about. Reforms must be wrought gradually. They cannot be accomplished by force. Those that would engage in a reform should be convinced of its feasibility; and they must have an *earnest*, *sincere* belief in the advantage gained by such a reform. They must convince their hearers of this advantage by a clear, logical course of reasoning; then enlist their energies and zeal by an earnest appeal for their assistance.

A great influence may be exerted over brothers, husbands, fathers, and sons, by the gentler sex, in advancing reforms. They may do much in moulding the tone of thought and feeling. They may bring their influence to bear in preparing the young for viewing correctly, and investigating, various reforms, and thereby enlisting them, as they become older, in advancing and carrying forward remedies for evils that are too deeply rooted, far extended, or of a nature not fitted for woman's efforts.

One of the errors of the present age lies in the neglect of means to *prevent* evil. They have been overlooked in the effort to establish remedial measures.

There ought to be voluntary orders of nurses, of work-house teachers, asylum attendants, clothes distributors, &c. Individual members of these societies may have a tact or fondness for some special kind of work. Some may have money, some leisure, some opportunities; so that a concerted body may accomplish far more than the same individuals working separately. These women could accomplish much good by visiting the female department of workhouses and prisons, and conversing with the inmates, reading the Bible to them, and praying with them. By their sympathy and kindness they may be the means of leading many an unfortunate wanderer into the paths of truth, honor, and virtue.

No individual of time and means need be unoccupied in benevolent works. There is labor for all. Let not the charitable fear the diseases to be found among some of the squalid poor. It is a rare thing that a disease is contracted by the usual ministrations of kindness to the destitute sick. Alas, alas! how sad a thing for women, that are loved and provided for, to look with contempt upon the poor and oppressed of their own sex! What a stony, selfish heart it betrays! Many of the poor feel as if they were intruders on this bright, and beautiful earth; many would gladly lay down their lives if they could, when suffering from hunger, and shivering half clad over their smouldering coals. And yet they are as good, or better, than thousands enjoying all the luxuries of life.

Every effort at reform should be carried on in a spirit of charity and moderation so far as expedient. It is probably more difficult to introduce a mental reform in society than a moral reform; but with an individual a permanent moral reform is perhaps as difficult to accomplish as to overcome a prejudice, or remove an erroneous opinion.

The great object in all conditions of life should be to subdue the animal propensities by cultivating the higher powers of the mind, and the better qualities of the heart. Some people hold the opinion that efforts at reform should first be internal. We beg leave to differ. First make the body comfortable, then elevate the soul; or, if possible, accomplish both at the same time. But pray, tell me, ye who would commence with the inner exaltation, and leave the other neglected, in what time you would advise the poor seamstress, worn and wearied, who has toiled from break of day till past midnight, and drops exhausted on her straw pallet — *at what time* you would advise her to read, and think, and improve herself. Of the sixteen hours out of the twenty-four engaged in life-consuming labor, what can be spared for mental and moral culture? To none is poverty so terrible as to educated and refined women. In their unceasing struggle with the world, to obtain the necessaries of life, they have no time for recreation.

One great trouble in matters pertaining to women is, they are not true to each other. Men sustain each other; women do not. It is a radical defect, arising either from their constitution, education, or circumstances. Many oppress and undermine each other. Perhaps one, with a husband, will go around and get work for a mere trifle, that she may have a little pocket money. In that way she cuts down the wages of those that work for bread. A girl, with parents able and willing to support her, will apply for work, and offer to do it for something less than it is being done, that she may have extra laces and ribbons.

Educated and cultivated women are a part of almost every community, and their thoughts and efforts are needed to bring about many reforms. Keeping house and taking care of children will not fully satisfy the nature of any educated woman.

To speak, write, or act for the good of our sex is to do so for the good of the race; it is calling for a heartier and fuller humanity than exists.

Let women go into all the occupations of men they are capable of carrying on, and then demand fair prices. The influence they gain thereby will enable them to acquire political power. This will do away with their social and political inferiority. Undoubtedly much prejudice has been done away, and much good accomplished, by Woman's Rights' Conventions. Attention has thereby been called to social wrongs, civil disabilities, and unjust laws. Men have been talked of as human beings, not as gods. Injustice was attributed to thoughtlessness and ignorance in some, and to the cruel, selfish, unjust natures of others. While women's duties were kept in view, men's were not ignored. The views of many men respecting women's duties and proprieties were critically, and often sarcastically, treated. The agitation of the subject undoubtedly did good. Numberless domestic, social, educational, and civil errors were mentioned, that civilization, philanthropy, and justice had not eradicated. Many difficulties that stood high in the way of reform were enumerated, and a few plans offered to better the present condition of affairs. Claims were laid to all the rights that belong to a human being, and that men claim for themselves. The most important demand was the suffrage of women. The members of these conventions met to educe opinions, call out facts, discuss plans, and create power. They exhibited talent and intelligence, and have succeeded in awakening thought and drawing attention to existing evils. But the reformers are not sufficiently *practical*. They show how matters stand, but do not suggest, as fully as they might, how to remedy them.

As a people, they are much influenced by their prejudices. A desire for notoriety is the mainspring of action with some of the leaders. They make an effort for the promotion of their own individual interests, regardless of the general welfare of the sex. In order to receive more *éclat* themselves, they keep the public ignorant of those that have been quite as diligent, and more self-sacrificing, in the same cause, and have appropriated the result of their labors as the fruits of their own. But some of the members are undoubtedly honorable and conscientious women.

In woman's work and wages the times are a century or more behind the improvements made in science and art. Society is tardy, dragging, in the matter. The present state of affairs is a disgrace to the civilized world. America, proud and strong, goes forth in the freshness of a young and prosperous nation; but a cancer is consuming her life. Well may she blush for the disgrace that rests on her otherwise fair escutcheon, in the fact that hundreds, yes, thousands, of her women, and many of them educated women, are prostitutes this day from the want of remunerative labor.

Woman must have the right to accumulate and hold

property, and public opinion must accord her, without reflection, the right to enter any respectable employment, before she can occupy her true position.

Men who are in occupations suitable for women should be taxed fifty per cent. of their profits, to support poor women whom they have thus selfishly elbowed out of places where they might earn a living, and who must subsist on alms, or starve.

One of the most dreadful features in war has ceased. Women are no longer made slaves, and subjected to dishonor, if their country is conquered, or their husbands, fathers, and brothers taken prisoners.

We have seen it suggested that much good might be done, as opportunities offer, by clergymen and physicians, for kind and worthy employers, by inspiring the confidence of their work-people in them, thereby carrying out the suggestion made by Bacon, that a friend may say for another what he would not like to say for himself.

Since 1850 the laws respecting woman have been changed in a large number of states. In several of the states women can now transact business in their own names. We have more than once seen the announcement of gentlemen taking their daughters into partnership in the mercantile business. There is a woollen manufactory carried on in Worcester County, Mass., by some ladies and gentlemen, each owning his and her portion of the stock, and drawing his and her individual proportion of the profits. The ladies are sisters of two of the gentlemen partners. The citizens of Erving, Mass., elected, not long ago, a woman as a member of the school committee. In some places women have the privilege of voting for school commissioners, or trustees; but they have not often used the privilege. The right to vote on church matters is permitted women in some churches. At a railroad meeting in Pennsylvania, a lady, who owned stock, cast her vote, and the president expressed himself much gratified.

There are some people who sneer at an attempt to make any reformatory change in domestic, social, or civil life.

They are generally those who are very fond of their ease and self-indulgence, and fear they may be called upon to make some exertion or sacrifice.

Woman is expected to be a moral reformer. It is by moral influence that the greatest amount of good can be accomplished; and this can be most effectually exerted on the rising generation by woman. Women must be united in their efforts to overcome opinions and customs prejudicial to their welfare. If they work persistently, but gradually, they will meet with but little opposition from reasonable men.

Let not any good cause fail and languish for want of right management and due support. Those that advance its interests will ever have a place in the hearts of others that can appreciate what is noble, and pure, and elevating. Read, talk, lecture, and write upon every good subject you are interested in. Consider that every rational person knows something, and, perhaps, you will not make a statement, upon general subjects, that has not entered the mind, at some time, of one or more of your hearers. The laws pertaining to women, and their work and wages, offer a wide field for thought and effort. Many ideas on these subjects that you advance may be entirely new to those you meet with. Express your ideas slowly and carefully, that they may be taken in fully by your hearers. Judgment is required in your zeal for doing good. Without it the very cause may fail that you wish to prosper. Courage and judgment can conquer evils otherwise insurmountable. Duty calls to activity. Obey the mandate, and go forward, trusting in God, the great and everlasting God.

WOMEN SHOULD BE USEFUL AS WELL AS ORNAMENTAL.

THE ideas of beauty and utility are closely associated in the minds of Americans. Providence designed that women should render themselves useful. We draw the inference from the fact that all the rest of creation was designed for some special purpose.

Much stress is laid upon genius. Men and women of genius are rare. Seldom does the wild, erratic course of genius avail much of itself. It usually generates the materials for more methodical minds to work upon. They must be collected together, cut, smoothed, and formed into a fabric. Brilliancy of mind is not required to build the structure. An ability to systematize and render substantial is more wanted. Some women are peculiarly fitted for this work. They can so mould and finish the materials collected as to bring them into beautiful and graceful form. The strength, vigor, and power of endurance required to prosecute literary pursuits are possessed by few women. In some cases their intellects far exceed their bodily powers, and they fret and wear themselves away, from inability to carry out their plans and wishes. With the failure of health is the loss of that elasticity and freshness of mind so necessary for good writing. A few acquire excellence who have not that kind of physical strength required for manual labor. Few women, until within the last twenty years, have made literature a profession. With most it was, and is, a pastime.

Women that labor hard physically, and are much exposed to the changes of the weather, lose some of the fineness and delicacy that Nature originally gave them ; yet, if they possess strong constitutions, and do not labor in excess, they have an equivalent in better health.

ACHIEVEMENTS UNDER DIFFICULTIES.

THE more we know of any object or phenomena in nature, any chemical or mechanical process, the liberal arts, any scientific, or literary pursuit, in short, the more we know of any subject, the better we like it.

What we obtain by our own exertions ennobles us, what we receive as a gift, or by inheritance, tends to enervate. Necessity sharpens the faculties of a person not naturally obtuse.

The great body of women seem to be in a chrysalis state. They do not feel satisfied longer to be mere "hewers of wood, and drawers of water." Yet they seem to lack either talent, industry, opportunity, or moral courage, to fit themselves for a desirable and definite calling.

Many women have been without sufficient general intelligence to mark out for themselves any distinct plan, and some have been without the means, or self-reliance, to carry out such a plan. Yet the aspirations of women are pointing to a higher position. This is a favorable indication. If women can only be impressed with their want of fitness for occupying more honorable and lucrative positions, they will make the effort to acquire the requisite fitness. A few, to their honor, be it said, have already done so.

As a general thing, women place too low an estimate on their work, while the reverse is true of men. It probably arises from the unjust compensation hitherto rendered woman.

M. Maistre says, "Women, who want to distinguish themselves, only make themselves enemies of both sexes; of man, because he don't want woman to be his equal — of woman, because she does not want to be surpassed by a woman, &c." If woman has so much to contend with in gaining distinction, she deserves the more credit when successful.

FEMALE INVENTORS.

"MAN, having excluded woman from all opportunity of mechanical education, turns and reproaches her with having invented nothing. But one remarkable fact is overlooked. Society limits woman's sphere to the needle, the scissors, the spindle, the distaff, and the basket; and tradition reports that *she herself invented all.* If she has invented her tools as fast as she has found opportunity to use them, can more be asked?"

The "Newark Advertiser" mentions a woman near Trenton that is a skillful mechanic. She has made a carriage, and can make a violin, or a gun. She is only twenty-five years old. The mechanical genius of women has never been exercised to any extent. It may lie dormant in woman, but when it is awakened and cultivated, though the present generation of women may not accomplish anything, the next will.

The imagination and taste of women are superior to those of men. Women display ingenuity in designs for dress goods, wall paper, and such articles; why may they not in the mechanical department, if called to exercise their talents in that way? Centuries have rolled by, and woman has never been engaged in anything of the kind. Is it to be expected that she could, *at once*, bring in play as great inventive talent as man, whose ancestors, for centuries back, have been so occupied? No; such rapid development would be marvelous, if not miraculous.

So much has been done for popular education in our country — the education of the masses — that we may confidently look forward to many discoveries and inventions having their origin among us, and when encouragement is given to the ingenuity, and enterprise, of woman, the number, we hope, will greatly increase.

We will quote at length an article on the subject of female inventors, by Miss Mary L. Booth. "When woman's power to work is called in question, men almost always remark, that she has shown no *inventive* genius whatever. Should a proper history of the arts ever be written, this will be found to be an entire mistake. Patentees are not always inventors; and many of these, after hopeless labor carried on for years, have owed a final success to some woman's power of adaptation. We need not, however, take refuge in general statement, nor in the traditional fact that she invented spindle, distaff, needle, and scissors. Any newborn barbarian, pressed by necessity, might accomplish so much. The most delicate and beautiful obstetrical instruments were invented by Madame Boivin. Madame Ducoudray invented the manikin; Madame Breton, the system of artificial nourishment for babes; Morandi and Biheron adapted wax to the purposes of medical illustration; and it was to the observations of Mademoiselle Biheron, recorded in wax, that Dr. Hunter owed the illustrations of his best work. He was her generous friend; but she preceded him seven years in this direction, and may possibly have given him the right to use her observations as his own. Madame Roudet has, in the present century, invented a tube to be used in cases of restoration from asphyxia. It is easy to quote these cases from the history of medicine, because an honest French physician has taken pains to preserve them; but the following instances of inventive and mechanical power may be less known.

"In 1823, *the first patent of invention* was taken out in Paris, by Madame Dutillet, for the formation of artificial marble. This was so successful a patent, that she sold it in 1824; and the purchaser renewed it with still further improvements.

"In 1836, Burrows, an Englishman, took out a patent for cement. Madame Bex, of Paris, found this cement a failure in damp places, and published a method of less limited application, in which bitumen was employed.

"In 1840, Mrs. Marshall, once of Manchester, England, and now of Edinburgh, was struck with the idea, that the electric forces evolved by decaying animal and vegetable matter, acting upon calcareous substances, must have much to do with the natural formation of marble. In five years, by upwards of ten thousand experiments, she perfected an artificial marble, whose constituents and manufacture were entirely within control, and which could be made in hours or months, at the maker's volition. To this cement she gave the simple Italian name of *intonuca*. It is singular that she should so intuitively have seized this secret; for, under Madame Dutillet's patent, we are expressly informed that all vegetable matter must be removed from the composition, if we would have the cement indestructible. The example is an interesting one; for the ten thousand disagreeable experiments show that one woman, at least, possessed the power of persistent application, of long protracted labor, so often denied."

WOMEN NEED TO EXERT THEMSELVES.

WOMEN who wish to advance the welfare of their sex must exert themselves. Their influence and their pens must be brought to bear on the subject. In the progress of such matters, a great deal depends on the firm, amiable, and judicious action of women. The waves they set in motion may roll until thousands have felt their influence. Through others they may also do much.

Nervous, sensitive, delicate women may have their condition greatly ameliorated by the efforts of those more highly favored. They are more likely to suffer than those who, with good health and strong muscles, are able to perform severe physical labor.

One of the great troubles in the middle class of women is, they are too proud. They are not willing to engage in any honest labor that offers. They must do the kind they are accustomed to, or none. Another class of women are idle, and will not work, offering the excuse they cannot obtain employment. Women do not rely enough on themselves, nor keep sufficiently impressed with the consciousness that one must have a *stout heart* and a *ready hand* to succeed. A large number are deficient in perseverance, without which nothing of importance can be accomplished.

The principal reason that women do not effect more in reformatory movements and other good works is, they do not meet and consult about the matter as men do. Perhaps half a dozen ladies of narrow views and strong prejudices, unaccustomed to business, meet, and talk over, and squabble about, the work to be done, the plans to be laid, the money to be spent, and so forth. If they held a public meeting, as men do, and had the various opinions of well-matured minds, and the benevolence of a liberal philanthropy to act upon, different results would be produced. Others, on seeing that the talkers and organizers knew what they were about, and were qualified to advance, would give of their time and money.

If every woman, who desires to see justice done her sex, would not purchase at stores and shops attended by men, and would influence her friends to pursue the same plan, an immense amount of good might be accomplished by directing labor in its proper channels.

DEPENDENT WOMEN.

SOMETIMES fathers die, brothers marry, and sisters are left to take care of themselves as best they can. The state of their health, their support, and standing in society, devolve on themselves. Some become dependent on relatives or friends, that would gladly free themselves from the obligation if they only knew what to do — how they might successfully labor. The dull, sluggish stream of life would run leaping and bounding through their veins were the mist on their paths thus dissipated. A woman of honorable and independent feeling would rather be placed in the way of doing something for herself by her own exertions than receive charitable aid forever. To be dependent produces an abject feeling, and often must freedom of opinion and speech be sacrificed out of respect to the donor. A noble independence will give vigor and energy, to body and mind, when the way for exercising that independence is open.

Some people think it is more honorable for a single lady to be dependent on a father, with a salary of twelve or fifteen hundred dollars, and a large family to support, or on a married brother or sister, than employ her own energies. But it is not pleasant for adults to accept a home even with their parents, unless they are good, true, and kind people; unless they feel that they are welcome, and know that their parents have an ample supply of this world's goods.

Some women are at a loss to know how to earn even the food that nature craves. They know not where to go. All is vague uncertainty. They are like children groping in the dark, bewildered and helpless. A mother's thoughts are quickened, her wits sharpened, when hungry children appeal to her for bread. Yet her thoughts and wits may be brought to a stand for the lack of remunerative employment.

Some women have no relatives, a number have relatives that they would not be under obligation to, and a few have relatives that they would be better off without. Some people aid female relatives from a sense of duty or affection, or both, some because they would not be respected by the best portion of the community if they did not, and some do so because they think it reflects credit on themselves; but the amount of injustice and unkind treatment towards many such will never be revealed until, at the judgment bar of God, all hearts and actions are made known. Many women fear to offend their relatives by exerting themselves to earn a livelihood (because it may reflect on them), while, at the same time, they receive a mere pittance, grudgingly given. Their pride is galled, and their feelings hurt; but the uncertainty whether they can always maintain themselves decides their course. The obligation of many men to support female relatives who are unable to support themselves, is frightfully ignored in the United States; also the obligation to fit female relatives of health and strength for taking care of themselves. Let a woman have a regular occupation, and be properly compensated for her labor, and she will be as well cared for as if she depends on others. With such practical training, and correct principles, a woman will have a reliable capital. She may find the advice of kind, judicious friends valuable. If a more sensible, matter-of-fact view were taken of the reverses to which people are liable in our country, it would be rather a source of pride than mortification, that one has some pursuit that can be turned to account in case of emergency.

It would be well for women who have been engaged in non-domestic pursuits, and who have an opportunity, and wish to marry, to fit themselves for housekeeping by taking lessons in a school of cookery, and learning how to cut out and make clothes. Such institutions exist in Germany.

WOMEN'S RIGHTS AND WRONGS.

SOCIETY has deprived women of the best employments for earning a livelihood, and so far it has wronged them. No one could convince us that a *large portion* of the workwomen in New York city are not *wronged* and *persecuted*. They are wronged in the contemptible wages paid them. They are wronged in the size and arrangement of their work-rooms. They are persecuted in the close, tyrannizing oversight to which they are subjected while at work.

Instead of encouraging women in being virtuous, the tendency of society has been to develop what in them is weak and sinful, and to keep them in ignorance. The result has been to make women more dependent on men, and more thorough drudges.

Some women are censured, as the result of bearing wrong from others and not making it known. They are forced by circumstances to do things that seem improper, but which in reality are good and just, and cost a great sacrifice of time, money, and health. They do it rather than expose their persecutors. The harassing, life-corroding annoyances, are many, to which some women are subjected by unprincipled, selfish, or bad-tempered relatives or connections — annoyances that fret and chafe the spirit, and which they must bear in secret, or, by making known, subject themselves to the remarks of those who have neither the *heart*, nor the *courage*, to protect them in either *words*, or *deeds*.

If as much had been said about the rights and wrongs of women as about their duties, and by the same kind of writers, an incomparable amount of good might have been accomplished.

We have heard of a Bishop of London remarking that

God sent two angels to earth — one to sweep the streets, and the other to sit on a throne. As we have watched the woman drudge, and then turned to gaze at the fashionable lady, we have thought the remark well applied to women in different conditions of life.

In no country, and at no time, have women been placed on an equality with men by legislative enactment, except in Sparta, by Lycurgus. But the legislation and administration of most governments are, and ever have been, but the expression of the interest, prejudice, passion, and error of those in office.

"It was the design of Dalrymple — a deep enthusiast, but a man of some ability — in a colony which he attempted to form, that women should be admitted into a similar participation of political rights, and should possess an equal voice in the legislature, with the other sex."

By punishing women, men acknowledge them rational and responsible beings; and if so, they certainly have a right to assist in making laws, and assist in enforcing them, if so disposed; at any rate, aid in electing those who will. They have the right to impartial inquiry and free discussion. They have a right to the advantages of such colleges as they help, by taxation, to support for the other sex.

It is not just to trust any person with *limitless* power over the life and property of any human being, whether child or adult, whether man or woman, whether rational or irrational.

How little we know of the under-current of thought and feeling of those with whom we every day associate! How the heart may be wrung with anguish, while the face must be calm! How unutterable loneliness and desolation may be endured, and life still hang like an incubus on the sufferer!

When I consider the neglect, suspicion, and unkindness, that a woman, of education, worth and some means, may suffer, in a large city, where she has expended her strength, time, money, and efforts to benefit others, I am not surprised at any amount of imposition, fraud, even cruelty, to which many working women may be, and undoubtedly are, subjected. God help them!

And to these trials of business life there are, in many cases, to be added the terrible one of domestic trouble. Many a woman returns home after her day's labors to receive unjust and irritating treatment from those to whom she is related by marriage or blood. She sees hypocrisy and untruthfulness practiced by them in their homes. She sees them, corrupt in principle and character, before the world, pleasing in their address, and uttering smooth, fair words, and she sees that because the world never looks beneath the surface, they are enabled to command attention, influence and position. Where can the victim of such conduct turn for the covert of a home? where seek protection? Is it strange that the brain turns, and reels, and grows dizzy? Is it strange that the heart breaks, and that suicide, or insanity, terminates the unhappy woman's career?

Public opinion has always been unjust in not granting some and sustaining other privileges, liberties, and rights due to women. Public opinion is like an oak tree. Every leaf may be scattered, every bough broken, and limb after limb torn away, but the body has been made strong by these leaves, boughs, and limbs. Let us, then, destroy the leaves of error, break the boughs of prejudice, and tear away every limb, that ignorance, false reasoning, and unjust laws, have combined to make strong this oak — the growth of ages.

BRIEF REVIEW OF LAWS UNJUST TO WOMEN.

HOW often do we hear women say, when these matters are referred to, "O, I am well enough off; I wish for nothing better." Some of these are too indolent, and some have not the time, or inclination, to investigate the subject. Others fear losing the admiration of the other sex by expressing the opinion that some of the laws do not afford to women the rights and privileges that men would very speedily claim, if the matter was reversed. Others again are prosperous and happy, and care not to know of existing wrongs, and how they may rectify them. Women satisfied to endure, or see endured, such wrongs, exhibit the enervating effects of the false system under which they have lived. They manifest that servile condition that always attends subserviency. They exhibit either selfishness, conscious inferiority, or moral cowardice. The complacent, politic, and selfish spirit of the women described above is not that of the unhappy woman divorced from her husband, whose children are all taken and kept by him who is trifling and worthless, and who sets them a wretched example. Nor is it that of the woman whose husband oppresses her, and denies her the comforts of life, or furnishes her with only a scanty subsistence, while he spends hundreds and thousands on himself, and squanders his estate, leaving his children helpless on a cold, heartless world. Nor is it so with the wife who, by labor and self-denial, *has assisted in acquiring* property, and whose husband may transfer all the property acquired to those that have no claim on his kindness. 'Tis true she may, at his death, *if application is made in time*, receive her *thirds* for the *remainder of her life;* but the children may be deprived of every cent.

Massachusetts, Maine, Pennsylvania, New York, Ohio, California, and some of the other states, have, within the last twenty years, entitled married women to their own earnings. Previous to that there was no law to prevent a man from collecting the money due his wife for labor, and in some of the states it can now be done. The author of "Woman in America" says, "The wisest of men adds, 'Give her of the fruit of her hands, and let her own works praise her in the gates,' therein laying down a rule of justice, in regard to woman's rights over her own property, far more correct than any recognized by our modern laws." In some of the states, a woman's property, on marriage, passes into the hands of the husband. So by marrying a rich woman a man will come in possession of her property, which he can squander in the gratification of his own pleasures, thereby plunging her into poverty and ruin. She cannot bequeath any of the real estate she owned at the time of her marriage. If a married woman has by her labor secured property, in some of the states, she cannot, at her death, leave it to her children, without permission from her husband. If some friend leaves to a woman with a trifling husband a legacy, unless it is expressed to be for her separate use, he may claim and use it. She cannot even secure it to her children without his consent. A married woman cannot even claim the clothes she wears; nor can she attend upon any church service, if her husband forbids it. "If a man chooses, by way of tormenting his wife, to separate her children from her, or direct their lives in a manner that she conceives to be detrimental to them, she has no sufficient or satisfactory redress."

Women are taxed without representation, liable to be put in prison, and executed under laws they had no voice in making. They are subject to those in office, yet never can hold office. A woman, in some *Christian* countries, cannot obtain a divorce from her husband because of his intemperance, though he may have sunk as low as a beast; nor can she for the exercise, in her husband, of a malicious temper.

In England sixty thousand women, last May, signed petitions for the alteration of the law respecting married women's property. The alteration required is to give married women a right to their own earnings. This decides whether women desire to possess the fruits of their labor.

A remissness, corresponding in extent to the stringencies referred to, lies in the fact that if a woman has property, the laws and the courts expect her to have sense enough to know what property she has, and firmness enough to hold it, no matter what her age or circumstances. It matters not if her judgment is impaired by old age; it matters not if she is weak and silly, yielding to the selfish whims of a spoiled favorite, and withholding the just claims of those more worthy.

Many barbarous customs in relation to women continue to exist. A man can spend his wife's earnings for drink — in England can even whip his wife with impunity. I have seen accounts, now and then, within the last twenty years, of women being sold in the markets of England by their husbands; and George Borrow, in his singular narrative, "The Romany Rye," mentions the sale of a wife with a halter around her neck. The *legality* or *illegality* of the matter I leave others to ascertain; but the fact that such transactions are *permitted* is not very creditable to a country ruled by a queen.

From a work, entitled "Woman and her Master," by J. Frederick Smith, we read, "Strange that man should choose for a mate something to tyrannize over and oppress — to exhaust his ill-humor on in secret — a sort of human conductor, to dissipate the spleen which cowardice or interest prevents his venting on his fellow-man. The inferior creature, as an animal is unjustly called, might teach him a lesson. 'Nonsense!' some of our male readers will probably exclaim. 'Is there not the law?' Of course there is — law for the blow, law for the broken limb; but where is the law for the broken heart? for the cold word, the bitter sneer, the daily outrage of unkind looks, which mocks the sufferer's patience? There is none. She is his property — his slave. In puritanical Christian England, we affect to pity the women of the East, who are bought and sold in the public markets. But they at least possess one advantage over their sisters in Europe; their husbands treat them well. They know the price of them. O, man! man! it is glorious to possess thy strength, but cowardice to abuse it." Some men seem to ignore the truth that "woman was not taken out of man's head to rule over him, nor out of his feet to be trampled upon, but she was taken from under his arm to be protected, and from near his heart to love, and be loved."

Amid all the changes that have taken place, as mankind has advanced from a state of barbarism, to one of the highest enlightenment and refinement, few and slight are the changes in law respecting woman. The laws lag behind. They are the relics of a coarse, unformed, unjust, ignorant, and prejudiced age, when might made right; when physical power decided the correctness of a question in morals. The dust and mire of those savage times still come up, and defile the laws, that a more spiritual, and intellectual condition, might be supposed to bring about. A married woman in the eyes of the law is a nonentity. Her existence, and her interests, are merged in those of her husband. She is entirely at his disposal — at his mercy. And the terrible effects are seen in the low "cunning, the deceit, the pandering to appetites, and passions, of many women."

The small amount of woman's earnings is a disgrace to men that pay them. And worse still, a majority of feminine occupations are usurped by men. Remarked Mr. Chapin in a lecture in New York, "In this country, (America), we reverse the law that the strong should support the weak, as we oppress the weak, and we, the strong, prevent their earning a support." At one period of Grecian history, "society then, as now, excluded women from all legitimate sources by which they might provide for their subsistence, and opened its portals only to reward the exercise of their frailties;" but Lycurgus, in his laws for Sparta, raised women to an equality with men, and they were universally known as most exemplary wives.

A law should be made enforcing a man of health to support his wife during her life, and his children until they are fully competent to provide for themselves. "The laws should be so amended, that a woman, ill-treated by her husband, should be permitted to leave him, and to retain the custody of her children; that married women who come into possession of property by their own acquisition, by inheritance, or by gifts, should be permitted to use, retain, or dispose of them in their own right, and that at the death of her husband, the wife should have the same rights over the property and children, that the husband has when he is the survivor." A distinguished artist is said to have remarked, "The world will never be better till men subject themselves to the laws which they impose on women."

Women most severe in their judgments, and bitter in their feelings, towards men, are generally made so by suffering from the idleness, bad conduct, or unjust treatment of male relatives, or connections. There should be a law prohibiting the cruelty and harsh treatment of some parents to their children, particularly daughters. The crushing out of hope, the agony of spirit, that attend it, followed by mistrust, and bitterness of temper, are a curse, that should sink the perpetrator into the lowest depths of perdition. The injustice that the laws permit to an individual from coarse, selfish, unprincipled and dissipated relatives, or marriage connections, is greater than would be credited, by some well-bred Christian people who have not investigated the laws. The tyranny and avariciousness of men, and the tardiness, subserviency, and selfishness of women, are at the bottom of a great deal of domestic and social trouble.

As public opinion changes, the customs of society will become more liberal, and in time, will follow a corresponding change in the laws. The construction of society in the United States should be based upon more free, liberal, and sensible principles. We expect it. We look for it. It is, or should be, a natural result of the foundation on which the structure is erected. Its base lies more in nature, less in the conventionalities of men, than those of most other nations. The mouldy archives of centuries back will not answer for the present time. We often see decisions made by courts and juries not exactly in accordance with the written laws. Why is it? Probably because people are wiser now than when some laws were made, and because the unwritten law is the impartial expression of genuine feeling and opinion.

It is because of the helpless condition of women, brought about by unjust laws, and the customs induced thereby, that wicked men are enabled to tyrannize over and oppress women. To men both law and nature seem to have given the advantage. Bad laws affect the welfare of all who are governed by them, whether directly or indirectly.

A great change is certainly needed, not for those who do right, of course, but for those who do not. We know that we are better off with our laws than without any. Yet there is room for improvement in the making of new laws, and the amendment of old ones. Women always suffer most, and are the first to suffer, under a bad government. The poor suffer more than the rich. Bad laws bring back the darkness of past ages, and with it, the ignorance and degradation of those ages. We believe the French laws have, until the recent changes in our own, been considered most liberal to women. The statesmen of France have been mostly literary men, and we do not see but the statesmanship of France equals, in every respect, that of any other country. We ask for women that they be permitted to assist in making laws where they are involved. It is only fair. Men cannot fully understand the nature, the temptations, the trials of women. If they could, and were perfect, they might be able to make proper laws for women, for they would then act justly. As it is, they are not. In making laws to protect the interests of their sex, women could prevent an immense amount of sin and misery, and not have to confine their labors, as now, to remedying the individual consequences of unjust, and oppressive laws.

SUFFRAGE OF WOMEN.

MANY men are very jealous of the right of suffrage. Some sneer as if the thought itself of a woman voting were contemptible. It is a matter they will not listen to. Yet such think it all right for a freshly-imported foreigner, that knows nothing of our institutions, and cares nothing for the comparative merits of the candidates, to vote. Is it consistent? Are not the intelligent portion of our American ladies superior in mind and cultivation to thousands of men that do vote? Have they not a better knowledge of our laws and institutions, than one half of those that now appear at the ballot-box? Are they not in every respect more competent than most of the Germans and Irish that are in this country? And are they not greatly superior to the majority of Africans lately freed, and for whose right to suffrage so many white people are clamoring, particularly the anti-slavery, equal rights women of the North? Many of those women seem, if possible, more anxious to obtain the right of suffrage for negro men, than for themselves.

"The shrewd New Englander, the luxurious Southerner, the positive Englishman, the metaphysical Scotchman, the jovial Irishman, the excitable Frenchman, the passionate Spaniard, the voluptuous Italian, the plodding German, the debased African, the Russian, the Pole, the Norwegian, the Dane, are all flung together in this mighty crucible, each with his own language, his own plans, his own prejudices, his own religion. The antagonistic elements are in contact, but refuse to unite," save at the ballot-box, where all, with one exception, can, after three years' residence in our country, cast in their vote. A man, though unable to read or write, can vote. Drunkards, gamblers, and even idiots, and lunatics, *if men*, can vote.

Some say women would neglect home duties of they engage in matters of this kind. We think not. The time spent in gossiping, novel-reading, and such pastimes, would be given to an intelligent investigation of our laws. Some contend that domestic unhappiness might be produced if married women were allowed to vote, by a difference of opinion between them and their husbands. We reply, no more than by a difference of religious opinion.

A married woman is as likely, if not more so, to have a knowledge of political matters, and fitness of candidates, as unmarried women. Candidates think, and others say, that wives influence their husbands greatly in the exercise of the right of suffrage — that to gain the good opinion of a wife is a pretty sure avenue to the vote of the husband. If they have so much influence indirectly, why not let them give a direct and positive expression of it by casting their own votes?

Some approve of single women voting, but not married women. Single women generally have more time at their disposal, and consequently more for studying politics. If women were allowed to vote, their reading would be of a higher character, and more general; their thinking, and talking, of a more refined and improving nature. Some age at which women could begin to vote, say eighteen or twenty-one, it would be necessary to specify, if they acquire the privilege, unless the qualification is made educational.

The property of single women is taxed the same as if they were men. Yet they are not allowed a representation in making the laws of the country. This principle was the foundation of the Revolutionary war of 1776. Women that are taxed and legislated for, certainly have, in the name of justice, a right to vote. Yet they cannot vote, however useful they are in society, possessing an unblemished character, and even paying enormous taxes. Lucy Stone and Harriet K. Hunt, resisted taxation, because denied the privilege of the ballot-box. They were right. Their property was an inalienable claim to the privilege; their education, and morality, a still higher one.

Wives, by their labor and economy, in domestic matters, really earn, on an average, as much as their husbands. Yet, we think, unless the property of man and wife were distinct, it would not do to relieve the property of married women from taxation, for some husbands would be mean enough to put their property in their wives' names, and the public coffers would after a while become empty.

If women are to be tried for offenses, why should they not assist in making the laws to which they are amenable? There cannot be a just government without the consent of the governed. Why not be permitted to sit in judgment, in cases they can best appreciate, by similarity of thought and feeling? For, cannot a woman better understand the trials and temptations to which one of her sex is exposed, than a man possibly could? In time past, in England, in some special cases, juries were even constituted entirely of women.

If women had power in the making and execution of laws, and in the selection of candidates for office, there would be less corruption than there is.

Said Lucy Stone, "It has been stated that men are too vile and wicked for women to mingle with them; then certainly, if that is true, they are too vile and wicked to make laws for us."

H. F. Lee says, "Gentlemen have no objection to ladies being politicians, if they embrace the right side; to wit, that to which they themselves belong."

Wendell Phillips says, "Social life begins to-day where legal life began long ago. A woman may be hung; therefore she should be permitted to vote. Some men say many women don't know enough, have not sense enough to vote. A woman that has sense enough to work has sense enough to vote. In Great Britain the rich man says, 'I have wealth; so I will see that you are taken care of' to the poor man; but it proves a selfish protection. In America every man is permitted to take care of himself. The ballot-box is not based on brains. If women are like men, they should certainly have the same privileges; if they are not, men are not capable of representing them. To object to women going to the polls because they will see men, is absurd. Do they not see them in the street, in stages, churches, &c., and at home? Men have acquired both social and political superiority over women, and are likely to retain them, without effort on the part of woman. It is for this reason they have better wages, follow any calling they wish, go where and when they please, without reproach, and have laws to promote their own interests."

Dr. W. said to me, "If women find themselves fitted to exercise the elective franchise, let them — no harm will result. If not, they will soon drop it." All women would not wish to vote if they had the privilege. All men do not vote. They never do unless they wish to. There is no compulsion. There is no distinction made in the Bible between the privileges of men and women, except by St. Paul, who made that distinction merely to suit the people of those times.

My opinion is, that the majority of good and intelligent men, will not willingly debar women of just privileges, if they seek them. If women knew their power intellectually, and were united in demanding the ballot, it would not be withheld from them.

If women were granted the privilege of voting, it would be desirable to have separate polls, that they might go, and cast in their votes, as quietly as they now go to a sewing circle, or to a meeting of some charitable institution.

"Daniel O'Connell, in England, in 1840, showed that women exercised the right there to vote, as holders of bank stock, and as members of the East India Company, and some other institutions of that country."

It is well known that over nine thousand votes were cast for the suffrage of women, a year ago, in Kansas. In Massachusetts, and in the District of Columbia, the right of suffrage is granted to negro men, but not to white women.

"The moment that woman is intrusted with the power to shape the state by the right of suffrage, the community will see to it that she has the broadest opportunities for education. If woman has a direct share in the government, that very responsibility will educate her."

One kind of government is suited for one people, and another kind for another people. A republic would do better in the United States if the people were more willing to make sacrifices for their country, less grasping as individuals, more humble, more honest, more wise, and more God-fearing.

To sum up what I have said: I think laws should be made for the protection of the persons and property of women. I advocate the opening of all occupations to them. I insist on fair wages being paid for their labor. Married women, as well as unmarried ones, should be entitled to their earnings. Mothers should have the custody of their children, in all cases, except when mentally incapacitated, or unfitted by intemperance, or other immorality. I would ask for women the privileges of the ballot-box, and trial by their own peers. In short, I wish to see them possessing equal rights with men — domestic, social, educational, industrial, civil, and religious.

PROGRESS.

WONDERFUL disorder prevails in social life, and unquestionable wrong in the business world. New, and better, systems of education, need to be carried out, correct principles more generally instilled in children, and a radical change wrought in the nature of the great mass of adults. Such processes are slow; but they may serve to bring about a better organization of society, and business. Men may remodel their laws, and institutions, so as to encourage virtue and punish vice; they may even do a great deal to prevent vice; but they can never, of their own efforts, again make an Eden of earth. They may do something towards bringing about a millennium; but a higher power must assist and direct.

The time when woman was defined to be an animal that loves finery has passed away, how much soever the propensity may remain. Many women have so cultivated their minds, and hearts, as to find but little room for thoughts of the kind, and so the sex has been redeemed from the keen and cutting, but too general satire. Time was when woman was denied the possession of a soul — consequently of a place in heaven. Religiously, woman's condition is improved. Now she is acknowledged to have a soul, and as good a right to a place in heaven as man. Time was when woman was the toy of man — when she was ignorant as the birds of the air. But civilization has, to some extent, banished the mental darkness through which woman groped. Time was when woman was a beast of burden — when she was the "hewer of wood and drawer of water" — when she was required to labor in the fields. More shame that all this is still true of some Christian lands. Woman is no longer generally considered as she was formerly, and is now in Turkey, an object valued but for her personal beauty. No, her mental and moral powers are considered. It is not requisite that she have only a bright eye, a fair complexion, a mild countenance, but in that eye must speak an intellect, in that complexion a knowledge of the laws of health, in that countenance a good heart. Her condition mentally is improved. Woman is just beginning to take her proper place in the world. Hitherto her power has been almost entirely of a moral character, now it is assuming more of an intellectual tone. The next phase, we hope, will be a lovely blending of the two. Time was when woman stood before man merely as a slave to minister to his physical wants. Woman's social position is no longer such, in enlightened nations. As the mass of mankind are better educated, each individual will better know his and her own place. Ignorance will lose its presumption, conceit its inflation. The really superior will govern by the tacit, or expressed consent of the inferior, but they will need to exercise common sense, and wisdom.

Society seems to be undergoing a change favorable to the advancement of women, by a few of the sex entering higher, and more respectable, channels of employment. The selfishness, and prejudices, of men, have, since the creation of the world, formed the popular opinion until a century back. Since that time, in what are deemed enlightened countries, woman has exerted some little influence over the better educated, and more refined, and liberal class of men, thereby modifying and tempering, to some extent, their selfish usurpation. As woman becomes more generally educated, society will advance, the spirit of the times will be more liberal. There will be a corresponding change of views, new rules of action, and a more generous regard to the variety of occupations, and pastimes, suitable to the sex. Reflection, observation, intelligence, and morality, will serve to raise woman, as well as man, in the scale of being. Laws more favorable to the welfare of woman will be made, and others will be amended. New phases of society will call for different influences.

The present age is one of reformation, and benevolent plans. Temperance societies, mechanical unions, lectures before the working men, are of the first character. Homes for the destitute and desolate, and organizations for furnishing such as are able, with employment, are of the second kind.

Women have more persistency in carrying out a benevolent undertaking than men. In carrying out any special benevolence, an individual, or association, should consider, that few people (even of those whose sympathies they enlist,) will be likely to give the time and efforts to fully comprehend, and appreciate, said work of benevolence — consequently they will give sparingly of their means, thoughts, prayers, and influence. When disheartened, the benevolent enterprisers will need to summon their courage, and fight against any feelings of contempt for others, and still labor on carefully, judiciously. They must choke down murmurings, and overcome vexations, and when opposed by selfishness, and falsehood, and treachery, speak out boldly and fearlessly. When there is a possibility of their efforts succeeding, they should work on more diligently than ever, and repine not if it may not be accomplished in their lifetime. Truths should be uttered with simplicity, and earnestness, and those who speak them should be fearless of ridicule, and able to live without sympathy, and encouragement, to secure even a partial reform.

The rules that govern society to-day, would not have answered fifty years ago, nor would the rules that govern to-day be likely to answer fifty years hence. If the diffusion of knowledge, and the education of the masses, in this country, during the next fifty years are proportioned to the advances of the last fifty years, we not only predict a great elevation in the scale of intelligence, and a higher moral tone in society, but that such benefit will particularly accrue to the female sex. Woman's influence, soft as the balmy dew, will then be bracing as the mountain air. Her praise then will not be merely the elegance of her attire, as a bird is admired for the richness of its plumage. Symmetry of form, and regularity of features, may receive their due meed of praise, but the mind that gives them expression will better charm. She may be admired as the gazelle for her beautiful eyes, but the soul that speaks through them will be better appreciated. Her motions may be very graceful; but the loving heart, chastened by high-toned principle, will refine them inconceivably. The time will come when fashion will not rule with an iron sway, when each person will consult his or her taste, and judgment, in the selection, and making up, of raiment, and in furnishing dwellings.

A change in public opinion is slow in regard to the condition of women, and their improvement. Women must be patient, therefore, but not the less active in bringing the change about in a quiet way. Nor must they be discouraged. There is more or less, interruption, to every extended human effort. Slowly is the hour of woman's redemption approaching. When that has arrived she may throw off the shackles that have so long fettered her. She may indulge in more varied and original ideas. She may express her thoughts freely, and feel that she is entitled to a hearing as well as her brother — man. This gives rise to hope in the heart of woman. She is ever looking forward to some time in the future — some good to get or do — some enjoyment for herself or others — some hope to be realized — some wish to be gratified.

So long as people possess different minds, and bodies, so long must there be a difference in their condition. Without some incentive to activity, there would be a complete stagnation of business and society. Doubt leads to inquiry, and inquiry to truth. Every reform must be gradually accomplished — step at a time. How few of us realize that every event in life has its effect on the mind, and heart! Comparative freedom from care and anxiety is essential to success in business matters. In the past man wrote with a diamond pen on the imperishable rocks of time; but the tracings of woman's pencil were faint and imperfect. Yet in Christian nations she is now making her impress for eternity. On the tablets of the soul she is writing characters never to be effaced. The young and susceptible are molded by her example and precepts.

The results of woman's literary labor, and mechanical ingenuity, can scarcely be said to furnish a correct estimate of her abilities. For, until within the last fifty years, the efforts of the first kind were not encouraged, but rather scorned and ridiculed, and for less time than that, the exercise of mechanical talent has been considered as entirely without her province. It is not so with men, who for centuries have been encouraged, stimulated, and rewarded, with honors and pecuniary profits.

One great trouble is, women are too dainty about their work. A man of good sense will go at anything; but a woman objects to this, that, and the other. A man will go anywhere; a woman will object that she cannot go among strangers, she may be deprived of her own church service, she would not like the society, or something else of the kind. When women are not extremely difficult to please, they should be encouraged, and sustained in their labor.

The last, and greatest change, we ask for woman, is that her political condition be improved. Give her to feel the freedom of an American citizen. Her property is taxed. Give her the privilege of assisting to select those that will protect her person, and property, and rights, and privileges. It is her inalienable right. She is amenable to the laws of her country. Let her assist in selecting such as she thinks proper to make those laws, or even assist in forming them herself. Release woman from political bondage. As our laws exist, she is deprived of political power. If woman is as much entitled to the privileges of heaven as man, why should she not be to the privileges of earth? Your human laws are professedly founded on divine laws. Then carry the principle out. Do you think if there is ever any voting done in heaven, women will be pushed to one side, and excluded from the privilege? But perhaps you will say, sex will not be known, or recognized in heaven. Well, is it not the spirit that makes us what we are — immortal beings? Does spirit recognize sex here? Certainly not.

Then allow the spirit of woman the same privilege as that of man. Let her consult her abilities, and inclinations, in the selection of an employment. Let her quietly drop her vote at the polls set aside for women exclusively. Be assured if you pursue this course, our country will be more prosperous, and longer continue so. Improvements are going on; but it is by the unflinching perseverance of clear-headed men, and energetic women.

Men can do much towards bringing about a favorable result in all matters pertaining to woman's good, but women can do more. It must be done by a change in public opinion, by bringing about a right appreciation of the state of affairs — by exciting thought and inquiry on the subject. It cannot and should not be attempted by other than mental, and moral force. Moral influence, and the result of good sense, and correct principles, will prove the great lever by which the mass of the male mind is to be turned. In woman's influence consists her power.

When women are more sought as the coöperators of men in philanthropic works, more efficient means will be taken to prevent evil. Their foresight, and keener perceptive powers, will come into play. Their sympathetic nature will be called as fully into exercise; but its operations will be more judicious. Women will thus prevent an immense amount of suffering, wretchedness, and woe, that they are now merely expected to palliate, and relieve. When women have a voice in the administration of affairs, they will see that women, who alone can understand, and appreciate the trials, and temptations of their own sex, are the arbiters, to some extent, of those who are charged with offenses, social, or civil. They will see that justice, in some degree, is done to their own sex, and that mercy tempers justice. When women assist in making laws they will not have one code of morals for men, and another for women, but all will be alike amenable to the same laws. A stricter morality will be required; law will be divested of its technicalities, and circumlocutions; many laws now in existence will be annulled, and many new ones made, while some will be modified to suit the times, and circumstances,

OPPOSITION.

SOME men will not work for those that employ women. Most men are too selfish, too sensitive to anything that concerns their pecuniary interest, to make any sacrifice for the advancement of women. They are not willing to assist them, if it will cost them a dollar. Some employers will not even take women to work for them, lest they be subjected to ridicule, or accused of doing it that they may have their work done for less pay, or be disliked by the employers, and workmen, of other establishments, who will say they are driving men out of employment by substituting women. Until the novelty wears off, of the introduction of women into new occupations, there will be opposition, envy, and jealousy, among some of the men in those pursuits. There are some men that sneer at all women undertake. Let such sneer on. It will do them no good, and women no harm. So there is no cause for discouragement.

The prejudice that has so long existed, in regard to women entering any other field of labor, than that of a housewife, is wearing away. Women that attempt to open new fields of labor for their sex — to elevate their condition — in short to benefit them — must not be surprised to find a strong opposing force in their own sex. Some are blinded to their own interests, and some misjudge the motives of those who would do them good. The credulity of ignorant people, their inability to read motives, and be reasoned with, are sad detriments to their intellectual advancement. The prejudiced, the uneducated, the unthinking mass, will form a barrier to daunt any destitute of a *brave* heart.

One of the greatest sources of trouble of the present time, in our country, arises from the fact that the majority of people think they have fulfilled their duty to others, if they have treated them kindly and politely, without any regard to the more important qualities of truth, honesty, and justice.

The envy of men keeps women out of many occupations that are decidedly feminine in their character. We find greater opposition to the entrance of women into the lighter, and more artistic industrial branches, made by men so employed, than we do from men in vocations of a more ordinary kind. Probably because there is more physical ease, and a more handsome profit attending the first. "The jealousy which keeps women from the employment of engraving the brass work of a watch, and from pasting patterns of floss silk upon cards for trade purposes, long kept the doors of the School of Design in London closed against female pupils, and renders it almost impossible for an English woman to qualify herself for treating the diseases of women and children. The same jealousy cost many lives in the Crimean war, by delaying the reception of the nurses into the hospitals in the East, and by restricting their action when there. In the Staffordshire potteries women are largely employed in painting porcelain — an art which they are better qualified to practice than men. It will hardly be credited, but we can vouch for the fact, that such is the jealousy of the men, that they compel the women *to paint without a rest for the hand*, and the masters are obliged by their own workmen to sanction this absurd act of injustice." Could not her Majesty, Queen Victoria, bring about a better state of affairs, if she were so disposed, by having the police arrest, and imprison men, who would offend, and harm women, because engaged in such work? and might she not uphold masters in their efforts to do justice to woman's work? Such arbitrary opposition should certainly be checked. It is unfortunate for women when their work competes with that of young people, particularly boys.

The objection urged by some merchants, to the employment of women in their stores, is that they would have to change frequently. How often does Stewart change on an average his salesmen? No doubt as often as Sharpless, and

Evans, of Philadelphia, do their saleswomen, except where the loss arises from the marriage of saleswomen.

Some one writes me, he is a women's wrongs man. If women had their rights they would not have wrongs to be corrected. I believe "an ounce of prevention is better than a pound of cure."

"Generally speaking, woman is denied her humanity and her equality; yet she is none the less *exposed* to all the burdens of existence. But let her receive a vigorous physical education to develop her body — let her have a latitude of *public opinion* sufficient to expand her soul in the presence of great thoughts — do as you would be done by, and give to woman all the rights, liberties, advantages, emoluments which her organizational needs suggest, and quite certain am I, that the lords of creation would no longer question the adaptedness of the female nature to the various intellectual professions, which a despotic custom, and masculine selfishness, have for centuries assigned to the supposed stronger body, and better prepared brain."

"Persecution for opinion, punishment for all manifestations of intellectual, and moral strength, are still as common as women who have opinions, and who manifest strength; but some things are easy, and many are possible of achievement, to women of ordinary powers, which it would have required genius to accomplish a few years ago."

Dr. Walker, the author of a work on woman, denies to her the ability to generalize ideas — considers her incapable of abstract and connected thought. Walker says, "It is well known, that, when women are capable of some degree of mental exertion, this, by directing the blood towards the brain, makes it a centre of activity at the expense of the vital organs, which are much more important to them." It depends on circumstances whether they are more important. If they remain single, and do not desire a long life, they might as well enjoy it by intellectual exercise. Walker goes on to say, "If the vital organs suffer from the activity of the brain, their chief value as women is destroyed, and it is certain that great fecundity of the brain in women usually accompanies sterility, or disorder of the matrix." What of that unless a woman is married, and wishes to have children. From my limited knowledge, diseases of the womb are as common among ignorant, as among learned women.

If Walker's ideas are correct, women would be incapable of using, and appreciating, knowledge, even if it were diluted, and presented in the most simple form. We infer from what Walker says that he thinks all intellectual exertion is to provide for the animal wants, and nothing more. "The natural sensibility, feebleness and timidity of woman lead her instinctively, and with little aid from reasoning, to observe the circumstances which prompt mankind to act." So, Dr. Walker, you would say that instinct gives to woman a little penetration.

"Women," says Walker, "are peculiarly sensitive to ridicule." We reply, not more so than men.

He remarks, "They attach great importance to little faults." Can anything else be expected, if their intellects are made barren deserts, such as you would have them? "It is the instinctive faculties of women," he continues, "as well as the other qualities already described, that fit them, better than men, for passing from the lowest to the highest ranks." Ranks of what? of society do you mean? certainly not of intellect, as that in your opinion is impossible.

We would infer from some portions of Walker's book, that he had been jilted by some learned woman, and so acquired the distaste for such that he now vents his hatred and envy on them. Walker's ideas of women are about on a par with Michelet's. He makes woman out a nonenity intellectually — a lump of animal pulsation physically, and a weak and sickly being morally. He seems to think woman merely a creature of emotions, incapable of anything deep and strong.

Most men would have women without a will or spirit, with no aspirations above being a good housekeeper, and seamstress. They will not recognize in her a yearning for something higher, and better, that she has a soul needing nourishment, a mind whose fire requires to be replenished and kept burning. When conscious that the soul life, the heart life is being crushed, the divinity of mind materialized, by sad circumstances over which we have no control, of what avail are wealth and luxury? They are too external to reach the yearning abyss within. If Nature smiles it mocks the misery it cannot heal, if it frowns it only reflects the gloom within.

Custom and prejudice are the barriers to most works for the amelioration of the race, especially for the feminine part of it.

"In the eighteenth century, a learned and elaborate treatise was written, to prove that women were not of the same species with men, and that they had no souls, and a solemn council was held at Macon, composed of bishops, &c., wherein the question was gravely put, whether women were human creatures."

Most men that are not highly educated, fear, and some even hate, a learned woman, and many men that are highly educated dread the power, and influence, and competition, of a learned woman, but it is not so with all. If the earth were rid of all knaves, and fools, there might be a long and unceasing jubilee among the few people left. Yet to make a line of demarcation between those who are, and those who are not, would be puzzling, as almost everybody is considered either a knave, or a fool, by somebody else.

The remark was once made to me, "Women will not help themselves, and you only make enemies by trying to help them." We have not found this the case with all. We should be sorry if all women were so ungrateful and perverse.

The circumstances that oppose women's advancement, are as much of an indirect, as of a direct character.

M. Comté has proposed that all women be withdrawn from industrial (other than domestic) pursuits, but with the condition that all those who have neither husband, nor parents, to provide for them, be supported by the state. Surely it is but just, unless women are permitted to enter all industrial pursuits, and earn a livelihood for themselves.

PROGRESS RETARDED BY WOMEN.

MANY women are so blind to the interests of their own sex that they retard, rather than assist, in any movement, having for its aim the opening of employments. They think, as too many men do, the sphere of every woman is at home. They forget that poverty, loss of relatives, and other circumstances, deprive many women of the comforts, and freedom, of a home. The fact that they are provided for, and taken care of, should make them desirous to see those differently situated, placed in the way of being helped, or helping themselves. Some women of wealth, treat those who earn a livelihood by their exertions, as if they were doing something improper; as if they were transgressing the limit of "woman's sphere." What a shame that it should be so! How unreasonable! how absurd! how sinful!

Some women, from want of judgment, defeat plans intended for their own good. The great difficulty in bringing about reforms, among the working women of the United States, arises from their false pride. Most of them are ashamed of their occupation. We have heard of girls in some of the cities, learning trades, that carry books with them, to give the impression that they are attending school. They do not consider that every person in the nation, from the President to a boot-black, works for money. More false pride is probably cherished in the United States than in any other country. It is founded on a desire to be thought what we are not, and the silly belief, with many, that not to work makes a lady. Consequently, it leads them to an improper estimate of the standing of their occupation. Its issue is a false pride, dangerous in its tendencies, and sometimes fatal in its results.

Until much of that heartless selfishness ceases to exist, that now characterizes most women of means, who scorn labor, so long must freezing, starving, desolate, homeless women continue to perish. The loneliness of women in the middle ranks, who support themselves, is owing to the selfishness, or want of kindness and sympathy, of people in their own, and those in a higher rank. Nor are those living without labor any better off, for, to the majority, their aimless, useless lives, are a burden.

Some women have been so shocked by the sentiments, and movements, of ultra reformers, that they close their ears to any information on the subject. They prefer remaining in utter ignorance. Of course we make exception of the intelligent, educated, and liberal, that are willing to investigate any matter before they condemn it.

The working class of women could accomplish far more if they would unite in efforts to have their wages advanced. What union can do was accomplished a few years since in the shoe strike of Massachusetts. But generally women have not sufficient intelligence to combine and demand higher wages. They have none to point out to them how they may better their condition, and take the matter in hand, and lead them. Many are timid and fear losing their places as workers by taking such a stand. Add to this, that very few women are practical, because they have never had the opportunity, occasion, or ability, to cultivate their business talents.

Women are often accused of being less generous than men. We think, in most cases, it is because they have less to be generous with. Other people cannot always study us better than we can study ourselves. Yet it is a lamentable fact, that selfishness and ingratitude mar the character of many women in the learned professions, as authors, physicians, and teachers. It pains us to see a selfish, grasping spirit manifested by women in the lower grades of labor, but far more to see it manifested by women deriving a handsome income from their professional services.

Many men and women are the slaves of custom and prejudice; many have no ideas beyond those so acquired, and the most of those that have, are without the moral courage to express and uphold them. It is surprising with what credulity people receive statements that chime in with their prejudices.

The opposition of women to each other arises in many cases from rivalry, a want of principle, jealousy, or envy. "Woman's inhumanity to woman makes countless thousands mourn." The majority of women talk much — do little. Some women are jealous of other women that would enter the literary field, and therefore would not hesitate to force them from the field. They would sneer at their efforts, and cast contempt on their achievements. They have no real interest in the welfare of their sex.

From the moment a thought is expressed it becomes a something tangible — it takes form. We may in our minds picture a beautiful scene, but when we place it on canvas it at once becomes visible to the eyes of others — so with thought.

All women have not alike the tact to secure favorable opportunities that open in business. It looks badly to see a woman discouraging employers from engaging the services of women, in preference to men, when she must have some knowledge of the great necessity that exists for openings by which women can earn a support. It looks badly for any one of the number, who has made a fortune off of workwomen, to make severe strictures through the press on their ability, and to write disparagingly of them as a class. It shows a want of sensibility, and sympathy, for the hundreds, yes, thousands, of women, quite the equal, if not the superior of herself, striving to earn an honest livelihood. Such an influence is discouraging to workwomen, and such statements greedily received by selfish men and heartless women.

INJUSTICE OF WOMEN PARTLY ACCOUNTED FOR.

"A RIGHT over my *subsistence* is a power over all my thoughts and actions." When woman is taught to know what is due her, she will resist oppression; and when she is taught not to exact more of others than she, under the same circumstances, would be willing to grant, then will she be more likely to render entire justice to others. The injustice of women in business transactions with each other has been a hobby with some snarling, surly men, who, by the way, are always on the lookout themselves to take advantage of their fellow-men. And if women are unjust, it is usually the fault of the very men that sneer at the result of what they themselves occasion. It is well known that, generally, those people are most oppressive who have been most oppressed.

The spirit that prompts a married woman to beat down the prices, and contend for a bargain, in making a purchase, arises mostly from the consciousness that her husband, in whose hands the purse is very likely to be, will expect the ultimatum of the money's worth. And most men are ignorant of the vast number of purchases that must be made by a housekeeper, and the prices that must be paid. In some cases money is doled out to a wife with a hard, mean parsimony. Perhaps the husband calls the same day, at the same counter where his wife has cautiously expended her meager sum, and purchases some article of dress for himself. He would not, for the world, haggle about the price. It might give the impression that he is miserly. What a man gets easily he spends freely; what a woman earns dearly she parts with sparingly. Besides, a man is less willing to be troubled by small matters, and has less time for them; that accounts, to some extent, for men paying better prices for what they buy. "The husband who deserts his home, in nine cases out of ten, is pitied. The wife who abandons her's is universally condemned; and by none more severely than by her own sex, who have done most to rivet the chain which binds them, by the want of charity they show to their unhappy sisters." The question arises, Can a conscientious woman prove recreant to the interest and happiness of her own sex?

If a woman's purse is her own, and she has earned what she spends, she well knows that for the same amount of work, as well done as by a man, she has received a less remuneration. This may prompt her to drive close bargains. But a single woman that has always had, and still has, a free, full purse of her own, and has not herself been subjected to oppression, or witnessed it in those about her, will, we think, very rarely be seen beating down the prices of her dress-maker, milliner, and laundress. No, we cannot, and will not, believe such a spirit of meanness exists in many of our sex. Circumstances have created it, where it does exist. "Women who have their own peculiar world, and so many secrets in common, ought certainly to love each other a little, and sustain each other, instead of warring among themselves. They inflict mutual injury, in a thousand cases, indirectly."

The exercise of certain faculties is involved in different vocations. These faculties must be cultivated, to attain to excellence. If a woman possesses certain faculties in a high degree, she should fit herself for that vocation in which her talents will be best employed. Women should preserve their identity intellectually as well as men.

A jealousy and rivalry in business do exist, to some extent, among women. Some female writers are more jealous of others of their own sex gaining a foothold in the literary world than men are. Perhaps men think they have less to fear from competition with women.

One reason women have less patience with each other

than with men is, that they are more thrown together in the house, and see each other's faults, while the desire of most women for the admiration of men makes them conceal every fault.

The supremacy of physical power, in past ages, may have created, in some women, a sense of inferiority, of dependence on men, that led them to be unjust to women.

The great foundation of woman's injustice is, that she is destitute of the moral courage that enables her to do right, fearless of consequences; that she is the victim of public opinion — the opinion of men whose selfishness has ever sought the best for themselves, and established the impression that it was merely their due. These women have not the moral courage to declare themselves advocates of woman's social, civil, and political rights. They fear the disapproval of men, and the want of support from their own sex. They are unwilling to risk popularity. Some are destitute of a sense of justice, and act upon the principle that might makes right. Others are favorably situated themselves, and do not wish to do anything they find unpleasant, in order to benefit others. They are not willing to sacrifice the ease, and quiet, and peace that might be involved.

If it be true that women are to a greater extent false to the interests of their sex than men, one cause of it is the great competition in the labor market for women; — that causes women to undersell each other. An intelligent shoe-binder told me she knew of many a woman that would be working for a store, but another woman would come in and say, "I will do the same work for fifty cents less." So the work is given to her. And another will come in and say, "I will do the work for still less;" and so it is given to her. But when we consider that many of these women must do their work at starvation prices, or lie down and die, or sell their virtue, where, we ask, does the fault lie? Not at their door. One might suggest trades' unions, and established wages for work; but that, it is said, can never be done in New York, because of the starving foreigners that come in, and are willing to work at half price. Yet this objection is not thoroughly grounded.

Many poor male foreigners enter our ports, to come in competition with American men; but they are acquainted with a greater variety of employments, and consequently more fields are open for their work. Every occupation in this country that has elicited female industry has been filled to excess. The crowded condition of those now open for female labor will drive women into others. The cry cannot be in vain. It must be heard. When that is done, a standard of wages can as well be established by them as by tradesmen, or by that number of superior workmen who wish to establish a reputation as such. But, then, may not a false pride come in? Some women of education, who have been reduced in fortune, may not wish to be known as workwomen. All the fancy-work done by wealthy young ladies as a pastime lowers the estimate placed on woman's labor. Woman's labor is also depreciated, to some extent, by women in the country, in comfortable circumstances, taking away their sister woman's work by doing it in leisure hours, for pocket-money, at lower prices than it would be possible to do it, if they were entirely dependent on their labor. Milliners and dress-makers have those of their own sex to compete with who are not engaged in any non-domestic employments, and also those who follow the business without any preparation, while men engaged in making men's clothing have no reason to fear like competition.

A reform should commence with women of position and wealth. How often may you see a well-dressed woman cheapening the price of an article, and that article very likely the workmanship of one of her own sex! Perhaps the merchant favors her, and falls in his prices; but he does not lose; — no, he deducts from his work-people's wages; they are the ones to suffer. And there, I think, is the need of producers and consumers being brought more together, not separated by those who come in as a medium, accommodating — *particularly to themselves*. Not that we object to men who do business honorably, but to middlemen and shavers.

One reason why men succeed better than women in what they undertake, of a personal kind, is, that they are likely to have more friends that are willing to exert themselves, and make sacrifices for their advancement. Look, for instance, at what is done for politicians. Another thing is, that men apply themselves more closely, make greater effort, risk more, and have more to risk. Women in business are apt to be very selfish and jealous of their business interests. There is much harshness and oppression, a great bearing down and crushing out of the life spirit. Particularly is it so from married to single women. I have been told in New York that if a single woman goes alone to apply for boarding, at some houses, the doors are shut in her face. Is it not a shame to the housekeeper, and an insult to the virtuous single woman? I have seen such a motto as this: "Am I not a woman and a sister?" Would to Heaven every woman, particularly those that employ work-women, would study the question.

The impositions and oppressions to which women have been subjected, the severe struggles of those engaged in business life, their limited means, and long-continued labor, will account for the greater injustice of women to women, *if it be true* that more does exist, than with the other sex. One person rarely hates another without having been wronged by the individual, or having wronged the individual.

I think that when workwomen are *convinced* that efforts are being made for their good, they are able to somewhat appreciate them, and in most cases, are not ungrateful. Yet gratitude and truth are not often permanent growths, unless the seeds are planted in childhood.

PREPARATION FOR USEFULNESS.

LET a girl be raised with a thorough, practical, but limited knowledge of household duties. It will not then be difficult, if she becomes a wife, or takes charge of a house, to improve and extend her knowledge. But let her by all means gain a knowledge of some employment that she can turn to account, if remaining a single lady, or left a penniless widow. The steady pursuit of some definite plan will greatly promote interest and happiness. Her knowledge of such a pursuit will be no disadvantage, even if always a happy and prosperous wife.

Why should not girls have a definite preparation made for usefulness? Are boys possessed of more, or higher faculties? Are they more gifted by nature? If so they less need the advantages of education. In the progress of the age, the education of woman is becoming, and deservedly so, a distinctive feature. In the heyday of life, when all is bright and sunny, the time is best to plant the seed for future growth.

Let girls examine the different employments, and then study their capabilities, and adaptedness, and when they have selected a pursuit, follow it with unflinching perseverance. They should not permit obstacles to daunt, and turn them aside. Common sense, a resolute will, decision of character, promptness of action, uniformity of temper, self-control, and good judgment, will fit most women for their duties, whatever they be.

The circumstances in which a young girl approaches, and enters, womanhood, are never twice the same. For that reason it behooves her to be prepared by education, and the exercise of judgment, united with a delicate sense of propriety and independence of character, to act as a lady, and a Christian. The happiness and usefulness of the future woman should be considered in her education. The principles and conduct of a young girl at home, and among her schoolmates, are a pretty fair criterion of what she will be when a wife and mother. With the enthusiastic nature of most young ladies, the period of entering into society, is one of peculiar temptation. Most girls need to be withheld to some extent from the excitements, and frivolities, that are really intoxicating, by the careful hand of a judicious mother. How much danger there is that all religious impressions be lost! There is danger of self-love too much engrossing the young girl. She is apt to see herself in a light too favorable, and others in one too unfavorable. So varied, so irregular, and so unlooked-for, are many of the events of life, that she is often puzzled to know the best course to pursue. Therefore it is well for her to feel the superiority of mental, and moral, over personal beauty, to rightly appreciate the vast influence for good and evil woman wields, and her noble destiny for time and eternity. If homely, she may consider how many women have, by means of their personal beauty, been lured and won from the path of virtue — how many have fallen victims to the wily snares of wicked men — how many have sunk in wretchedness, in degradation and ruin. Then may she feel resigned that she received not that too often fatal gift. "It is a fact," says Madame Necker de Saussure, "that must be acknowledged, that the second education, that which we give to ourselves when the moral and physical powers are developed, is the one which really bears fruit; the only one of which the traces are never obliterated."

If women were furnished with a trade or profession, they would not be so dependent on men. They would not be so much trained with the view of marrying, and feeling that to be the only resource by which to secure a livelihood. It would not be the aim, the scheme of so many mothers and daughters. There would be greater dignity in the female character, more nobleness, candor and purity. Greater ease, independence, and decision would prevail.

A woman should be educated under all circumstances. She will need an education to be the companion of man intellectually. If she is a wife, how can she, if ignorant, charm him in his leisure moments, and render his home a place of genial companionship? If he cannot find society in his own home, he is apt to seek it elsewhere. How vast — how powerful is the influence of a wife, and mother! Her impress is made for eternity, as well as time.

The increasing wants of mankind multiply the number of employments, but discretion needs to be used that each employment is filled according to its wants — not that some departments be crowded to excess, and others lack laborers. This needs to be thought of by those who select occupations for young people, and by young people themselves. The professions of law and medicine are now crowded, and many a young man must endure privations for years, before he can establish himself, while some mechanical departments of labor are not sufficiently filled to meet existing wants. The most steady, industrious, and skillful laborers, are ever most sure of employment, and such rarely fail of obtaining it, for it is to the interest of the employer to retain such. A serviceable direction should be given to the powers of industry.

We cannot urge too often upon parents to cultivate to the utmost, the talents of their children, and give them a right direction and free scope. The character of a nation depends on its people, and that depends on their home lives. A nation has not arrived at its highest state of perfection until each member of the community has every faculty and energy developed, and fully employed. Undoubtedly many are possessed of capabilities they never dreamed of possessing until some embarrassment, or disaster, brought them out. But the active exercise of their other powers had given them energy that led to the development of these.

The machinery of the human mind should be kept in

proper working order to accomplish much. The framework in which it rests, should not be worn out by use, or decayed by premature age, induced by any avoidable cause. If you would make yourselves essential to others, you must do something for their comfort, or interest, which they have not the ability or the inclination to do. That you can do so must be proved in many cases by personal effort, or by the evidence of what you have done for others. Many people estimate others exactly in proportion to what they do for them, not in proportion to their moral worth. Let your work, whether mental or manual, be *practical* — something that will benefit yourselves or others. You may put in operation a cause, the results of which will be limitless. You may, perhaps, advance ideas that will benefit all Christendom. Amid provocations and ill health, endeavor to retain your self-control, and so far as you can, consistently with your conscience, agree with those among whom you live, and, in doing so, cultivate a sympathetic nature. Express and maintain, so far as you can, an interest in everybody, yet without permitting your spirit-nature to be exhausted. Do not let the faults of those connected with you sour your temper. Be as careful to observe truthfulness when talking to your inferiors as to those above you. Acquire that knowledge and discernment, that will serve as a safeguard amid the temptations of a deceitful world. By your indefatigable efforts, and the results, be individually a practical illustration, a living memorial of what one woman may accomplish when she has a definite purpose in view.

OPPORTUNITIES OF DOING GOOD.

TO benefit any class of people, thought, time, money, and strength must be given. Some injudicious, but kind-hearted people, do not consider that by trying to correct certain minor errors in society they may drive the victims into greater poverty and evil.

If some single lady, or widow of wealth, would like to devote her time, talents, and some of her means, to the good of her sex, let her prepare herself for carrying on one of the pursuits, presenting a prospect of success, set forth in my work entitled "The Employments of Women." She might, in time, receive back all, or more than she had expended, and by her goodness win the love and gratitude of many that she would personally benefit, by furnishing employment and wages. She would possess, too, the admiration and approbation of those who only hear of her. The blessings of many will rest upon her in life, and when she is gone to her long home her memory will be cherished. She may set in action a series of causes that shall be followed by an indefinite number of advantages being gained for women. If she did not succeed in realizing her expectations, it might lead others to experiment, and exert themselves, until something is accomplished. Very few of the great discoveries and inventions were made perfect at first. One commenced, another discovered some defect, and remedied it, another added some improvement, and so on, until the acme of perfection has been attained in many, at first, crude inventions.

If wealthy women would bequeath their money to establish colleges for women, to aid them in getting into new branches of labor, to establish homes for those out of employment, hospitals for the sick, and asylums for the aged, it would be much to their credit. Seldom, if ever, is an effort for good lost. The very effort brings with it a blessing to the individual. Besides, there is a luxury in doing good. If you go forward, and succeed, cheerfully extend the benefit to others. Be not too hasty to reap the fruit of your toil. It is not in the bright hours of spring that the trees are filled with fruit, but in the long, burning days of summer; so time and experience must ripen the fruit of your toil. Work, and leave the result to Heaven.

Both in the country and in town opportunities offer constantly for doing good. Probably more opportunities offer in a city, on account of the great collection of people, and their wants not being so generally known. But the mind is so much divided by the vanities, and varieties of a city, and there are so many impositions, that the heart loses much of its tenderness, and desire to expend upon others its warm, generous impulses. Besides, in a city there are constant temptations to waste time and opportunity of doing good. But, by overcoming these temptations, and working while it is day with all the energies and faculties, character is ennobled and purified, and the Christian receives an additional lustre to his already bright profession. Woman's agency in the success of the world, her influence on its destiny for weal or woe, her efforts to make labor honorable or degrading, her ability to open new occupations to women, her power to save thousands of her sex from ruin of soul and body, or add to their degradation, seem to form the problem now to be solved in England, and in our own country.

The duties of a married woman may not employ all her energies. Why, then, should she not visit the sick and poor? The true glory of a woman lies in her usefulness. Mental and moral labors are to be wrought, and who so fit as woman? The sick are to be nursed, the poor clothed, the orphan provided for; the helplessness of childhood and old age is to be looked after; misery, wretchedness, and want are to be banished — and who so competent as woman? Vice and crime are to give way to virtue, and purity, and love, and holiness — and who a more powerful champion than woman?

An obligation rests on those in easy circumstances to render as comfortable as possible those not so highly favored. It is their duty to see that those able to work have it, and are well paid, and that the aged and orphans unable to work be fed and clothed. Very many ladies in our large cities might gladden the hearts of the homeless and desolate. What is the probable proportion of single women of wealth and leisure who have their faculties fully and profitably brought into use? Is it not small?

Quiet, unobtrusive charity is not less precious in the sight of God than the most public. "The poor ye have always with you." The condition of the poor should be investigated, and such assistance given as discretion dictates. It will do the rich good; it will warm their hearts, remind them of the fickleness of fortune, and impress on them a consciousness of their common origin. Money is of no value to the possessor, or any one else, unless in circulation. If hoarded up, it cannot do any one good.

Of what avail is talent or genius unless profitably used? As well be without. Then develop your physical and mental powers to their fullest extent, and seek for opportunities to use them. You will not have occasion to seek long. More evil, perhaps, might be prevented by encouraging hope in the poor and distressed. Hope is a strong principle of our nature, and without it an appeal to the energies is almost useless. We should often be unable to support the tax levied upon our sympathies, by the suffering that surrounds us, were it not for the exertions called forth to alleviate. And, O, how often should we sink under discouragement, in our efforts to overcome wrong, were it not for a reliance upon a higher power!

Much evil might be prevented by offering rewards for virtuous and useful actions. Morality can be greatly promoted among the lower classes by the encouragement and example of those in better conditions. You may excite their feelings, arouse their impulses, and restore that vitality which has long slumbered. The voice, the words, the manners of refined and amiable women will do much to influence the ignorant or degraded of their own sex. It will accomplish more than aught else. And the very fact that one whom they respect manifests an interest in them will, of itself, be a safeguard. Make them feel that they can be, and do, something, and when they come to respect themselves, and feel that they are worthy of respect, they will bless you who kindly encouraged them, and pointed them to the path of truth and virtue. Love of our fellow-beings is but a reflection of that higher and purer love we experience for the Author of all good. There will be much that is disagreeable to the sight, and sickening to the heart, in your labors, but do not mind that. Your efforts to do good will not be lost, though you see not the result. "In addressing persons of inferior station, do not be prone to suppose that there is much occasion for intellectual condescension on your part; at any rate, do not be careless in what you say, as if anything would do for them. Observe the almost infinite fleetness of your own powers of thought, and then consider whether it is likely that education has much to do with this. Use simple language, but do not fear to put substance in it. Choose, if you like, common materials, but make the best structure you can of them; and be assured that method and logical order are not thrown away upon any one."

The isolation that exists between families, and between individuals without relatives, forming the society of a large city, is a barrier to much of the good that might otherwise be done. Many are totally ignorant of the poor, it may be, in the adjoining square. Individual effort may accomplish much, but in cities, when merged into a society or organization, it may accomplish a more than proportionate amount. Organize societies for furnishing destitute women with remunerative employment, and homes for such women when out of employment. Let your heart be about it, and, our word for it, you will find enough to do. Establish industrial schools. See to it that girls are trained to some honest pursuit, and we will venture to say there will not be one fiftieth as much misery, and vice, and degradation, among women so trained, as among those that are not. Thousands of your sex are this night on the road to ruin. Souls are too precious to be sacrificed. Let them not linger on the shores of eternal death. Go to their rescue, and point them to a Savior of love and pity. To save from degradation your sisters (for are you not all of the same stock, having the same origin?) is a duty you owe, not merely as Christians, but as women. You are responsible to God, your country, your friends, and yourselves, for exertion in this matter.

Your acquaintance with people, your own wants, and reflection, may impress you with other means of usefulness to be accomplished than those that have been mentioned. At first the idea may seem but a seed. You may plant the seed. The germ, by sunlight, moisture, earth, and air, expands and bursts; a stem rises, leaves grow out, blossoms come forth, and there it is — a whole, living, and beautiful plant. So your idea may gradually develop and take form, until it is no longer the dry, dark seed of a few months back, but a bright, glowing, and spreading plant, beneath which many may rest, when wearied by the hard and hurried tramp of life. Let your work be woman's work — one of the head and heart. Let the knowledge you acquire be the assistant to others you have sought for yourself.

Among other methods of doing good, I would beg of ladies to patronize or encourage establishments where the workwomen are not underpaid or overworked. They could, without much trouble, learn where such is the case. In some of our large cities are houses where girls are required to labor for their employers every moment of their waking hours, except when eating a hurried meal. Feel for those poor girls as you would for a sister, and, O, how vast the amount of good you may accomplish! Every Christian man and woman possessed of reason, and the comforts of life, should, if they have a moment of leisure, or a spare dollar, be up and doing, for "the night cometh, when none can work." Truly "*the harvest is plenteous, and the laborers few.*"

People of wealth and leisure, with judgment and inventive skill, could confer a benefit on hand-workers by increasing the value of that work, instructing them in the best methods of performing it, in adding to the facilities for prosecuting it efficiently and expeditiously, and in making known the inventions for preventing disease from certain employments. The rich can thus help to save themselves from idle, enervated, aimless lives. Any surplus of worldly possessions they have might be advantageously used in carrying out such benevolent suggestions. It would be a good investment with the rich — a deposit in the bank of heaven.

LADIES' BENEVOLENT ORGANIZATIONS.

IN our largest cities there are thousands of females engaged in various employments, and day after day more come in. Many of them are without friends or even acquaintances. Perhaps they think, as the city is large, there must be many openings for employment, and to get there is all that is sufficient. My attention has been drawn to this subject by cases that came immediately under my observation. And to the ladies of our cities, that are champions in a good cause, I would call attention.

About ten years ago I met with one case referred to. I was on a boat coming to St. Louis. Among the lady passengers I observed a girl about sixteen, I presume, plainly and neatly dressed. She looked sad and lonely, but, I supposed, was traveling with some one. While standing on the guard, as the boat drew near St. Louis, a pleasant little lady pointed out to me her father's residence. Then I made some inquiry in regard to the different buildings, whose spires loomed above that great and proud city. Our desultory talk ran from one subject to another, until the lady remarked, "There is a young lady on the boat that has aroused my sympathy. She tells me she is coming to St. Louis to seek employment as a seamstress, and on inquiry, I learned from her she has not a friend or acquaintance in the place." I asked a description, and found it was the sad, quiet-looking girl I had observed. Well, thought I, if there were only a Ladies' Aid Association to which I might direct her, how grateful I should be! She might go there and make known her wants and abilities, and perhaps be cheered and helped on her rough, lonely road. A word of sympathy, advice, and assistance might relieve her anxious mind.

While traveling in a stage-coach from St. Louis, I learned, accidentally, of a different, but somewhat similar case, from the conversation of some passengers — the relater of the incident being a man that I knew by reputation as a man of influence, standing and piety.

Last summer, while traveling on the Ohio River, two other cases were incidentally brought to my immediate knowledge — one an orphan girl — the other with a trifling, drunken father. They were going to new places to seek employment. In those places they had no friends or acquaintances, and as to letters of introduction, or credentials, they scarcely knew what they were. Poor girls! I thought then, if in Louisville, St. Louis, Chicago and New Orleans, there existed Protestant institutions, of a charitable kind, for seeking and furnishing employment to young women, what a great blessing it would be. Young ladies that have leisure, might do an immense amount of good by interesting themselves in such a work. Ah! my friends, you, who enjoy the comforts and pleasures of life, little know the hardships, sufferings and temptations of the poor. Perhaps some say we should be imposed upon. Better bear imposition occasionally than permit one soul to be lost. I appeal to you, kind women in towns and cities. How many a weary, homeless one of your sex might be saved, if some kind guardian were at hand to guide and direct her in obtaining employment. If every liberal and benevolent woman would take each one of the kind that came to her knowledge, by the hand, and say, "Friend, here is a home and employment for you," how many might be saved from the snare of the tempter! Here is a work for your hands and hearts. Form associations and build up asylums where these poor lone wanderers may come until they get employment. Furnish them with remunerative work if you can — if not, assist them in their efforts to obtain employment, and ever keep a kind and watchful eye over them, and you will be blessed by your heavenly Father. Let the enterprise have for its object the good of humanity. The coöperation of educated and noble men will give spirit and strength to the Association. Let such rally their powers. "Gently scan your brother man. Still gentler, sister woman." The few flowers that bloom in the desert of life — kindness, sympathy and love — the lone, sad ones, you would benefit, may not have known. Palliate their misery. Calm their souls wrung by anguish. Exchange the dark and stormy path they have trod for a quiet and peaceful one. Your personal efforts and influence can do much. Wearied and worn, it may be, these homeless wanderers find not a resting-place in this dark, gloomy world. Like a bird of passage, they flit from place to place, and like the first dove Noah sent forth, find not a resting-place for the sole of their foot.

Say not there are none such. Skeptics, there are such, and many such; and those that have lived any time in large cities can testify to such cases having fallen under their own observation. What is wrong in woman is wrong in man, and what is right in woman is right in man; but the injustice of society permits that to be right in a man which would be considered very bad in woman. There is not in the Bible a code of morals for man and another for woman; but some men, self-indulgent to themselves and harsh in their judgment of women, have made one which, to some extent, regulates the general opinion of society. Custom blinds to the error of many things in civilized life.

HOUSES OF REFUGE AND INDUSTRIAL SCHOOLS.

HAVE pity on homeless, neglected children. To them life is a long, dark void, broken only by wails and sobs. No parent's love has warmed their hearts. The kind voice, the soft gleam of the eye, the warm pressure of the hand, are unknown to them. Affection has not provided them with a home. Their young hearts, frozen by neglect and vice, might be softened by tenderness, and their feet directed in the path of duty by kindness. Their griefs are hard to be borne. They are oppressed and degraded. O, raise poor neglected children from their sad and low condition. They hear not the music of a loved one's voice, nor watch the tender love-lit eyes. The Angel of Love long since ceased to spread his pinions above them. On the young brow is the impress of sorrow. The young face is lined with marks of care. The tear of sorrow and grief falls from the eye. How eloquently it speaks! It tells of anguish of spirit and a bleeding heart. The life-blood of that young heart is curdled. It has been accustomed to see that evil of nature, and blackness of heart, which, of all others, a child should never know. Then gladden the lonely path of young wanderers. Give them sympathy and companionship. Encourage them in the performance of duty — stimulate them to persevere in overcoming difficulties. Fill their hearts with a love of justice, truth, and mercy. When the sensitive nature of childhood is chilled by coldness and neglect, when the buoyant spirit is shadowed, and the outgushing affection of a warm, loving heart is checked, or cast back on itself, it proves a hard, bitter lesson. Distrust follows, and its whole retinue of gloomy attendants.

Many persons of enlarged views, and extended observation, think it a fault of the present age that the remedial schemes exceed the preventive. No power is more effectual for the world's reform than proper attention to the rising generation. The mind is as much developed as the physical being by action. We think our orphan asylums, industrial, and reformatory schools, have generally confined their pupils too much to books, and not enough to the acquisition of a pursuit for after-support. Children need to be taught to labor intelligently, and to use the best and most approved means for accomplishing the results. The discipline so acquired, and the habits formed, would be ever after an invaluable acquisition.

A mighty work has been commenced and carried on in the North in the rescuing of children from bad influences, and placing them in homes where they will be cared for, and religiously trained. Institutions for the reform of juvenile criminals, are very much needed in our Western States. At Wilson's Industrial School, New York, some of the older girls are taught dress-making by a practical dress-maker, who receives a salary. When they have learned, they can remain, and for their sewing receive four dollars per month and their dinners, but they must attend school in the morning. They receive, as others do, a penny for each good mark in school. Opportunities that offer for getting them situations where they can do better are effectually used. The school has most girls in winter. In summer many go to the country and pick berries, put up pickles, &c. Many of the summer inmates are fur-sewers. In New York some Sisters of Charity conduct an Industrial School, where an orphan girl, for one hundred dollars, is supported for three years, and during the time is taught a trade, and some book learning. In houses of refuge at the North, for boys, different trades are taught — shoe-making, broom-making, whip-making, chair-seating, the weaving of wire-cloth, &c. A reformatory school of Boston, has originated the plan of employing the boys in the different occupations requisite for navigating vessels. The institution has one or more boats of its own, manned, and conducted almost entirely by its boys. Many a child is saved from ruin by being provided with a pleasant reformatory home. In a few orphan asylums, just as a girl has reached the age when she most needs protection and counsel, companionship and sympathy, and the possession of some regular occupation by which to earn a livelihood, she is, by rules limiting the advantages of the institution to those of specified ages, excluded from the shelter of said institution; its doors are closed upon her, and she must go forth into the cold world to fight the battle of life alone and unarmed. But in most charitable institutions care is taken to secure good homes to the inmates when they leave.

* * * * *

Poor young pilgrim, may strangers care for thee and bless thee. May they give thee a home — a cheerful fireside. May they practice lessons of virtue and charity, as well as teach them. May they carry out the wish of a young poet:

> "A little life-boat I will be —
> And where'er the storms have raged,
> That made a wreck of peace and happiness,
> I'll cruise to pick the lost ones up, and save,
> And give them food and drink for sustenance."

And mayst thou, young pilgrim, though grateful for earthly blessings, not forget to look forward "to thy better rest in heaven."

BOARDING-HOUSES FOR WORKWOMEN.

IN all large cities boarding-houses should be established for workwomen. They should be under the supervision of the various churches, or conducted by organizations of humane and benevolent ladies. The price of board should be such as to place it within the power of all workers, receiving moderate wages, to avail themselves of the comforts of the house. To establish such houses would require judgment and peculiar tact. They must be adapted to the social position and education of the occupants, yet of such a character as to elevate and improve them. The houses should be in healthy and respectable locations, kept neat and comfortable; plain, wholesome, well-prepared food, furnished at regular hours, and a purely moral and religious influence exerted. It would be well to have a flower garden attached. It would be well to have family worship, and, on Sunday evening, a Bible class for those who choose to attend. Lectures by distinguished men, social gatherings occasionally, a library and reading-room, magic-lantern exhibitions, paintings, statuary, musical instruments, innocent and instructive games, drawing and singing classes, would tend to the elevation, and contribute to the recreation of the inmates. A pleasant change, now and then, might be to assemble and sew, while one of the number reads aloud from a selected book or magazine. A matron should be secured that would exert a good influence, and show the boarders attention in sickness and distress. By such kindness, some may be saved from the snares and pitfalls that beset the weary, heart-sick pilgrim.

Connected with the bookbindery of the Appletons, in New York, is a society formed of the women who work in it, that contribute a small sum weekly to the care of the sick of their number. It is a wise regulation, and one we would love to see adopted by all establishments where women are employed. In several of the large stores of New York and Philadelphia, the saleswomen and lady book-keepers have lunch at twelve or half past twelve. The arrangements are such that they can have tea or coffee made. It is the case at Evans's and Sharpless's stores, Philadelphia, and at Harpers' bookbindery, New York. At the Mission Rooms opposite the Methodist Book Concern, New York, prayer-meeting is held every Thursday, at noon, for the work-people of the establishment. A city missionary told me he thought about one half of the workwomen of New York board, and one half live at home. They pay, in ordinary times, for board, from fifty cents to five dollars and fifty cents a week. The wages of some workwomen are such that they can only get board of the most common kind. The majority of those in the lower walks of life, in New York city, sleep in a room with from ten to twenty persons, and, in many cases, not all of their own sex. Some, owing to the crowded condition of the house, are obliged to sleep in the same room with the man and woman of the house. When human beings are huddled together in that way, is it strange that crime, misery, degradation, and disease are rife among them? A lady connected with the Magdalen Society of New York told me that she knew of several girls who had been ruined by getting into boarding-houses they were told were respectable, but found, to their sorrow, were not. An intelligent young girl told me there is great corruption in many of the boarding-houses for work-girls in New York. Some men, able to pay good prices, board in those cheap houses for the influence they may obtain over the girls, and finally ruin them. When the dread of becoming homeless and friendless enters the every thought of work-girls, and the dread of destitution and famine stares them in the face, is it strange they find it difficult to compose their minds to reflection, or anything else, or that they feel no interest in reading? Indeed, many of them cannot read; besides, how very few are able to get books! Add to this the fact that in a room where a dozen or more are variously engaged, it requires some practice to abstract one's self sufficiently to become absorbed in a book. And in the densely crowded portions of a city the rooms of some are between a rum-shop and a gambling-house, for poverty precludes a choice of locality. In New York there is a boarding-house the inmates of which are mostly young ladies attending the School of Design, where they acquire a knowledge of wood engraving, china decorating, designing for wall-paper, &c., by which to earn a livelihood in those departments of art. They are well educated — many of them have been teachers, and most of them are orphans, but have very limited means. They are plainly but comfortably accommodated, and receive their boarding at a low rate. A few teachers, dress-makers, and store-girls, whose incomes are small, are also accommodated.

Three boarding-houses of a kindred nature have recently been established there, in two of which women of all pursuits and all ages are received; two are also in operation in Philadelphia, two in Boston, and one in Chicago.

Would it not be a noble work for some wealthy person, or persons, to establish a home for virtuous, worthy women, when out of employment, and where facilities would be afforded for securing them some respectable reumerative employment? Such a temporary home would prove a blessing to many a good but homeless woman. It would be American women, of some education, for whose benefit I would especially suggest the enterprise, and at the present time, when hundreds and thousands have lost, by the war, property and friends on whom they depended for support.

LADIES' EMPLOYMENT AGENCY.

THE object of such an agency as I suggest is to furnish employment to women, and to be the means of opening more occupations, particularly to educated women, and, in so doing, increase their ways of earning a respectable livelihood, and also bring about a better remuneration for women's work. That there is a necessity for such an agency, is very evident from the vast number of dependent women.

It surely cannot be that more women have been placed upon earth than there is any use for. If not, their faculties should be healthily and fully developed, and it cannot be done without employment.

In conducting this agency it is necessary to have an organization of ladies and gentlemen, whose aid, advice and encouragement will be given. Meetings should be held by them at least once a fortnight, until the agency is well established, to talk over matters connected with it. The judgment and tact of any one individual are insufficient to direct the varied cases that are submitted. It would be well to interest wealthy and influential ladies in the cause. By explaining in person the object in view, a deeper impression is made than by writing. People interested in this matter could do much to secure employees of a good class.

The enterprise can be made a matter of mutual advantage to employers and employees, and every portion of the country be thereby benefited.

Great efforts must be made, and every precaution used, to prevent imposition. No woman should have the privileges of the agency who cannot bring a letter of introduction and recommendation, or present testimonials of character from some respectable and responsible person in the city, or out of it. If from a person out of the city, the character of *that* person is to be ascertained, if possible, and, if found reliable, he or she is to be written to immediately, to ascertain if the reference is genuine. Much care should be exercised in the selection of a person to take charge of the office. A character of the highest moral tone, influenced by religious principles, united with agreeable manners, business habits, and a good knowledge of the French and German languages, is *desideratum* of the first importance. The duties of the office should be performed in a faithful Christian spirit.

Some partiality should be shown in selecting situations offered to workers. A choice must always be made, where different locations offer, of those best adapted to health, and furnishing the best advantages religiously, socially, and educationally. These advantages alone should make a distinction.

When application is made to the agency for lady copyists, secretaries, book-keepers, &c., by persons living out of the city, they should furnish satisfactory references, unless they are known to some members of the board.

The difficulty of sending women from the agency to employers in other places might, I think, be obviated in this way. The employers might pay the traveling expenses to the place on condition the individual gives a written agreement to remain six months, and work for specified wages, or work a certain length of time without charge, until traveling expenses are defrayed. If the applicant pays her expenses, she should be at liberty to leave as soon as she pleases. If funds to convey the lady whose services are required to her place of destination are to be furnished by the employer, they must be received prior to the lady starting on her journey. Money can be sent by mail, by express, or in any other safe way, and as soon as received, the agent, or one of the committee, will purchase tickets for the place of destination, and supply enough money out of that sum to purchase such refreshments as will be needed on the journey, and furnish an additional item to use in case of detention on the way by accident or sickness. A sum should be paid by the applicant as a registration fee, and something by employers. The amount can be determined on by the committee. I would suggest a fee of two dollars under professional, artistic, or mercantile pursuits; in other avocations, one dollar and fifty cents. A percentage may also be charged on the salary when the place is secured.

An annual report of the agency should be published. Donations or legacies left to the agency should be accepted if they do not conflict with its spirit and intention. They might form a fund to aid those unable to secure the services of the agency. As stated before, the benefits of the agency should accrue to women in any part of the United States from which application is made, if the cases are found worthy of attention. After the most deserving belonging to the city have been accommodated, others should be, so far as the means of the agency will admit. Such applicants as are exceedingly fastidious about the places offered them, and very difficult to please, after proper effort has been made to give them satisfaction, should be set aside for other applicants.

If keepers of fancy stores, dry goods merchants, druggists, &c., would employ women, it would help to bring the enterprise more directly into operation.

The field for the establishment of such an agency is clear. Many men, now having female relatives or connections dependent on them, would avail themselves of the privileges of the agency, and many employers would take women because their labor is cheaper. Many lady teachers would prefer to come to a lady to get a situation.

SECRET SOCIETIES.

I HAVE much faith in organizations for accomplishing good when conducted by people of integrity and judgment. The united thought, ingenuity, and effort, of a number, are brought to bear upon one subject, or in pursuance of one object. The benefit accruing is similar to that of a division of labor in mechanical employments. But never, under any circumstances, or in any climate, can we tolerate in such societies a want of personal freedom. What are considered such societies by some people exist in the Roman Catholic church. One of their forms is of a secret nature — that of confession. Rigid Protestants consider it a blot upon their religion, a curse that should not be suffered. Like everything else, it has its merits and demerits. In some respects it has an advantage that no Protestant church possesses. A virtuous, judicious, and honorable confessor, may be a guide, and counselor, to the lonely and desolate. He will advise with, upon *temporal*, as well as spiritual matters, and give that friendly aid, and those valuable suggestions, that many a poor mortal in a Protestant church *needs*, but *never receives*. I doubt not but the confessional has saved many a woman from ruin, and insanity, and many a man from deeds of desperation, and even suicide. The Roman Catholic church has made a wise provision for its single women by establishing sisterhoods. The property of those who become members goes into the common fund; those that are without means are provided for. All give their time, and efforts, to the performance of specified duties, selected with reference to the capabilities of each individual. A full equivalent, and in many cases more than an equivalent, is thus given in the services of even those members that enter without means, for the material comforts they receive; yet it relieves thousands of women from the fear that they will not be provided for, and taken care of in old age. Protestants are beginning to see its advantages, and are establishing orders of Deaconesses, which are similar in their nature. The restrictions of Protestant organizations are not so great, they not requiring the entire surrender of property, nor a vow of eternal celibacy, nor a life-long servitude. Such a course better accords with our ideas of liberty. Let women leave the orders when they wish. Many women become nuns partially ignorant of the sacrifices to be incurred, the hardships endured. The vows once taken, they are forever cut off from intercourse with every human being, save their sister nuns, and the priests to whom they confess. If we are rightly informed, the members of the *inclosed sisterhoods* are debarred intercourse even with each other. They are immured in prison walls, unable to leave, or even escape if they desire. They are deprived of breathing the pure air, and treading the green earth. Their buildings are the only ones in this country that are exempt from the eye of civil scrutiny, and they ought not to be.

WOMEN WITHOUT A HOME.

TO girls that have their own way to make through the world, life presents but little that is inviting. A girl is left destitute. She looks about her, and on reflection or inquiry, perhaps, finds she may engage in some labor, but fears that the propriety of her course may be questioned. Naturally timid, and wanting encouragement, she shrinks back, and perhaps becomes, the rest of her life, a helpless, soured woman, clinging as she can to some relative or friend for a support. If we analyze her feelings, we find her inefficiency arose from the *want of self-reliance, and a morbid sensitiveness.* The last-mentioned bane to success is one for which many parents are accountable. They raise their children as they would hot-house plants, instead of preparing them for the chilling winds and stormy tempests of life. If there is one feeling, above all others, I would implant in a girl, it is *self-reliance*, particularly if I had reason to think her path in life would be single and alone. And to those whose faith in humanity has been shaken, who have discovered the heartless selfishness that characterizes the generality of mankind, woe, woe to their sad hearts. Bleeding and sore, may their feet tread the highway of life, with none to comfort and cheer. Yet look up, sad ones, your Father in heaven counts your tears and hears your every sigh. Angels are hovering near, and would direct your thoughts to the land of blessedness above.

Says Miss Beecher, of young ladies, after completing their school education, before becoming settled in life, "That restless longing for excitement, that craving for unattainable good, that morbid action of the imagination, that dissatisfaction with the world, that fictitious interest in trifles, and those alternations of high excitement and brooding apathy — these are the secret history of many a gifted, and highly cultivated female mind."

The fears, uncertainties, and anxieties, that disturb single women, are greater than those of married women. It may be that they have not greater cause. But they have more time to yield to such apprehensions. Their feelings are generally more acute, and their thoughts more centered in self. The fear of not being provided for in old age is one source of disquietude to single women. If such would only consider how many women marry men who fail in health, or lose their energies, or who are improvident, and run through with all they have, without the business ability to replace as they go; that many women marry men who prove unkind, trifling, and dissipated — who do nothing to aid their wives — in many cases are supported by them, while a vast number become widows, and must support, not only themselves, but a family of children, we think the fear might quickly give way to the consciousness that a woman, with time, and means to sustain her, may fortify herself against this difficulty, by acquiring a practical knowledge of some pursuit that she may, if necessary, turn to account.

Many a single woman becomes an auxiliary to a family. There are many ways in which such a one can make herself useful. A woman so situated needs much delicacy and tact. She should be careful not to offer advice unasked, and not to assume authority, (unless delegated,) over children and servants.

The woman who is cast alone and unprotected on the world, without means, or a home, for no fault of her own, has a claim upon Christian men and women to provide her with a respectable home, and aid her in obtaining employment by which to earn her living. But it is a lamentable fact that a woman so situated is often neglected — yea, looked upon suspiciously, and avoided, even by those men and women *calling themselves Christians.*

WOMEN IN DIFFERENT STAGES OF SOCIETY.

WOMEN in primitive states of society, cook, tend the flocks, spin, and weave cloth for garments and tents. Yet they enjoy as great personal freedom as those in more improved conditions of society.

When women are cramped, restrained, and oppressed, they never can attain a full development of their mental and moral nature. As society improves, women rise in rank, and are more valued for their mental and moral powers. Consequently they become cultivated. A corresponding change takes place among men, but the change among men is prior to that of women. The estimate placed upon men and women ceases to be proportioned to their physical force. The body sinks in significance beneath the mind, and its attainments. Woman becomes less profitable as a slave, but a more entertaining and instructive companion.

In a country where a free expression of religious and political opinions is prohibited, where the energies of the press are unduly curbed, woman must suffer, like man, the bad effects. Domestic tyranny will follow in the wake of civil and religious intolerance, mind will be fettered, and woman will become degraded. That strong family attachment which springs from a similarity of moral sentiments, or intellectual companionship, will be rarely known.

We learn from the writings of Solomon, that the Hebrew women under the early monarchy, transacted business, carried on commercial speculations, and performed all agencies in which forethought and judgment were necessary. Such were the women who " considered a field, and bought it, and planted a vineyard; who made fine linen and sold it, and delivered girdles to the merchants; who purchased wool and flax, and worked diligently with their own hands."

MODERN SOCIETY.

"IT is plain that, naturally, woman has more *curiosity* than man; that she is more *imitative* and more *communicative*, and that her *ambition* is not less. In her present condition, these faculties, demanding of their possessor plenty of out-door exercise, are employed to the disadvantage of society. Now, living unnaturally, she keeps whole communities in hot water. Her eagerness *to know*, her native *inquisitiveness*, leads to innumerable troubles. Her *communicative* attribute produces domestic turmoil. This evil results from the misplacement of woman in the mission of life. Woman is still the *angel* of poets, the *drudge* of tyrants, the *charm* of home, the *compound mystery* of philosophers, the *necessary evil* of politicians, the *flower* of society, the *victim* of masculine patronage, the *savior* of men, and the *terror* of bachelors. There are no legal prohibitions against women in regard to education or profession; but there is a despotism to which universally she is a slave, namely, the despotism of public opinion. Public opinion is her rule of faith and practice. She fails to draw a line of demarcation between public opinion and living principle. It is opinion, not law, that keeps woman out of pursuits whereby she could distinguish herself for talent and skill, could employ those mental faculties for the world's good which now *afflict* society, and could procure an independence in worldly goods — elevating her above the necessity of making marriage the only refuge against want. The popular structure of society develops four distinct types of female situations — the *fashionable woman* and the *drudge woman*, the *noble housewife* and the *abandoned female*."

It is a sad fact, that in all stages of society, even the

most enlightened, the pleasures of the body are more sought for, and enjoyed, than those of the mind. A splendid style of living is, in a city particularly, the ultimatum of most people's aspirations. In that way talent and moral worth are often overlooked, and forever hid in obscurity, unless some fortunate circumstance brings them to light.

Fashionable women are subject to extremes. Pretty women that indulge in frippery and frivolity, whose thoughts are of themselves only, and whose great delight is in a flirtation, rarely have the respect of sensible men, and are more rarely sought in marriage by them. Their principal admirers are men of gallantry, who care not to marry at all, or if they do, seek a woman of fortune, or a fashionable beauty, whose charms will draw about the husband a circle of wealthy people, or gay society.

Some weak, silly, artful women are as amiable as an angel before those they wish to please; as pliant as a willow-bough, apparently, yet in fact bent on their own aims and purposes; as obedient as a child, to observation, yet as perverse as a mule in reality; with a scrupulous regard to minor proprieties, but a total disregard to correct principles of honor. Sad is the moral history of such a woman, and lamentable her teachings!

Women not very fashionable, in moderate circumstances, are much cramped by the restraints of society. They are much influenced by what the world will say; they depend not enough on their own judgment and sense of propriety; their feelings are checked, and forced back upon themselves — they are not permitted to gush forth freely, and without interruption; their thoughts suffer in the same way. Their motives are apt to be misguided, and too low an estimate placed on their worth. A number run into the opposite extreme. They assume a haughty, indifferent manner, and care nothing for the opinion of others; they are vain and frivolous; pleasure-seeking is the aim of their existence; they are subject to the gossip and tattle of those like themselves. Women would not be so shallow and sensitive, if they mixed more with the world — men would not treat them as if they were dolls, but more as if they were rational beings.

Of woman in the middle classes of society in England, the author of "Woman's Industrial and Social Position" writes, "Isolated from the world, a stranger to the other sex, her faculties dulled by seclusion, she is regarded as incapable of forming a judgment, except on household affairs, and is content to lead the life of an upper servant."

Most men in the middle, or lower walks of life, like to see women work, but not to enter their occupations, unless it be their wives, sisters, and daughters, who, by assisting in their specific labor, will aid them in making money. Most proud, wealthy men do not object to women, in general, working, nor to their wives and sisters engaging in household labor, but would consider it a disgrace that they should work for money, particularly for others. Some cultivated men would prefer the women of their own families devoting themselves exclusively to the improvement of their minds, to the acquisition of accomplishments, and to benevolent works.

Why should the nature of a woman's education and training differ from that of a man's? Does she not require as much strength, breadth, discipline, and forethought of mind, to fulfill the duties of life?

Romanism would keep women in ignorance. Thereby the priests may govern the women, and the women the men. From politic motives, the priests may profess to advocate the education of females; but what is that education? Is it a training of the moral and mental powers? No! it is needlework, music, drawing, a smattering of the languages, and other showy accomplishments.

The time required for a high cultivation of mind precludes the attention to dress of a fashionable woman without fortune. In most cases, it is the youth, beauty, and vivacity of a woman, in the higher circles, that gain her the title of *angel*, and not her virtues, or superiority of mind.

Many people float too much on the surface. They do not dive into the facts and condition of every-day life. They attempt display, they ape gentility, they study to make a show before the world.

In New York, most women in the first, second, and third class hotels, and boarding-houses, have husbands to support them, and do not want the occupations and labors of a profession. Some are wealthy single women, who devote part of their time to benevolent works, and some spend their time visiting, reading novels, shopping, and in all the trivial pastimes of fashionable life pertaining to a city.

Most Americans are too ambitious. They are not satisfied with what they possess; they continually wish for more. Health may extend her beneficent influence, wealth may lavish her richest gifts, friends may surround, and honor crown their course; hope may gleam with its brilliant light, to cheer their pathway, but still some wish is ungratified. On the contrary, others are racked by pain, and distressed in mind, the present darkened by affliction, and the future yet darker; honor departs, wealth vanishes, friends forsake, yet their subjects desire not to exchange places with others. They humbly submit, and look with pious resignation to their heavenly Father, as the author of their afflictions, and yet the all-wise God.

We have heard some ladies say they would prefer being waited on in a store by men — they did not like saleswomen. But they were probably exceptions; or might it not have been that those ladies asked to see more goods, occupied more time, in short, were themselves more troublesome, and expected more attention, than if they had been claiming it at the hands of some of the opposite sex? Or is it that such women like the gossip and effeminacy of most dry goods salesmen? We have reason to think shop-women are generally as obliging as men in the same capacity, and have as much genuine politeness. Besides, they are quite as truthful and conscientious.

As society is artificial, so must domestic life partake of the same character. A higher, nobler existence should be sought. The problem of domestic and social reform is a difficult one to solve. It requires fresh and vigorous thought, moral courage, and independence of action. Many a struggle is made at the expense of principle to climb the ladder of fame, wealth, or position.

The claim that a person of wealth or talents has to the admiration of others depends on the use to which said wealth or talents are put, whether to a selfish or benevolent one. A man may deserve credit for the application to business and enterprise which has accumulated property; but, aside from this, his wealth should have no weight in determining the place he should hold in the estimation of others.

Says Madame de Héricourt,* "The progress hitherto made by humanity is that love has now for its end the perpetuation of the species, the modification of man by woman, and the production of labor. In a higher ideal of justice, *the sexes being equal in rights*, love will have a higher end; the spouses will unite on account of conformity of principles, union of hearts, wedding of intellects, common labor. Love will join them to double their strength, to modify them by each other. From the friction of their hearts will be struck out sentiments which neither would have had alone; from the union of their intellects will be born thoughts which neither would have had alone; from the aid that they will lend to each other, in their common labor, will proceed works that neither would have accomplished alone, as from the union of their whole being will be born new generations more perfect than the preceding, because they will be the product of the greatest possible harmony."

* "A Woman's Philosophy of Woman" should be read by every lady physician.

GIRLS RAISED WITH THE EXPECTATION OF MARRYING.

TOO many girls are educated with a view to married life. We are sorry that so many mothers who raise their daughters intending them to marry, do not fit them for married life, by forming in them active and industrious habits. But I would ask why girls should be educated to be wives more than industrial workers? Why be impressed with views that may not be realized? The present education of girls has a tendency to make them desire the admiration of the indiscriminate many, rather than the esteem of a few superior people. A great desire in a woman for the admiration of men, produces an indifference to the opinions and interests of her own sex. She cares not whether she is interesting to women, or beloved by them. How sad the history of such a one, if she fails to secure the love of any man whom she admires, or if she fails to realize her extravagant matrimonial expectations! She will feel that her hopes have proved "the baseless fabric of a vision that leaves not a trace behind." To one of strong feelings it is a death-knell to happiness. One of a light, changeable nature, may laugh off her disappointment, with the other (to her) trifles of life.

Even if certain that a majority of the girls being educated were to be wives, it would not be an easy task to direct their studies with that in view. Suppose a girl with a fondness for scientific pursuits married a learned man. It might be agreeable to him to have her continue the pursuit of such studies, or it might be altogether distasteful. If she married one with a plain education, he might, or he might not, desire to see his wife devote her time to the cultivation of her mind. Or even admitting his willingness, she might find her time otherwise so occupied, that she could not spare enough for that purpose. If her husband is a man that desires her to continue to cultivate her mind, and is able to afford her the means of doing so, she will be much favored.

Marriage in the higher circles of society has become, we fear, more a human than a divine institution. Many young ladies, whose parents are wealthy, know little else than how to spend money. When they marry they become in many cases burdens to their husbands, instead of assistants, and in time bring bankruptcy and ruin upon their families.

We would not for a moment make the relations of life less dear, or take from a virtuous home that holy sanctity which it deserves. Nor would we disincline those of our sex who would seek for usefulness and enjoyment in the domestic relationship of life. But we would love to see marriage regarded as the pure and holy sacrament it is, and entered into from unselfish motives, prompted by love alone. When a marriage is founded on right principles, and congenial tastes and opinions, with the exercise of patience and forbearance, it is the most contented condition in life. To marry badly is far worse than not to marry at all. What discord arises from an uncongenial alliance, what constant jarring, what discontent, what disorder of mind, wretchedness, and, eventually, idiocy, or insanity, and death! To the parties, the present is gloomy, the future hopeless. Not only is the welfare of the parties sacrificed in this world by it, but their interest in a better one jeopardized. Besides, what a wreck to the happiness of the offspring of such a marriage!

Marriage where one, or both, of the parties is deformed, or defective in mind, morals, or physique, should be prohibited by legislation. So should the marriage of those closely allied by relationship. Our asylums, for the insane, and demented, are a sad testimony to the recklessness of public opinion, and public action, on this subject.

Most marriages take place in times of peace and national prosperity. Cheerfulness and hope tend to produce love and marriage. Warm, genial seasons also have their influence. A low, or moderate price for the necessaries of life, is also conducive to marriage; likewise an increase of income. Fashion, too, has an influence in increasing, or diminishing, the number of marriages.

Some women marry for a position in society, but the majority of women probably marry to be with those they love. The influences are perhaps more varied that lead men to marry than women. Some men marry that they may have a comfortable home — some that they may receive more respect as members of society — some because they are lonely, and want companionship — some from affection, and some from passion — some for wealth — some because they think it a duty — some from one cause, and some from another.

"In some countries women enter into matrimony more readily than men, even where their affections are not concerned. The reasons are obvious. Women are more restrained by the laws and usages of society, than men, and the scope of their ambition is much more limited. Though marriage subjects them to many cares and privations, it gives them, in some respects, a greater degree of freedom and consideration; it likewise generally insures protection and support, and is almost the only way in which a woman can rise above her natural condition, with regard to wealth and rank."

Many a woman is tempted by her low wages to marry for a home. If a woman marries advantageously from proper motives, it is well, but if because she wants self-dependence in earning a livelihood, we fear it may be her lot to earn one when she has a family. It is often the case.

We fear the extravagant habits of some of our young ladies may do something to retard their matrimonial advancement. At one time, in Germany, so few ladies were solicited in marriage that the mothers got together, discussed the subject, and came to the conclusion that it was caused by their extravagant style of living and dressing. They made an agreement, and carried it out, that they, and their households, would retrench their expenses, as young men were frightened at the expenditure requisite to keep up an establishment, many of them being conscious their means would not permit it. As was expected — a change — a favorable change, in the matrimonial line, was the result. Indeed we think were a less tenacious hold made of fashion, less money spent, and more taste exercised on dress, most ladies would be better satisfied with themselves and their purses. The efforts made, by some mothers of the higher classes in England, to marry off their daughters, are ludicrously set forth, in the article styled Pigeons in "Modern Women."

Few women like to receive all, and give nothing. Consequently such wish to be prepared at the time of marriage for helping to bear the burden of life. A girl is as unfitted for the duties of a housekeeper, without some preparation, as a man pursuing a business that he has not learned. In addition to a knowledge of housekeeping, we would again recommend to women a practical acquaintance with a regular occupation. A man will then have this capital in addition to his wife, and she will, no doubt, cheerfully bring it into requisition, in case unforeseen changes call for it. Not that we would suppose men so mercenary as to seek in a wife such capital; yet it is not to be ignored, on the same ground that a snug little fortune is not objectionable to lay by for contingencies, although the present occupation yields sufficient income for present wants. Many women will revolt at the idea here thrown out. To such we would say, Acquire the capital referred to — an occupation — for your own personal good, in case your husband dies, or fails in business. The presence of mind, activity, and practical knowledge acquired, will be invaluable.

Some women impress upon their daughters the idea that the end and aim of their existence is to secure an advantageous marriage. In it must center all their efforts and attainments. The principle is deleterious. Silly girls, whose minds are filled with the thought that they are some day to lay aside their books, and as a matter of course marry, become frivolous and trifling in their manners, and talk, and fritter away their minds. The very fact that they look forward to marriage as the only aim in life, must have a tendency to preclude them from undertaking any definite pursuit, and from acquiring that strength and elevated tone of character, so essential to success in any great undertaking. It creates a feeling of anxiety and uncertainty, not favorable either to useful reflection or action. It checks independence of thought and expression; it mars purity and integrity of character. It causes some women to marry those not congenial, and as a consequence, domestic discord follows, with its ten thousand attendant evils and sorrows.

Unless a woman has an occupation, or some property, her chances for marriage are not great, because there are more marriageable women than men, and a great many men never marry. A middle-aged woman is rarely sought in marriage by a man of means, unless she has some property, or the practical knowledge of a pursuit. With some women the chance lies open, so far as they can see, to live single and work, or marry a man that they may have to support, and live wretchedly with. They had better marry plain, industrious, honest, moral farmers, than salesmen, with little to recommend them but their lily-white hands and fair speech.

Marriage makes no difference with a man's business. He goes on with it just the same as before. It is different with a woman. It interferes sadly with her business. In fact, the very nature of her occupation is changed.

Many young women marry before their constitutions become firm and well settled. It is sad to see a woman, just at the age when she is most capable of enjoying life, have her mind dwarfed, and her character belittled, with the petty details of housekeeping. Is it not better for young ladies, when they leave school, to spend a few years in the innocent amusements, and improving studies, that impressible and cultivated minds enjoy, and so gain strength for the performance of heavier duties? It will give time for the character to develop, the mind to mature. A woman will not then be so likely to marry a man without business habits, or who is trifling, and dissipated. How often it is that parents die, money becomes exhausted, the husband dissipated, and without any prospect of earning a decent support for herself the heart-broken wife is soon laid in her cold, cheerless grave. Or perhaps a woman marries well, but her husband suffers a reverse of fortune, and dies. She is left a widow with small children to support. Her education has been neglected, and she cannot teach. The needle offers a precarious subsistence, and toiling, and struggling, she lives on a prey to care, and anxiety, and dread, until exhausted nature gives way, and she is counted among the dead. Or perhaps she becomes an auxiliary to a family where she is considered a burden, or where there are not peace, and love, and harmony — where she has the cares, and not the comforts, of a home. There she is discontented, and her dependence makes her more so. Or, it may be, she enters a kind, agreeable family, that love her as a friend, and prize her as one of their own. There she may become a useful and agreeable acquisition to the family, and be happy in her adopted home. She may care for the children, attend on the family when sick, be a companion for the wife, and enliven the leisure hours of the husband by social intercourse. In such a home, under such circumstances, the ease and freedom of a single, or widowed life, can be enjoyed, while the heart is warmed by friendship.

Employers have told me that they can rarely get women to learn a trade that requires much time, and they do not learn so thoroughly what they undertake, and are not so industrious and efficient as men, because they look forward to marriage, and to laying aside their trade when married. We do not know to what extent this is a fact, but we are inclined to think that women, who are careless and inefficient in business, would be so in household duties. That they pursue their vocation merely as an expedient, does not, in our opinion, justify a neglect to acquire proficiency, or work industriously, and conscientiously. We have been told by employers that the most skillful, efficient, and industrious workwomen are always the first married.

The reproach some men cast on old maids, as they are pleased to term them, arises from a dread of seeing women independent of men. Most of such men would rather see dependent women become prostitutes than direct them how to earn an honest livelihood. In the eyes of such men a single woman who has passed the flower of youth is odious. Her virtue, intelligence, and usefulness pass for nothing.

FRIVOLITIES OF THE YOUNG.

THOUGHTLESSNESS is a common fault with many young people, particularly with those who have been much indulged, and had no great sorrow.

Dress and fashion usually occupy too much time with young ladies. Their constitutions become enfeebled — and is it strange? The hours that should be given to balmy sleep are passed in a routine of gay amusements. Frivolity is almost a characteristic of the minds of fashionable women. Many are as destitute of stability as froth, as unstable as water, and their thoughts like the mountain mist. They lack strength and discipline.

The mere negative existence of most young ladies in our cities may be attributed to circumstances. These are custom, and the out-door sameness of scene, with late hours, and irregular meals. If my young friends would consider the number of souls around them sinking into perdition, the number of sick and suffering bodies that require attention, the desolate and homeless ones that need comfort and protection, surely they would not complain that time passes slowly, that it hangs heavily on their hands. The mere calls of suffering humanity forbid a waste of time.

Some people, in years past, objected to the cultivation of a taste for music, on the ground that it enlivens the sensibilities of woman, and deepens her passions. Such objections are rarely made now, as the fashion of the day has rendered music an almost indispensable accomplishment. The effect produced in young people by hearing great admiration expressed of foreigners, particularly public singers and performers, is very pernicious. The airs they assume, their affected manners, and artificial graces, are imitated. And why should they not be, if they are worthy of admiration? But can they be admired by those of a strong, elevated nature?

I wish to see my sex honored, not merely because they are women, but because they have minds and hearts of such cultivation and goodness as must entitle them to honor and respect.

The influence of mind over mind is for eternity, as well as time. There is no influence, short of God's, equal to it. The murder of Time is beautifully portrayed by Miss Muloch, on page 17 of her "Woman's Thoughts about Women."

Things that appear trivial in the eyes of God may to us seem very important, and such as are trivial to us may to the Almighty be very important. He does not see as we do.

Some young people are filled with a yearning desire to see and know whatever is useful and valuable. They are capable of the most exquisite delight from the sight of a beautiful object, from reading a fine poem, from learning some useful fact, from enjoying the society of a friend.

To those young ladies who would have their pastime profitable, as well as pleasant, and are fond of flowers, I would suggest experiments to be made by them in the kinds of soil adapted to various plants, the amount of water, light, and heat they require, and their organization, as discovered by the microscope. To those fond of animal life, an inviting field might offer itself in an examination of the habits of insects and worms, their constitution, modes of living, &c. Those to whom minerals afford an interest, would find an engrossing study in their structures, forms, localities, and characters. Atmospheric and meteorological investigations might be made by women, and prove profitable contributions to science.

It is said that nothing is more absorbing than the exercise of a talent for writing, to such as write from the love of it — because they feel impelled by an onward something — *je ne sais quoi* — to do so. All else is forgotten, lost to sight. The excitement attending it is very great, dangerously so, if indulged in to excess. To such we recommend the pastime, but, at the same time, for health's sake, urge moderation.

REMARKS TO PARENTS.

MANY people are incapable of rightly discharging the solemn obligations and responsibilities of married life. Some cannot appreciate its duties, some are unfitted by bad health, some by want of moral qualities, and many others are mentally incapacitated.

It is not unfrequently the case that we see a woman, who has by her own industry and perseverance earned a livelihood, marry a man in moderate circumstances. Both toil and save, that they may bring up their children respectably. The sons are spared all the labor possible, or else toil and strive to dress their sisters handsomely. And as for the girls — bless me! — they dress like queens, and show off the expensive accomplishments they have acquired. Their hands are kept gloved, and tenderly cared for, until they vie with the snow-flake in whiteness. Their days are spent in shopping, calling, reading novels, and keeping in practice their costly and superficial acquirements. As to obtaining a knowledge of some employment by which they may support themselves (as their mothers did), if it became necessary, they would scorn the mention of it. They would consider it beneath their dignity.

Mrs. Graves writes, in her "Woman in America," "As soon as children are of sufficient age to minister to the wants of their parents, they should be required to do so. These services should always be proportioned to their years and their strength; but when time has at length brought their powers to maturity, the father and mother should then retire from laborious duty to the undisturbed quiet and repose of their firesides, and leave their sons to provide for their necessities, and their daughters to take upon themselves the burden of household management. It is a fatal mistake in parents to continue, throughout their lives, to be the ministering servants of their offspring. Fathers should be the patriarchal sovereigns, and mothers the queens of their households; and every child should be so trained as to yield them the willing homage of attention and respect, no less than of affection. And they who abdicate the throne legitimately belonging to them, either through neglect or weak indulgence, will find, in their old age, that there will be none to rise up and do them reverence."

A family isolated from relatives and connections, labors under many difficulties, particularly if the family is not a happy and united one.

Parents, give your children a comfortable home, where they may have a good influence and example. What is fame or wealth, without the pleasures of a happy home, whose inmates respect, love, and have confidence in each other? It is a bubble, a passing sunbeam. It cannot give substantial comfort.

Teach your children, by example, as well as by precept, to be good and useful. An influence, an example, may change the entire destinies of a child — and of all influences and examples that of the parent is the greatest. Teach your children to sacrifice their selfish desires in the effort to make others happy. When selfishness reigns in a family, is the governing principle, there must be envy, discord, hatred, and injustice. Selfishness and injustice are at the bottom of nearly, or quite, all family feuds. It is a parent's duty to check selfishness, petulance, and self-will, when first they display themselves in a child. Where love reigns there will be self-denial, forbearance, kindness, and harmony.

Encourage pure and elevated conversation; make companions of your children; encourage inquiry, and originate thought — the warm, impressive mind of youth receives ideas as readily as the earth absorbs water. Read with your children, and talk to them; encourage in them freedom of speech; to the best of your judgment, select proper books for their reading; put them under the influence of good people; never permit discontented, fault-finding, quarrelsome persons to make a home in your family — they will sow seed of the same nature in your children, which will ripen into poisonous fruit ere you are aware. The forming of an amiable disposition in children cannot be commenced too early; but the culture of the judgment should begin as early, and be as carefully pursued. Then may the affections and passions be subdued, and moderated, and regulated by the exercise of reason. One stronghold the Roman Catholics are gaining upon Protestants is through the influence of teachers and nurses of their own persuasion. It is a vast opening for their influence and power, in forming the religious predilections of youth. Refine the feelings and elevate the tastes of your children. Talk not too much of what they must eat, and drink, and wear, and yet enough to make them feel life is real. It is well for children to learn early to keep an account of their expenses. It accustoms them to figures, and often proves an economizer. Many poor parents might bind their children out to Western farmers, who would raise them to industrious habits, and teach them to work. If placed in proper families, their minds, morals, and manners would also be cared for. Already has this plan been carried into effect quite extensively by the Five Points Mission of New York.

A kind but firm control needs to be judiciously exercised by parents. A mother is likely to be too tender with her children, a father too severe. Subdue the temper, so far as you can, of your children by kindness — when you cannot in that way, use the rod. The want of subordination in American children has been loudly cried against by both foreign and American writers. Seek for your children associates that will make them better, not worse. Children require companionship. It is natural to them, and should be encouraged; but great care should be taken in guiding the selection of associates. Fit your children for active and pleasant pursuits. We beseech you, by the interest you feel in your daughters, to give them industrious habits, and the knowledge of an employment which they may profitably use, should they ever have occasion to do so. Your daughters have by nature as good a right to seek and follow an occupation, if they desire it, as your sons. I want to see the individuality of women more brought out. I want to see their personal characteristics and attainments more distinctly defined. They have by nature as distinct latent powers as men; but these powers are not developed. As a general thing, the studies they pursue, the tastes they cultivate, the style of dress, manners, and conversation they assume, are almost exactly the same. What a loss to society, what a failure in the economy of Nature, what a mystery in the plans of the Almighty, that parents are at the trouble and expense of raising and educating daughters, to be of no use in the world to themselves, or anybody else — ay, even worse, to fret, and murmur, and render unhappy themselves, and all about them! "To give education without giving an object, is but to strengthen the wings of a caged bird." The minds of most children, girls particularly, are not turned to the future in a business way — that is, their attention is not called at home, nor school, to what occupation they shall fit themselves for. It is a great oversight on the part of parents. The future is before them, and none can say what it may be. Women's physical wants are as great as those of men, and it requires as much to meet them; and that much must be paid for as dearly, though women are not paid half as well for their services. If parents do not provide their daughters with the ability to meet those wants honorably, by their exertions, they deserve the disgrace that, in many cases, will come upon them, as the authors of their own children's ruin. That women are endowed with the same faculties as men, and equal in every respect, is proof positive that they need, and should have, the same range for the development and use of those faculties, and that they should yield them the same privileges and profits.

I think it would be better if the prejudice against industrial laborers was done away at our public schools, the majority of whose male pupils become mechanics. It would familiarize them to the prospect, and increase their facilities for gaining information on the vocation they select. The remark will apply also to girls, who might have in view maintaining themselves as compositors, type-rubbers, fruit-raisers, poulterers, &c. Stimulate your children to constant and untiring exertion, to principles of honor, to acts of virtue, and worthy pursuits. Animate them in their search for truth and knowledge, until their countenances are lighted with the glow from virtuous principles and extensive knowledge. The seed of parents' sowing must sooner or later mature, and bring forth either good or evil fruit. Children are being molded by their parents' hands; they can make them good members of society, patriots, and philosophers, or raise them to be curses to themselves and their race — debased and vicious outcasts. The children of uneducated parents are rarely taught to use their faculties fully and efficiently. This accounts for the greater part of the stupidity existing — this, with idleness and natural listlessness, induced by the mental torpor of the children's ancestors, for generations past. We have seen it stated that "a crowd of persons, of both sexes, have less intelligence at thirty than at fifteen years of age. They have seen more things, and know less of them; they reason higher, but they reason less justly. By increasing physically, they have decreased morally; intuition has declined in them, and has turned to purely bestial instinct. It is the fault of man, and his gross habits, and bad government." And here the question arises, Why should weak-minded, unprincipled, or brutish people be permitted to marry, and bring into the world children to suffer misery, vice, disease, idiocy, and insanity? Why should such people be permitted to have an influence over their own children, other people's, or orphans? Why should diseased, disfigured people, deprived of one or more senses, be permitted to entail such afflictions upon offspring? Surely legislative action should be taken on the subject.

I would impress upon parents the need of being sincere and truthful. If your children discover in you a want of these qualities, they will cease to respect you, and you will imperil their souls by the example. Truthfulness, sincerity, and honesty are the base-work of a noble character. Parents of truth, honor, and affection are very rarely neglected by their children, while those who have neglected to educate their children, and train them in virtuous ways, sometimes suffer indifference, neglect, and even dislike. Do not fear losing the love of your children by correcting them for the expression of erroneous views, or the performance of sinful acts. Never sacrifice principle to popularity. You will gain nothing in the end by it. A close adherence to duty requires perseverance and conscientiousness.

A few words to the heads of families, in reference to each other, before I close. Wife, always consult your husband in preference to any one else, in reference to business and family matters, if he is a sober, correct man. Next consult your children, if they are worthy, and of sufficiently matured judgments. Never permit a stranger, or even relative, to come in as counselor, or manager of family matters, unless there are good reasons why your husband and children cannot first be consulted. If the opinions and advice of people out of the family circle must be sought, be careful to learn who are people of sufficient fineness of feeling to understand your embarrassment, with sufficient interest in you to study what is for your good, and with enough wisdom to properly counsel and aid you. I have known cases where adult children have been entirely alienated from their parents by knowing that strangers were permitted to take the place they should supply — that the advice of aliens had been sought when the advice of themselves was unsought. To a husband I would give the same advice. Consult with your wife and children, before, and in preference to, any one else. Sustain the authority of each other mildly, but firmly, that the children may know what to rely on, and that order and harmony may be preserved.

THOUGHTS FOR FATHERS.

THE social status of a family is, almost without exception, determined by the man. It is elevated not so much by what he is in himself, as by associating himself with worthy and respectable people, by his efforts to furnish his family with the comforts and refinements of life, giving to his children the advantages of a superior education, with opportunities to make the best use of those advantages, drawing about them influences of an elevating and purifying nature, instilling into them self-respect, and encouraging them in good words and deeds. It has long been a custom with the Prussian princes to learn a trade, by which, if they were ever thrown upon their own resources, they might earn their bread by manual labor. The young Prince Frederick William, who married the Princess of England, Queen Victoria's oldest daughter, learned the business of a compositor in a printing office. Every Emperor of China is, on his accession to the throne, obliged to give practical evidence of his knowledge of agriculture, by ploughing a designated piece of land. The plan may offer suggestions worth noting. The reverses of fortune are so frequent and so sudden in this country, that it behooves parents to prepare their daughters for them. Three plans are suggested by one of the most philanthropic women of the age, Miss Bessie R. Parkes, author of "Essays on Woman's Work." They are, that every father should give his daughter a practical business education, invest money in some permanent way for her support, or secure her a living by his life insurance. We would advise fathers to lay this to heart and act upon it. As the last two suggestions can be carried out where the parents are furnished with means, we will turn to the first suggestion, and consider it more fully. The individual and distinctive powers of women need to be more cultivated. Until the last few years the same studies were given them, the same tastes cultivated — in short, one pattern answered for all, notwithstanding their future duties, and positions in society, were to vary almost as much as the features of their faces. But if a daughter has one peculiar gift, why not cultivate it, as you would a son's? If she has a preference for one study, or one pursuit, why not give her the means and opportunity to attain excellence?

The self-reliance of females, that are timid, and likely to become dependent on their own resources, should be brought out as much as possible. This can be most efficiently done by kind encouragement. Give your daughters the power of self-support, and industrious habits, that they may, if necessary, earn a respectable living. You know not what may be their fate. Affluence and luxury may be yours now, but, ere you are forgotten beneath the sod, may come poverty, and distress, to the loved ones that gladden your heart. What then will become of your unmarried daughters? Perhaps you answer they will be taken care of in the homes of their brothers and sisters. Perhaps such homes will not be agreeable, either to themselves, or to those with whom they stay. Then give them a pursuit by which their own exertions will entitle them to a home, and free them from dependence. Have your daughters engage in such pastimes as will develop and strengthen their physical frames. Let them learn to swim, and shoot, to row a boat, and run a race. Wealth can procure almost any worldly enjoyment. Yet what good will the riches of Crœsus do one that has no mind to employ them to advantage, nor health to enjoy them?

SUGGESTIONS TO MOTHERS.

IT requires affection, and a serious sense of duty, to sanctify the home circle. A mother needs to possess sterling qualities of head and heart to perform her duties fully and faithfully. To guard associations, to direct the gradual unfolding of intellect, to inspire mental aptitude and activity, to awaken pure thoughts, and repress evil ones, to excite a thirst for knowledge, and cultivate a fondness for intellectual pleasures, are within the province of every sensible mother.

"Mothers," says Mrs. Sigourney, "whatever you wish your children to become, strive to exhibit in your own lives and conversation. Do not send them into an unexplored country, without a guide. Put yourself at their head. Lead the way like Moses through the wilderness to Pisgah. The most certain mode for you to fix their habits, is the silent ministry of example." A mother's every word is listened to, her tone and manners watched, her very principles imbibed, if not inherited. The impressions she makes are stamped indelibly on the child.

If there is an office on earth that requires the exercise of every good quality, it is that of a mother. Certainly no office in any government commands a more supreme and unbounded influence. A mother forms the tastes, disposition, and character of her children, and it may be of unborn generations through them. Nor is her influence limited to this world, for as they live and die here, so must they be hereafter. The most important period of life for forming impressions — the first ten years — is given to the mother. There is but little difficulty in making an impression on either the heart or the mind of children — more difficulty lies in fixing the impression.

Many mothers are ignorant and unqualified for their duties. The majority of mothers never devote as much time to acquiring a knowledge of the way in which to raise their children as they should. They will toil, and struggle, and labor, day after day, and year after year, to provide them fine clothes, and rich food, but the mere existence of the higher and nobler part of their nature, they seem unconscious of, or perhaps think the mind and morals need no training and guidance, except what are given at school. Many do not govern at all, and many that do, govern by impulse, not reason.

An ignorant woman at the head of a family, whose controlling motive is a desire to please, is productive of much evil. A mother of weak character and corrupt principles, spreads blight and desolation throughout her family. She is among human beings what the Upas tree is among plants. It is difficult to purify the streams from a corrupt fountain. I have known a woman sacrifice the morals and minds of her children, by giving way to the selfishness of a dissipated husband, whose impositions gradually grew into cruelty and brutishness.

It is useless for a mother to suppose her children, when they are possessed of moral education, and mature judgment, will respect her without virtuous principles, or admire her without intelligence.

A woman with a low grade of character will be more a curse than a blessing to her family. "How can a woman educate her children when she is not accustomed to reflect? How determine what is suited to them? How incline to virtue of which she is ignorant? to merit of which she has no idea? She will only know how to flatter and menace them — to render them insolent or fearful — imitative monkeys, careless and dishonest — never right-minded, amiable children." Eternity alone can unfold the evil, sorrow, and shame brought on a family by such a mother. A woman of that kind drives her husband from his home, to seek sympathy and companionship elsewhere, and in many cases artificial stimulus is resorted to, hoping to blunt wounded feelings, and produce oblivion of troubles that cannot be mitigated — that eat out health, and strength, and life.

There are places that from force of habit are called home — places where intemperance reigns, where ignorance rules, where the animal propensities preponderate, where the silence of dumb brutes is the hushing up of evil, where manual labor exhausts the vital force, and yet is the only labor recognized, where dishonesty in business relations exists, and untruthfulness in reference to social and domestic matters, where distrust, and bitterness, and hatred, make imbecile the strongest intellects, and corrupt the purest hearts. In such places the noblest aspirations, the most unselfish deeds, are cursed.

T. S. Arthur says, "A large proportion of the wrong woman suffers in the present constitution of society may be fairly set down as the fault of woman. Not so much to the women of this, as of the preceding generation; for the men of the times are, to a certain degree, either what their mothers have made them, or have, through ignorance, error, or neglect, permitted them to become. And the wrongs that women may suffer in the next generation, will, in a like measure, be chargeable to the women of this. The child is far more easily molded to a woman's will than the man."

Mothers by indulging a spirit of selfishness in their sons are paving the way for them to practice selfishness, exactions, and impositions, in their families. That the moral character of a mother is strongly impressed upon her children any one of observation will confirm. A good woman generally has good sons, while a woman, deficient in moral character, usually has bad sons. A mother's power is greatest in molding the character. The mothers of most great and good men have been women of common sense, education, and force of character, caring but little, if at all, for showy dress, and pomp of living.

Any one of observation is aware that the mental nature of sons is almost invariably derived from the mother. Her influence is also more constant. Especially is it so with men distinguished for their superior qualities. Franklin,

Washington, Bonaparte, and Byron, attribute their talents to their mother. If a man of ordinary talents has a wife of superior mind, their children will partake of the mother's superiority, while if a talented man has a wife of inferior intellect, their children will be like the mother. The physique of parents is also to a great extent transmitted. Small, delicate parents will have delicate and diseased offspring, while healthy, robust parents will have offspring of a similar kind. When the heads and hearts of women are more thoroughly and properly cultivated, we shall have a better race of people.

Foresight and judgment are absolutely essential to a woman in the right management of her family. A woman needs wisdom to guide her children, principle to demand their respect, and information to retain the favor of her husband. Self-control is the grand central power of a mother over her children. It is essential to the welfare of children that they be educated to habits of industry and activity. Indolence is the bane of progress.

Mothers should improve themselves by reading and conversation, for when their children are grown they will probably be better educated than they are, and the constant addition made to the repositories of art and science will leave them far in the background, if they do not find time to keep pace with those additions.

Inquiries may be started, and observations made, by a child, that will call into exercise the deepest thinking powers of a philosopher.

Miss Edgeworth recommends that a mother read the books she wishes her children to read, and mark out such passages as she thinks would have a bad effect, or cut out pages containing objectionable views, or influences — also to mark the stories, chapters, and divisions, suitable for different ages.

There is a class of women, (as well as men,) that insist upon it a woman's province is at home — whether she has a home or not. They are so charmed with married life that the rest of all womankind are ignored by them, though they form a pretty respectable body in numbers and quality.

They do sometimes — in their clemency — remember the existence of a certain portion of this body on which they are dependent — lady teachers.

Many women that are free from home cares devote themselves to religious duties. Especially is it so with pious ladies whose children have grown up, and no longer require their time.

Many daughters are tenderly cared for, and provided with all that heart can wish. But ofttimes the messenger of death comes unawares, and in his train may follow want and poverty. Then, mothers, provide for that time, in case it should come. Furnish your daughters with such knowledge of some one employment as may serve them in the hour of need. If you wish to fit your daughters for the practical experiences of life, educate them for its practical purposes. So live as to make your children love and respect you. If you do,

> "In sorrow's lonely hour,
> Your memory on their souls will steal,
> Like music strain, with magic power,
> To chase away each thought of ill."

A mother may inspire in her children sentiments that in future years will lead them to advance justice, to uphold truth, and sustain the rights of the weak and helpless. She may cultivate in them a love for the beautiful in nature, for the stars, flowers, and clouds, for the trees, and water, and for the varieties of landscape. She may teach them to detest treachery and meanness, and to check tyranny and oppression. She may inspire the moral courage that will lead them to act nobly under the most trying circumstances.

ADVICE TO BROTHERS.

BROTHERS, do you toil from morn till night for orphan or destitute sisters? If so, put it in their power to fit themselves for some useful employment, and they will be likely to feel more gratitude, than if remaining dependent on your labors, and they will more delight to help themselves, than see you exhausting mind and body, in the effort to provide for them.

Give your sisters remunerative employment to make them self-reliant and independent — that their self-respect may keep them from doing anything improper to gain a subsistence. You will thereby free them, to some extent, from that sense of dependence so crushing to proud spirits. Women need support, but nothing chills them more than the necessity of receiving it from those on whom they have but a slight claim. Not that I would intimate sisters have no claims on brothers, for they certainly have to a large extent, and brothers of self-respect, and proper principle, will feel and recognize that claim. But the kindest, and best, of brothers, may be removed by misfortune, or carried off by death, and sisters may be cast with those on whom they have no claims, save those of humanity.

Encourage not your sisters in the reading of fiction. How many of our magazines, edited by women of cultivation, are mere trash! The prose is only love dreams, and the poetry vague sentiment. It is cruel to offer such light froth to the souls of women — to furnish their minds with such ethereal, unsatisfactory diet.

Brothers, neglect not your sisters on the peril of your souls. Deal with them justly, honorably, tenderly. Never treat a female unkindly. You know not how much a woman needs kindness. Her nature demands it. Her duties are generally of a quiet, contemplative kind. Her thoughts and feelings are confined to the persons about her. A man, if engaged in manual labor, can forget his troubles in the noise and bustle around him. If a professional man, the varied duties of his sphere call his mind from the frequently trivial, yet vexatious difficulties, that annoy and harass a woman.

I believe all the improper conduct of a woman may be traced to a want of sympathy in her feelings, or a want of appreciation of her moral and mental worth. Then be careful, brothers, that you give to your sisters that love and sympathy which they require, for the full development of their higher and better nature. You will be well rewarded in so doing, by a return of affection and confidence.

WORDS TO YOUNG LADIES.

YOUTH is the time in which character is shaped. Then the habits are formed, and the principles fixed. Then good habits are easily acquired, and bad ones abandoned. Then the passions should be controlled, and self-government acquired. Then should endeavors be made to secure a well-balanced mind, and good moral character, for youth will decide the misery, or happiness, of old age.

The first ten years after leaving school are generally, with a young lady, the turning-point in her destiny. She leaves school with a warm heart, an active mind, and high hopes; but it may be, she finds nothing to fully occupy them. She becomes listless, inactive, selfish. Her sympathies and energies are not brought into play, and so she passes on the dull, "even tenor of her way." She occupies her waking hours in reading novels, practicing the accomplishments, and entertaining gay, thoughtless companions.

"Is there nothing to study, and nothing to learn,
No object to care for, no credit to earn,
No wisdom worth seeking, no aim to fulfill,
No hope to encourage, no motive for will,
No field unexplored, no pathway to aught,
That is worthy a being of reason, and thought?
Can it be there is nothing an interest possessing,
More worth than society, dashing, and dressing?"

We have often thought how little, to a casual observer, there *seems to be*, to occupy the time profitably of young ladies, in cities, whose circumstances are easy. It is sad that when there is so much work to do in the world, there should be so many young ladies wasting their hours in idleness, — sad there should be so many in bad health from the want of bodily exercise, and mental activity, when thousands are perishing for want of the attention they might give. Surely in this world of sin, misery, and poverty, they might find something to do, or their friends might find it for them. I fear that many of our sex, on their death-beds, will look back with bitter regret to the early years of womanhood, when idleness and listlessness, or thoughtlessness and dissipation, swept many hours into that great abyss from which they can never return. And yet, we know they were not so much to blame as the parents, who opened not to their daughters useful fields of employment, nor instilled into them high and worthy purposes.

Our capacities for enjoyment are great. If the affections take a right direction, they bring joy and happiness; if a wrong direction, sorrow and misery. Many young ladies have sentimental ideas of friendship and love, but they often find the experience mere lip service. If young ladies would refuse to accept the attentions of men that are immoral, it would be better for themselves, and society. It would work a glorious revolution. If women had more force of character, and sought the approbation of their God with more zeal, methinks there would not be such a lack of resolution when they are called on to express their opinions of fashionable immoralities — not such a smoothing over, and coating of vice with sugared words, not such a desire to excuse that which they know is evil. Principles of truth and honor should be dearer than life to a woman. We love to see a woman possess that virtue, which evil men quail before. Intercourse with the best authors will create a distaste for the society of the rude and ignorant. Wishes and tastes grow refined, or coarse, according to nature and cultivation.

In seeing a young lady, hour after hour, in the appliances of toilet mysteries, when she should be enriching her mind, to see her by little tricks of coquetry endeavoring to gain admiration, or, by envious words, increasing the disparity between herself and those of inferior claims, it makes in some plainer persons, honest simplicity, self-denial, and sacrifices, shine forth with increased lustre. It makes sincerity rank as a gem of the first water.

Young ladies — you, who revel in luxurious ease, and are decked with queenly robes, and costly ornaments — you, that fritter away your precious hours, and languidly dream away your time, in the easy elegance of drawing-room life, turn for a few moments, and lend a listening ear. Consider the old adage, "It is better to wear out than to rust out." Better in activity try to accomplish something, even though you fail. No labor is lost, for the very energy acquired thereby is valuable. Life is too short to spend a third, or thereabouts, in preparation at school, and then waste years in deciding what plan to pursue through life — what aim to keep in view to make yourself useful. If you undertake anything useful, do it with resolution and courage. On your road you may find success. 'Tis true you may tread on thorns and thistles now and then. Yet tell me the road where you will not. You cannot expect a path hedged in by roses, and strewed with beautiful flowers. Be prepared, then, for your journey. Active, untiring industry, perseverance, and self-reliance, are necessary for success. Fixedness of purpose, too, is essential. The uncertainty of life, and everything else, renders it desirable that the fulfillment of every intention, the performance of every duty, be attended to without delay. You must give an account to God for all your time — every month, week, day, hour. For doing good all have some ability, natural or acquired. One can give of their substance, another can wait on the sick, another visit the poor, another teach the ignorant, and another furnish a home to the orphan. These are blessed missions of woman.

So live that you may surrender with joy, and not with trembling, the talents committed to your care. "What you truly and earnestly aspire *to be*, that in some sense you *are*. The mere aspiration, by changing the frame of the mind, for the moment, realizes itself."

Two or three years might be profitably spent, after leaving school, in fitting yourselves for occupations. They will engage your time and talents, and may be a valuable resource in times of trial. Defer it not while time and opportunity are given. "Persevere in well doing, for in due season, you shall reap your reward, if you fail not." We would not have you live as the epicure, for present pleasure only, nor as the cynic, shunning society, nor as the stoic, lauding insensibility as a virtue, but in exercising the intellectual faculties, and preparing them for a higher and loftier sphere of action. Live for something better, and nobler, than the mere gratification of bodily wants, and pleasures. So live that when called away you may feel the world is better for your having lived in it.

In youth, real sorrow, if not too long continued, softens and subdues the feelings, yet strengthens and matures the character. But let not melancholy brood over your spirits. It saddens, it crushes every impulse, every energy. Use such opportunities as you have for social enjoyment; but work diligently. Cut your cable and sail out from the shores of indolence. Summon energy and industry to your rescue. If your vessel lies long in a calm, it will become unfit to bear the storms likely to come upon it. Its timbers will become so decayed, its sails so tender, its ropes so spliced, that it will be broken away, and wrecked, or dashed in a thousand pieces. Look to the Pilot that can direct you through this sea of vague uncertainty, and at last, after an active, useful life, safely moor you in the haven of eternal rest.

Do not suppose marriage is essential for happiness. If you see much of human life, you will learn that there is probably as much misery in married life as out of it.

Take such capital as nature and education have furnished you, and turn it to the best account. If you are beautiful, improve your mind to correspond with your person. We would not decry beauty. It is a gift from the Almighty. We admire it, and love to see it becomingly cherished; but with humility. Cultivate the beauty of the heart, then of the mind, then of the person. Pure and noble aims, high and holy purposes, are more beautiful than the most perfect symmetry of features and form. Women are too much flattered for their personal beauty—just as a pet fawn, a lamb, a rabbit, or bird would be. The soul, that noblest part of woman, is rarely taken into consideration. Her mind is overlooked as though she was not expected to possess any. And even her qualities of heart sink below beauty of face and form. And so woman is degraded. And her anxiety to please men will often lead her to feel, and think, that the most desirable thing to possess is personal beauty. She sees not that woman is thereby likely to be kept in ignorance, and a corresponding degradation, for knowledge guided by judgment is wisdom, and *wisdom is power.* She sees not that woman is flattered for what she deserves no credit, inasmuch as her beauty is an accidental property, while the learning she has acquired, the good she has done, are the fruits of industry and application. Miss Hannah More says, "Those blessed with beauty should have something to take up when beauty has to be laid down." Of all other beauties, the most lasting, the most exalted, is moral beauty. No other can compare with it. It is seen under every circumstance, in every condition of life. It glows in poverty as in wealth, in affliction as in happiness, in misfortune as in prosperity. It shines forth from the hovel as from the palace. It is not limited to time or place. It is not so much a gift of Nature as the result of training, and self-culture.

Then "work while it is day, for the night cometh wherein none can work." You are hastening to the grave, in which "there is no work, nor device, nor knowledge, nor wisdom."

THE FORMATION OF HABITS AND CHARACTER.

A WISE Providence, no doubt, orders all the events of our lives. Many of these events may be severe chastisements, but the devout Christian can generally trace the good effects that have followed them. In many cases they develop sterling qualities that are latent, and confirm those that exist.

We must suffer to bring us near to God. Without suffering we would live at too great a distance from him. We cannot fully realize any feeling without having experienced the opposite. We cannot appreciate pleasure without having suffered pain. We cannot enjoy a spirit of triumph if we have not known disappointment.

The mind of man is capable of infinite expansion, and is as immortal as the great I AM. Dr. Boynton says, "I do not envy men of superior intellects, like Clay and Webster, but I venerate them. I do not scorn people of inferior intellect. My benevolence prompts me to try and elevate them. My sense of justice and goodness leads me to raise them to a level with himself."

Some writer remarks, "The sentiment of *necessity*, strongly and liberally conceived by a reasonable being, is the only thing that imparts interest to human action, and thence energy to the character. That sentiment clothes with equal dignity the most varied occupations. It often gives to the young girl, who is compelled to fulfill duties, which seem abject in their nature, a more elevated inward existence, than her equal in age of the affluent class, who is occupied with trifles, or does nothing."

In the medical periodical, "Scalpel," I saw an article

containing an idea that I think is becoming fearfully prevalent — namely, "that bad habits are to a great extent constitutional, being derived from the parent." An individual impressed with that belief, whose parents are worthless or depraved, will give way to evil thoughts and feelings, and act them out, that might otherwise check and subdue them. He would feel that he was doomed to be wicked, and could not be different. In this respect we think the tendency of such a doctrine exceedingly pernicious. Some may bring as an argument against this that a person, by knowing to what sins he has an hereditary tendency, may guard against them. The "Scalpel" continues, "Poverty and crime depend on the organization of the body. The face is an index to the soul — so we can judge much of the character and disposition by the face. Impulses, whether good or evil, are born of the brain. Poverty in two or three generations becomes an organic disease. Unwholesome food, damp rooms, insufficient heat, and bad clothing, produce a low degree of life power. About one in one thousand may be an exception to the rule. They may discover the existence of superior powers, because in some way a spark of genius has dropped into their souls. It would seem as if some are designed, from the first moment of their existence, to direct and lead the rest. The contrary of this may be the case. Some, blessed with every advantage, and possessing strong, athletic, clear-minded parents, are weak, silly, and inefficient."

We are so constituted, and rendered so different by education and habit, that one person cannot possibly undergo the fatigue, mentally or physically, that another can. And the same causes make the hours required for rest to vary greatly. We, to a great extent, form ourselves as we are. Day after day serves to impress some idea incorporated into our soul's history, to develop some latent germ of thought, to mature some misty, half-formed plan.

Facts make people dry and hard. They extract the poetry from their natures. But facts are stubborn realities, and must be faced. It is a sad, yes, a terrible thing, to lose the freshness and vigor of life — to be conscious of it — to feel it in your soul. The dark shadows that haunt the spirit may not be dispelled. The cry of a breaking heart, the wail of an agonized soul, are, in many cases, heard only by God.

The different classes of society are not entirely separate and distinct in any civilized country except India. They have their influence everywhere, on each other, for good or evil. They mutually and constantly act and react. The follies and vices of one class are likely to become the follies and vices of another, while the virtues of one, in time, become the virtues of another.

We do wrong to judge others. We should always make some allowance, for we often do not know of circumstances that lead persons to do what may appear wrong. Learn, then, to forgive and forget. But at the same time be firm and decided when conscious that you are right. Never permit yourself to be led astray by any one — even if they are agreeable, or talented, or influential. Speak and act decidedly when any would tempt you to do wrong. Remember there is a God who sees us at all times, and who will judge us as rational beings. Heaven rarely lets merit and goodness go unrewarded, though it is often long before that reward is seen or felt.

Most people are anxious to be respected — some wish to be admired, and some desire to be loved. Few people, except when in authority, wish to be feared. Some proud, misguided people will not ask pardon for evil spoken, or wrong done, and so harm themselves, as well as others, by increasing the disorder of their brains, and the sinfulness of their hearts.

The changes are very great in opinion, feeling, disposition, and character, that take place in every individual, that resides in various places, among different people, and under a variety of circumstances. The individual of to-day, would be so changed in nature fifteen or twenty years hence, that he would not be recognized by the friends of to-day, nor even recognize himself.

Opinions are the result of our mental and moral training, observation, example, reading, the influence of others, and associations. We are responsible for them to some extent.

No two children ever enter life upon exactly the same footing. Some come into the possession of material wealth, some do not; some look forward to its possession, some do not; some are carefully trained to make the best of life, while some are allowed to vegetate in idleness; some are favored with the best society and best human institutions, others have no privileges of the kind.

I have seen it stated that those who were born and reared with wealth, were more amiable, charitable, and loving, than those who have acquired it by their own energies or talents. This is probable, but such people rarely possess so great force of character. They have not that decision, that determination of will, which overcome difficulties, and can only be gained by conflict in the battle of life.

The good and virtuous use to the best advantage the blessings conferred on them, the bad and vicious turn them into curses.

CONNECTION OF EDUCATION WITH HOME DUTIES.

EDUCATION, and the gratification of a literary taste, do not unfit women for the discharge of domestic duties. It is not necessary that a woman be a slovenly housekeeper because she is a woman of learning. Indeed, a certain discipline of the mind is acquired by an early and constant attention to domestic duties. Many of our most distinguished writers have been as faithful in performing the duties pertaining to the various relations of life as the illiterate. Education gives a definiteness to the mind, a clearness in making explanations, and giving orders, that facilitate the duties of housekeeping. Home life is as dear to the authoress as to the woman of a vacant mind. In her heart, as in that of any *good* mother, the springs of love are stronger and deeper, than those of life. By education we open the door to a wider field of usefulness. The more highly people are educated, the more reason have they for working. They hold a boon for which they are responsible. They know better how to work to some purpose. They are, in fact, more likely to work, for the increased consciousness of duty, arising from education, would make them desire to accomplish something worthy of the usefulness and dignity of their position. They thereby enjoy and increase the blessings of education and home refinement. The most ignorant and bigoted people, so far as I know, are the most despotic. A kind heart, influenced by an uncultivated mind, and a want of judgment, is more productive of unhappiness, injustice, and evil, than a less warm, impulsive heart, with a cool, clear judgment, and more intelligence. If women do lose any of their sweetness, and softness, of manner, and temper, by intellectual culture, they grow in force, influence, and variety of attractions. "We appeal to any one who has lived with cultivated persons of both sexes, whether he has not witnessed as much pedantry, as much wrong-headedness, as much annoyance, produced by learning, in men, as in women, and certainly a great deal more rudeness." If an educated woman marry a man whose want of culture may sometimes shock her sense of propriety and good taste, the happiness she will have in a superior education, and the ability thereby afforded for instructing her children, will do much to reconcile her. The effort required (if not too great) to bear patiently his coarseness, will be a strengthener of her virtues. If her husband should be a man of cultivated tastes, and superior attainments, she will greatly enjoy his society, and he will be blessed by her companionship. So, whether congenially married or not, she will suffer no disadvantage from being educated. Educate a woman properly in mind, heart, and manners, and she will generally know how to direct her course. It is rather a sad fact that most women are ready to learn the accomplishments, but after marriage neglect them, and, what is more to be lamented, fail to cultivate their mental powers. A good cabinet, a well-selected library, masterpieces of painting and sculpture, are objects that will improve, as well as entertain, and every mother should endeavor to make such collections for her children.

In a few schools domestic economy is now being taught practically, as well as theoretically. It was at a school of this kind, in Philadelphia, that Miss Leslie learned the rudiments of cooking, and so established the foundation of that information imparted in her cookery book. The only *educational* school of note in this country in which any knowledge of housewife duties is given, and that on a limited scale, is the one at Mount Holyoke, Mass., founded by one of the richest treasures of her sex — Miss Mary Lyon. There is one of considerable extent, *confined exclusively* to the various branches of cooking, in Stuttgard, Germany. Within a few years one has been established in London, and one is about to go into operation in New York city.

WOMEN'S WANT OF INCENTIVE TO STUDY AND ACTION.

THE question, What shall I be when I am grown? presents itself, again and again, to the mind of the boy, and the youth. But how seldom does it occur to the mind of the girl! And why? Because the same aspirations are not offered her — equal posts of honor are not presented. If the question ever occurs to her, it is in a moral light, not a mental one. She thinks of what lovely graces she will cultivate, not what powers of mind.

Why not afford women the same mental stimulus as men? Why may they not receive equal degrees of honor? Why may they not be encouraged to cultivate an aspiring nature, and feel that their talents and wisdom will be acknowledged? With them the buoyant spirits of youth may be crushed, and the fancy dimmed, by too close application to study. Yet, what does it avail, as matters now stand, save the personal gratification arising from the possession of knowledge? In the present state of society, women have but little encouragement to become highly cultivated, and well informed. It is true, culture may afford a limited advantage, by opening to such women the acquaintance, if they reside in a city, of a small circle of select and congenial friends.

The possession of knowledge, both theoretical and practical, should serve to give women influence. It certainly does much to mold character, and should, with moral stamina, fix a woman's position in society. It is capable of doing much to render her happy or miserable, and will make her conscious of her power and strength.

As a general thing, there is no distinct aim in view, in a female's education, but to fit her to make a show in society; consequently there is no selection of appropriate studies, no direction given to any particular bent of inclinations, talents, and tastes. And too frequently the only talent exercised is that of memory. It is very much like running a race without any object in view.

Did woman's education open, to her expectation, professions in which she might accomplish good, and earn a reputation, as her brothers do, there would then be a stimulus. Such mental capital would in that case be of pecuniary profit, in serving as publisher, proof-reader, engraver, lecturer, librarian, &c. It would encourage her to culture of mind in a business way, and to active exertion.

Make the occupations of women more honorable. The higher professions of men are at once a passport to the first class of society. Let it be so with those of women. Why should it not? Endow institutions for their education, that they may acquire instruction at a reasonable rate. Let the professors be ladies, well qualified, and receiving such a compensation as accords with the same office in male institutions. With the buoyancy of youth, and the ambition that fires her brothers, a woman may then accomplish something before her strength is wasted and her constitution shattered. By ambition, a woman's time and efforts would be so engrossed as to absorb minor griefs and annoyances.

A certain amount of self-reliance is necessary for every woman that would earn her own livelihood. Skill may be the chief requisite in an employment, or knowledge, or physical strength, or endurance, or capability of resisting extremes of heat and cold. But patience and constancy are desirable in all.

Women who devote themselves to literary pursuits, and works of philanthropy, will ever be respected by people of morality and cultivation; their influence and opinions will have weight.

A woman of education and talents must occupy herself

fully and freely, or she will be discontented, miserable. Such are the restrictions and prejudices of society that few can do so. Those womeh that can, should inaugurate a new state of affairs; they should, by speech and with their pens, endeavor to do away with unfounded prejudice and unreasonable restrictions.

The resources afforded in hours of loneliness have been the principal inducement to women to become well informed. All reading is done for either pleasure or profit. As the facilities become greater to women, for acquiring a livelihood by their learning, they will make more effort to obtain it. In education, a man rarely learns anything that he cannot use — a woman may learn much that she cannot use practically, unless she engages in business, or has the instruction of children.

It is to be hoped that the Sorosis of New York, and its branch in Chicago, with the New England Women's Club of Boston, will do much to ameliorate and elevate the condition of women. In the circular of the New York Sorosis the aims set forth are noble, the aspirations high. A vast and inviting field awaits its labors. May success crown the efforts of all who work *earnestly*, *practically*, and *judiciously* in the cause of woman.

UNMARRIED WOMEN AND WIDOWS.

THE extreme sensitiveness of youth, the fear of ridicule, the timidity that makes women shrink from observation, all tend to make them backward in every enterprise, however well calculated it may be to improve the condition of themselves, and of their sex. Women lose much of this as they grow older. They are therefore better fitted to be pioneers in new channels of employment. Many unmarried ladies and widows have time to reflect, and awaken thought in others, and assist in the promotion of schemes for the amelioration of their race. We will venture to assert that there are very few who have made themselves more useful in the world than single women. Their efficiency cannot be denied. They are an important part of society, and, in the raising of children, we do not see how they could be dispensed with. How many have supplied the place of careless, busy, or sickly mothers, and indifferent servants! Often are the arms of little ones twined about auntie's neck. And often is she called upon to take part in their childish sports. In all the diseases incident to childhood, who so ready and willing as the kind aunt? When the mother is sick, who so well able to take her place, if there be not a grown daughter? And in after years, how respectfully she is looked up to as a second mother! But if the aunt is not a good woman, she must not expect to be loved, and respected, by her nieces and nephews when they are grown. If she is a woman of a bad disposition, or incorrect principles, her presence had better be dispensed with in the family, for the children's dispositions will be formed to a great extent by hers, and the impress she will make upon their young minds will be, not only for time, but for eternity. It is well for single women to cultivate those graces that will render them agreeable, and attractive, when the bloom and freshness of youth are gone.

Woman must have courage to do what is right, let fashion and custom say what they will. She must have courage to act independently of the opinions of her fellow-beings when they conflict with the approbation of God. Whatever can be done for ameliorating the condition of the poor, ignorant, and degraded, should be one of woman's studies. The next thing should be to execute what thought and judgment dictate. Combine with others if you can — if not, work alone. Never let pleasure come before duty, nor feeling before judgment. Let the rich treasures of your heart be given to the desolate, the homeless, the orphan, the widow — let your time be given to instruct the ignorant, to attend the sick, to cheer the sad. Your freedom from family cares gives you time for the performance of such duties. Assist in building up and aiding benevolent institutions. If you are in connection with a church, your pastor will be able to point out to you fields of labor. If you have some worthy friend, who is a physician, he can tell you of sick and needy ones that require attention. If you have either means, or leisure, you can find enough to do. If you have leisure, and no means, perhaps, by devoting your energies to some branch of business, you may be enabled to assist young brothers, or sisters, to acquire an education, or fit them for business, or aid an aged parent. If you have means, and no leisure, I can only say, I hope your wealth is as profitably employed, as you would wish when you go to render a final account of property, and talents, and opportunities. Act wisely and faithfully in the relation you sustain to your neighbors, your fellow-beings, and your God.

"It requires less courage to live single now than it did twenty years ago," remarked an old lady to me. Public opinion has changed somewhat. No unmarried woman need feel that she is useless, and therefore be discontented. Work will open to her if she strives to learn her duties.

God in his wisdom has made even the lonely female, without home ties, to fulfill some end, to perform some work, to achieve some labor, that may glorify him, and benefit her fellow-creatures.

> "All the means of action,
> The shapeless masses — the materials,
> Lie everywhere about us.
> What we need is,
> The celestial fire, to change the flint
> Into transparent crystal, bright and clear."

So numerous are the cares and duties of mothers of families, that single women and widows need not fear competition with them, in business. Besides, the affection so natural to a mother would lead her to devote herself to the wants and comforts of her children before all other claims. I think the time of most married women is as much occupied as that of business men, and also the time of single women dependent on their own efforts for a livelihood.

Miss Muloch says, "The absolute power that a single woman of wealth possesses over her time and property gives an extensive range to her patriotic and charitable exertions. Ladies who are thus circumstanced are the properest patrons of public undertakings; they are the natural protectors of the friendless, and the proprietors of those funds to which genius and indigence have a right to apply. Destitute of nearer ties, and unfettered by primary obligations, the whole world of benevolence affords a sphere for their actions, and the whole circle of science offers to adorn their minds. It seems, indeed, difficult to portray a more enviable being, than a single woman possessed of affluence, who has passed through the tempest of youthful passions with unstained character, unvitiated temper, and unfettered heart. Let us allow her an active mind, sound judgment, good principles, and bodily activity; and we must rank her with those orders of superior beings, who, though they neither marry nor are given in marriage, are ever employed in executing the will and studying the works of God."

NEVER TOO OLD TO LEARN.

PERHAPS some will say, I am too old to learn a pursuit, or make myself useful in any special way. Miss Mary Lyon, the founder of Mount Holyoke Seminary, did not see any work to which she was particularly called until after twenty years of age, nor did the will of Providence respecting her own individual enterprise for his glory, and the good of her fellow-beings, develop itself until she was thirty-five.

"One of the ablest generals of the French revolution was a lawyer till the age of thirty-five. One of the most eloquent lawyers of the English bar, and who rose to lord chancellor, was a navy officer till he was forty. One of the most renowned admirals of the British navy was never on shipboard till he was fifty. When Dryden came up to London, over thirty years of age, he did not know that he could write a line of poetry. Milton was over fifty when he commenced 'Paradise Lost.' Cowper's 'Task' was not written until he was nearly fifty."

Pythagoras said, that "ability and necessity dwell near each other." So to those who are backward about commencing an undertaking, I would say, if you find it feasible, begin at once. Time and opportunities are passing. Life is short. We are blown away as leaves from the forest, we are lost to sight as pebbles in the stream.

If a woman defers to fit herself for an occupation, until every prospect of marriage is gone, it may be too late to qualify herself efficiently. Her faculties will be strengthened by beginning early, and habits of order and industry will be formed.

Woman should awake from that listless, weary apathy, in which she has so long slumbered. Without effort she can accomplish nothing. But with a right purpose, earnestly carried out, she will receive some encouragement, and when she has gained a triumph she will be sure to find plenty to befriend her.

WOMEN CAPABLE OF ATTAINING TO EXCELLENCY.

FOR the full development of a human being, the working faculties of mind must be taxed to the utmost; but not overtaxed, lest the bowstring, drawn too tightly, break.

Method is as necessary to success, in intellectual labor, as labor itself. More than half the labor and time of acquiring a good education can be saved by having a judicious and cultivated adviser.

Most highly educated women have a proud satisfaction in their superiority, but very little real satisfaction in general society, particularly of their own sex, whose tastes and pleasures are, in nine cases out of ten, uncultivated, trivial, and unimproving. "Literary women usually either go to the other sex for sympathy and support, or immure themselves, and live without congenial society."

The native strength and vigor of woman's mind are not developed and brought into full play constantly, like man's. Indeed, her education and circumstances have not hitherto seemed to call for it. But as the world advances in wisdom it becomes more and more requisite, and where there is a demand for anything there is generally a supply furnished; consequently the deficiency is being, to a great extent, remedied.

What has been done, in the world of mind, that was not accomplished as well by woman as man? 'Tis true the number is not so large that have accomplished anything to distinguish them; but that is because women, *en masse*, have not had as great advantages, and circumstances have not been such as to develop any special traits. But we think what women have done, in what has been considered their line of work, has been as well done. The success women attain as musicians and linguists is considered by some a proof of their ability to attain superiority in purely artistic and intellectual pursuits.

Some people have said women are incapable of concentrating their thoughts and efforts. There are sufficient reasons for it, aside from any natural inferiority, if any exists. Among them are the want of a thorough and extensive education, and the *discipline* acquired thereby, neglect of useful reflection, the light and frivolous talk and customs of fashionable society, the discouragement received by women until recently, from men, of anything noble and intellectual in their natures, and their timidity in undertaking anything averse to the popular opinion of *men*, the fear of seeming odd and conspicuous, the indolence of some women, and the poor health of others; also the habit cultivated in women of deferring to the judgment of others, not depending on their own sense of right and justice. In addition, women have not the advantages arising from that concentration of thought and action acquired by a regular and definite occupation.

Mrs. Jameson writes, "I have heard of a lady, now, or very lately, residing near Harvard University, who, amid the duties and cares of her own household, fitted many young men for those colleges which neither she, nor any of her sex, were, as students, ever allowed to enter. For twenty years this lady has been accustomed to receive under her roof those students of the university who were rusticated for various offenses. While kneading her bread, or plying her needle, she assisted them in their classical studies, and mended their manners at the same time."

"Not long ago, the daughter of a poor widowed seamstress was seen reading the Koran, in Arabic. There was but one man in the town who could do the same, and he was a learned blacksmith."

I think it is Horace Smith who says, "If our females have not yet attained that high and equal station in society to which they are assuredly destined, they have so far found their rank and influence, and established their capacity for the very highest efforts of intellect, that any attempt to revive the defunct jokes upon their inferiority would be reckoned, in every enlightened company, an evidence of supremely bad taste, or of the most egregious ignorance."

John Stuart Mill, the distinguished logician and political economist, in the preface to his new essay on "Liberty," which he dedicates to the memory of a wife whom he has lately lost, attributes to her all the inspiration, and part of the authorship, of all that is best in his writings, for many years past. A woman could scarcely ask better testimony to the capacity of the sex.

Ariosto says, "Women have attained to excellence in every art to which they have applied themselves." The disabilities through which they have acquired learning and fame do them credit.

In the ninth volume of Vasari, we find this article: "It is a notable fact that in every pursuit for which women have, at any time, chosen to prepare themselves by study, they have always succeeded marvelously, and rendered themselves more than famous. It would be easy to show this by examples; and certainly at no period can the fact be more easily recognized than in our own age, when women have acquired the most solid fame, not in letters only, but in every other department. It would almost seem as if they had resolved to strip our sex of its vaunt of superiority, by entering in the field of toil, with their white and tender hands, and forcing the rough marble, and the rugged iron, to aid them in accomplishing their object, and winning their laurels.

"Minerva, Diana, Ceres, Psyche, the Muses, the Graces, and the Fates were all women. When Pythagoras, in his desire to make proselytes of the ignorant, and extend the influence of his sect, opened his first school of philosophy in Italy, the friend of wisdom was accompanied by female disciples. His wife and daughter taught in his classes, and fifteen other women, of high capacities and attainments, —

his pupils, — gave grace to his stern truths, and became the persuasive missionaries of doctrines which preached restraint over all the passions, and the supremacy of reason in all things. Aspasia, who improved the eloquence, while she perverted the politics of Pericles, lisped her Atticisms in the ears of Socrates, till she became rather his teacher than his disciple."

"The commanding influence of Deborah, the poetic genius of Sappho, the martial spirit of Zenobia, the administrative ability of Queen Elizabeth, the statesman-like character of Margaret of Denmark, the heroic courage and achievements of Joan of Arc, Flora Macdonald, and Grace Darling, the versatile talents of Madame de Staël, the classical learning of Madame Dacier, the scientific attainments of Mrs. Somerville, not to mention a hundred others, stand, not only as an evidence of what woman has done in all the walks which man has claimed as his own, but as an argument for what she could do, if all those walks were as open to her as they are to him."

ADVICE TO READERS OF THIS BOOK.

WE would advise women about to engage in an occupation to consult one or more male friends, in whose judgment they can have confidence, and who, not being engaged in the business they wish to pursue, would not be influenced by motives of self-interest. We know that many of those who stand first in their vocation will pursue a straightforward, kind, and liberal line of conduct.

My young friends, it will be necessary in the selection of an employment to exercise your taste and judgment. Your health, your temperament and talents, with many other things, are to be taken into consideration. Remember you must advance gradually — as the child first crawls, then steps, then walks — so by long and patient labor you may reach your standard. But be not discouraged. There is no silent resting-place for the powers of the soul. You may make advances without being conscious of it yourself. Be courageous and strong. Let not false pride deter you from suitable fields of labor. Keep in view your object. If poor or afflicted relatives are dependent on you, let that stimulate, if dependent for your own support, let that buoy you up. Be kind to those that meet with you daily for the same purpose. Encourage and sustain each other. When weary and worn, faint not — bear up. Seriously review the past — fearlessly anticipate the future. If there be strangers in your number, deal gently with them. Encourage those striving to do right. Let time be measured by the good you do, not by hours and days. It requires labor, patience, and perseverance, to acquire proficiency in anything. Prepare yourselves to perform your duties well. Purity of heart, propriety of conduct, and self-respect, will earn for you, from any virtuous employer, a fair reputation. To any who select and enter upon a pursuit, with a determination to persevere, I bid you God speed. If you wish to maintain your proper position in society, to command the respect of your friends now, and those connected with you in future, you should read, think, study, try to be wise, to know your own plans and keep them, your own duties, and do them. You should try to understand everything you see and hear; to act and judge for yourselves; to remember you each have a soul of your own to account for, a mind of your own to improve. When you once get these ideas fixed, and learn to act upon them, "no man, or set of men, no laws, customs, or combinations of them, can seriously oppress you." By books, observation, and intercourse with well-informed and virtuous people, you will accumulate new thoughts. Store them up as incorruptible treasures. They will be to you more valuable than the costly gems of India, or the rich productions of a tropical clime. Cultivate the habit of close, continuous thought, on some profitable and pleasant subject. You must think and work, and work and think. In the crucible of the alchemist, by a wise and judicious use of minerals, and acids, and alkalies, a change is produced that furnishes most valuable results. Let your mind be the crucible in which acquisitions from the wise and great, united with your own reflections, shall generate sentiments, and make real their practicability. Do not go in debt, without some certain assurance that you can pay what you owe, at some definite time. If you do, the debt will hang as an incubus on your conscience, and either paralyze your exertions, or cause you to overtax them, and injure your health. Money matters have cut many a Gordian knot of love and friendship, and proved an eternal barrier between some of the nearest relatives. To labor for supplying the every-day wants of life may seem very material to some people, but in my opinion, it is the first thing to be considered. You will have more cause to despise yourself if you remain dependent on others than laboring to earn your own bread. I mean, if you have health and strength, and are able to employ your own powers.

VARIETY OF OCCUPATIONS DESIRABLE.

THE time required to obtain a thorough knowledge of any one branch of business determines the expediency of having the attention of the young early directed to the selection of an employment. Yet we would not advocate the plan adopted in some parts of Europe of setting aside children from the cradle to certain employments.

Many of the poor suffer from the want of information that might be given them by intelligent people. Especially is it so in regard to business matters. The selfishness manifested in this way is very great, and the indifference, when the most intelligent of the two individuals could experience no loss by it, is disheartening. But the poor often feel a delicacy about troubling others with their affairs, and in that way suffer unnecessarily.

We doubt whether there is any branch of business whose object is not to supply some want, either real or imaginary. The trades, and mercantile pursuits, are mostly devoted to supplying wants of the body — but the making and selling of books has for its object, supplying the necessities of mind. The professional devotee provides mostly for the wants of the mind — yet not exclusively — for the physician's province is to treat the body, and, so far as possible, the mind, if it be diseased.

The knowledge that a professional person needs, is different from that required for a merchant, and that of a merchant different from that essential to a mechanic, and that of a mechanic varies considerably from that necessary for a manufacturer, while that of a manufacturer is as far removed from that of a farmer.

No person in a civilized country confines himself in his

business to meet merely his own wants. If he did he would not be able to secure the products of other men's labor. Each one, as a general thing, engages in that business to which he finds himself best adapted, and in which circumstances throw him.

Different kinds of knowledge are adapted to different pursuits. We would not for a moment discourage the acquisition of varied knowledge by any one, but, as a man loves his own country best, so it is natural that he should best love to acquire knowledge pertaining to his own branch of business, thereby elevating himself, and it, and gaining the benefit arising from such knowledge.

Business people must, to some extent, be machines — yet not machines incapable of improvement. Spirit, ingenuity, and industry will gain for them many a patent.

The irregular performance of uncultivated talent rarely amounts to much. It is the persevering thought and labor that follow from day to day, that accomplish even the most of those great achievements that are often attributed to genius or talent.

The tastes, habits, and circumstances of women contribute to render a variety of employments desirable. The occupations of women vary somewhat in different cities, yet in all American cities the number is small.

Hitherto women have been confined almost entirely to teaching, keeping boarders, sewing, in factory work, or domestic service, for earning a livelihood. The first employment to which an educated woman resorts, as most genteel, and requiring no capital, is that of teaching. Hence the profession is crowded. We believe that the supply of teachers fully meets the demand. We are sorry to see the impression being so often given by editors and others, that teachers are needed and in demand; because we think many ladies of limited means are thereby induced to spend what little they have in preparing themselves to be teachers; and when they are qualified, ten chances to one, if they get a school, it is only for three months out of the twelve, and that not regularly. A precarious subsistence is obtained, and, to those without homes, certainly a most unreliable one. We love to see ladies educated, and would gladly see them all qualified to teach; but we do not like to see inducements thrown out to qualify themselves, under the impression that there are hundreds of places vacant only because teachers cannot be obtained. There is no employment more uncertain than that of a teacher. Many causes tend to produce this. Among them are low wages, dissatisfaction on the part of teacher or people, ignorant and inefficient school trustees, the fluctuating condition of country schools at different seasons of the year, a large mass of people not knowing the advantages of an education, and the want of endowed institutions of learning. If a lady has sufficient capital to establish herself in a school of her own, she will be far more likely to succeed. As new places are settled, and population advances, there will, no doubt, be some openings; but they will require teachers willing to endure the hardships and privations incident to a new country. Many educated women in the South, deprived by the war of former resources, will doubtless engage in teaching.

I should love to see thrown open to women the door of every trade and profession in which they are capable of expending their talents and energies. Women should not hesitate to enter any, and every lucrative occupation, that they consider suitable for them, and adapted to them.

PIONEERS.

"WITNESS that she who did these things, was born to do them; claims her license in her work."

The young need the advice and encouragement of those older and wiser, better established in character, and more determined in purpose. We fully believe that woman can attain excellence, and even distinction, by constant application in almost any branch of literature, or art, to which her talents may tend. Opportunities must be embraced, and circumstances seized upon, by those women who would be pioneers in new branches of employment.

Every great and good undertaking ordinarily begins, like the grain of mustard seed, with a humble, unnoticed growth; and the greater the enterprise to be achieved, the greater are the obstacles to be surmounted by its pioneer laborers.

Too long have women stood back, waiting for men to invite them to their comparatively easy vocations, expecting them to seek such as were more congenial to their stronger and more robust natures. And long may they continue to wait. To such I would say, Press on. If you see an employment suitable for a woman that you wish to enter, and that woman has not hitherto engaged in, get some female acquaintance to join you, and enter upon its duties without hesitation. Do not stand back for some one to lead the way.

"Who would be free
Themselves must strike the blow."

Dorothea Dix, Florence Nightingale, Mary Lyon, Mary Carpenter, Madame Luce, Caroline Chisholm, and Elizabeth Blackwell, struck out distinct paths for themselves.

Woman is less hampered by custom, by the conventionalities of society, and the distinctions of rank in this country than in most others. Consequently, she can with less surprise from the world, and less derogation, enter into such occupations as seem fitted for her.

Cheerfulness, and a desire to make every event wear the best face, will greatly promote good. An easy conscience will give you a foretaste of heavenly joys. If you feel that your mission is a noble, a heavenly one, *persevere*. It may involve many sacrifices, and much expense. It is better, however, if you can, to bear taunts and reproaches, than give up, if you may accomplish good thereby. We know not how to measure our souls until we have suffered. Even then the gauge is imperfect that measures their depths. Too many are apt to be discouraged in any new undertaking. It is only by experiment that the feasibility and advantage of any plan may be arrived at. But with lofty purposes, and noble aims, you may accomplish very much. Yet forget not that steady, and persevering industry, can alone lead to eminence of any kind. This is beautifully brought out by Dr. Johnson, in a dream of the Rambler, called "The Garden of Hope." It represents Hope as a garden, with two gates, kept by Reason and Fancy. The path from the gate of Reason is craggy, slippery and winding, and termed the "Strait of Difficulty." But few reach the throne of Hope. Some of those that do are disappointed when they receive the gift which Hope has promised. The rest retire with their prize, and are led by Wisdom to the bowers of Content. Any can enter the gate of Fancy, but unlike the rest, they enter the vale of Idleness. Here they rove about, a gay and happy party; but in a little while they are much frightened by the appearance of two dreadful monsters — Age and Want.

"If women," said a gentleman to me, "find themselves capable of conducting mercantile affairs, and have the capital, they can succeed. Men cannot prevent them, and will not; but women, to obtain a hold, must make the effort, and ask for it. It will not be granted from mere courtesy. It makes no difference what people think of your efforts.

Everybody is subject to criticism, all his or her life. If you succeed it is all right, if not it makes no difference — nobody cares. While using the means you must look with hope to success. If you are successful those that are not will envy you — if you are ambitious those that are not will hate you."

A woman satisfied with her own attainments is in a fair way to recede from her stand-point. With such a content her mind will lose its vigor, and her energies flag. That anything is merely so, because it has always been so, is no reason it should be so any longer. Changes are constantly taking place in opinions, habits, and customs. Men and women dread to undertake what is new and untried. Resolution, well directed, is a beacon light to guide us to happiness, virtue, wealth, influence, and position. Every act is a triumph, or a failure. Every man and every woman either conquer, or are conquered. Keep up your energy, and decision of character. Give not way to languor and nervousness. Form high resolves, and rest not until they are accomplished.

Of all other things I would impress upon women the necessity of holding their own — not submitting to imposition in the slightest degree, if it is possible to avoid it, for this will be increased to injustice, and oppression, until a woman's character is lost. If you have means, prosecute a slanderer; if not, get some one to give him a severe chastisement.

Some people were made for head work. Let such do head work. Let those that were not, do hand work. Some can and do combine the two. More progress could be made if women were more self-reliant. They will not decide, and do for themselves. Many of them want to live without labor. Yet in this respect they do not differ from some of the other sex. The strongest in physical force, have, until late years, always governed; but now that the world is getting rid of this disposition, woman may look up, and put in her claim to the consideration of justice.

Intelligent women will best succeed as pioneers in new

branches of labor, for they can more ably, and courageously, protect and sustain their rights.

A friend of mine, after citing many instances, within her personal knowledge, of women who have acquired a desirable position in society, and rendered themselves pecuniarily independent, says, "I have so much faith in women being able to do whatever they choose to undertake with earnestness, industry, and perseverance, that did my taste or my circumstances require it, I would go into any business whatever without the least fear of any man or men interfering to deprive me of any advantages my capital, energy, or talents might command."

Women of talent should not be content to occupy merely subordinate departments of labor, nor devote their time and talents to executing only mechanical drudgery. Let them qualify themselves for superior work, then take such a position as their abilities will command, and with dignity and firmness, maintain that position.

Dr. Channing says of man, — and he doubtless meant to some extent woman also, — "Man owes his growth, his energy, chiefly to that striving of the will, that conflict with difficulty, which we call effort. Easy, pleasant work does not make robust minds, does not give men a consciousness of their powers, does not train them to endurance, to perseverance, to steady force of will, that force without which all other acquisitions avail nothing. Manual labor is a school in which men are placed to get energy of purpose and character. I believe that difficulties are more important to the human mind than what we call assistants. Work we all must, if we mean to bring out our perfect nature."

Women must qualify themselves for the exercise of more important power, if they expect to wield it; they must better train their minds, and inform themselves, cultivate their higher and better nature, and submit to the guidance of heavenly power. When they would snatch from the Almighty the reins of government, their career is likely to be a more wild and dangerous one, than when Phaëthon attempted to manage the chariot of Helios. But with reliance upon our heavenly Father he will guard, and guide, and give that trustful obedience, quiet faith, and holy love, that may enable them to go on their way rejoicing.

By keeping one purpose in view, and striving perseveringly to accomplish it, you will be likely to succeed. If you fail, remember the good things of this world are not always proportioned to the merits of the recipient. Do not expect to effect a great deal at once. By benefiting the individual members of society you benefit society at large. Do not falter or sink because your ideas, or plans, are opposed, or ridiculed. The most valuable ideas, and important discoveries, have met with a similar fate, but in most cases eventually received the merit due them. When worn, weary, and fainting, under the trials and burdens of life, look, poor pilgrim, to thy better rest in heaven. Remember the Saviour, that trod a rough, weary pathway before you. Be not frightened by the storm cloud, but press on, and the sunlight will gladden your pathway. Place yourself as far as possible under good influences, and with such people as will encourage you in doing right. Cultivate calmness of mind, and firmness of nerve. If controlled only by impulse, not by reflection and judgment, success will be doubtful. Summon all your industry to labor, and your courage to bear privations. Be patient, and your reward will be likely to come at last.

" No privileged class shall say to thee, Touch not that honor, set not thy foot upon that eminence; it belongs to us. Thou art free, free to develop thyself as thy will shall prompt, and thy powers permit. This world is God's world, and He hath given thee so much of it as thou, with thy best faculties, canst conquer."

Contribute all in your power to the general harmony and happiness of society. Let not censure, or misfortune, or trouble, cast a shadow over your spirits; but bear up perseveringly, decidedly, and to the best of your ability, until, in the noontide glory of eternity, you may forget the past, and rapturously enjoy the present.

EMPLOYMENT OF WOMEN DOES NOT EXCUSE IDLENESS OF MEN.

THE flagrant sins of men, and neglect to provide for the wants of their families, deserve punishment in Christian countries. Too much license has been given to the bad passions of evil men. They should be controlled and restrained by the laws of good men, and therefore wise and good men only should be elected to the office of law-makers.

It is not necessary that men should be idle, and good for nothing, because their wives, sisters, and daughters are industrious. No, it should only incite them to more activity and energy.

Surely no conscientious person can yield to indolence, who considers how long it takes to prepare for efficient and well-directed labor, how much should be accomplished in the world, and how short life is.

I have been told that the French women, who do what has been considered men's work in this country, have lazy husbands, who spend their time roaming from one wine-shop, and place of amusement, to another. But this is true only to a limited extent. Many women, particularly storekeepers, prefer such occupation, and employ others to perform their household duties. The French women feel a warm interest in the business of their husbands, and have a better knowledge of that business than the women of most countries. We suppose there are few that will attribute that state existing among the *ouvrières* of Paris to women engaging in non-domestic pursuits. It arises from different causes. In France there is a surplus of females in the humbler classes, and these females are better educated and more refined than the men. The redundance of women makes the competition of female labor so great that it is impossible for them to support themselves decently on the proceeds of their labor. So the principal cause of their alleged immorality is *a want of constant employment at fair wages*. Another cause for the condition of the workwomen of France lies in the difference of their moral training. There is said to be as great a difference in the moral tone of the rich and influential classes of French and American women as in the lower classes of the two countries. Nor is it only to France that our remarks will apply in regard to labor and wages. In most parts of Europe many women are engaged in the most severe employments, because the wages of their fathers and husbands will not suffice to buy the necessaries of life. A nation will not inevitably fall into the French manner of turning most labor and business transactions into the hands of women because the majority of them are in possession of an employment by which to render themselves independent.

We think it is Thackrah who makes the following statement: "We imagined, from some general observations, that the lower the mental condition of a branch, the greater the proportion of shop-girls married by the artisans belonging to it. To determine this point, we made it a particular inquiry, and found such generally to be the fact. The shop-girls, from their ability to earn something, are regarded by the ignorant and thoughtless artisan as possessing peculiar advantages, worthy of his consideration."

That women can understand and assist a man in his occupation should be an incentive, not a drawback. Such women know the circumstances of their husbands, and how to regulate their expenditures accordingly. At the death of the husband they know exactly the condition of his business, and how to carry it on. If American women were kept acquainted, by their husbands, with the state of their pecuniary affairs, there might be less domestic trouble.

WOMEN SHOULD NOT TAKE MEN'S EMPLOYMENTS.

WE would not like to see *educated* women engage in any occupation that would call for the least sacrifice of delicacy or propriety, nor any at war with the ordinary physical weakness of the sex. But there are women who possess, or acquire, as great physical power as men. If such wish to engage in any of the pursuits of men, we say, let them by all means — that is, if men in the lighter occupations will continue to retain their places, and exclude women. With short-sighted selfishness, some men monopolize the labor market, and block up avenues of employment which women might well and worthily tread. Men have not given to women the protection and support that as a consequence are made necessary by this selfish monopoly; nor has government taken cognizance of the matter, or done anything to remedy it.

We ask why women are denied the benefits that accrue from a personal knowledge and prosecution of remunerative occupations? "The danger of driving men out," is the reply from some. It is only a plea for selfishness and injustice. Yet it is, and ever has been so, with reforms. Selfishness has said nothing ought to be done, nothing could be done — when it did not wish it done. It is a prompting of the Evil One. The moral courage produced in men by overcoming, to some extent, their selfishness, would be worth the effort of accomplishing it, aside from any other benefit.

As a general thing, "woman, no sooner than man, will enter vocations forbidden her by temperament, lack of aptitude, or want of time, and it is therefore quite as unnecessary to interdict them to her as to those who are unfit to enter them."

THE RESULT OF SUCH APPROPRIATION.

SHOULD women engage in many of the avocations now occupied by men, it would turn the energies of some men to agricultural pursuits. Trades and manufactures, it is well known, are more fluctuating in this country than agriculture. There is less pauperism in agricultural than in other communities. Vast tracts of land are lying waste for the want of cultivation, in the new states and territories of the West. Under the homestead law, a settler can enter one hundred and sixty acres of land, paying about eighteen dollars for office fees, and by cultivating it, at the end of five years receive it as his own, from the government. By preëmption, he can, after cultivating it a year, buy it at a low price. If single men would migrate, and engage in such labor, the profits, in a few years, would enable many of them to marry, that now cannot, from want of the wherewithal to support a wife.

The desire to live by some occupation, imagined genteel, having a fictitious estimate, because of its freedom from severe manual labor, is a fertile source of evil in the rising generation of our country.

To the number of men now engaged in marine expeditions, scientific researches, mining operations, and various other enterprises, many more could be added. They would bring, to hundreds so engaged, competency and independence. The mineral resources of America are vast, and as yet, but partially developed.

Both men and women of the working and middle class are now mostly supported by the wages paid for men's labor. If some women engage in industrial labor, the only difference will be, that they will earn what they have, instead of depending on the uncertainty of male relatives earning it for them.

"The real and only consequences of women engaging in men's pursuits would be, 1st, An increase of the productive power of the country; and, 2d, A slight readjustment of wages." For this increased production, there will probably be an increased demand, as many people will be able to purchase more, and the desire to purchase will increase with their ability to do so. It will be the means of either cheapening the results of labor, or of lessening the amount of labor performed by each individual; that is, the quantity done by each individual, will be more nearly equal. For instance, instead of one man working ten hours, and another two, each will work the average of ten and two, which are six hours. It has been estimated, that if every individual able to work spent four or five hours daily, in well-directed toil, it would be sufficient to meet the wants of all mankind; while if the same people should labor eight hours out of the twenty-four, and the proceeds of said work were evenly distributed, it would enable every laborer to command, not merely the comforts, but even the luxuries of life, and make comfortable the old, infirm, and sick.

The effeminate manners and habits, and fragile constitutions, in the United States, of young men, arise, to some extent, from the nature of their occupations. How can they become strong, healthy men, without exercise in the open air? Men were made for manly and vigorous pursuits.

There are some occupations we would like to see men deprived of — such as superintending a work-room where women only are employed. How a strong, well-dressed man, can watch over girls at work, taxing their strength until it fails; in short, be a regular slave-driver of women, is unaccountable to a person with any refinement of feeling. It far exceeds in degradation the employment of an overseer in the Southern States, when they were slave states.

The number of women engaged in domestic labor, equaled by the number of men in occupations, leaves but a comparatively small number of both sexes to come in competition in business life; added to this is the consideration that some of these non-domestic women have means of their own, and do not engage in business of any kind, while men, of equal or greater means, are so engaged.

Prejudice is very much diminished by education, observation, and general intelligence. Much of the prejudice that opposed the entrance of women into occupations new to them, has ceased to exist. Opinions are much influenced by feelings. We do not wish to see honest men deprived of their business profits, but we want women to have a fair chance.

The complaint is made that if women enter occupations now engaged in by men, the competition may lower the wages of the men in said occupations, and cause them to enter other occupations. If they enter those more suitable for them, and leave vacancies that women can profitably fill, where is the harm done to either men or women?

"With regard to educated women, their increased employments need not, and would not, have the effect of throwing men out of work, because the progress of civilization is continually opening fresh occupations to educated persons; great numbers of women could therefore find employment, if they were properly instructed, without displacing one solitary man."

One field that should be more extensively opened to women is that of selling dry goods, and fancy articles. Look at tall, bearded men behind counters, selling laces and ribbons to women; or exposing for sale hoop skirts; in millinery stores offering feathers and artificial flowers; in mantua-making establishments measuring the waists of women; in toy stores, handling dolls, and wooden horses; in bakeries selling pies; on sidewalks disposing of bouquets, or candies and fruit, — then tell me if the occupations look *manly*. Even men are employed, by many ladies, to dress their hair; and in California, they have been employed to do chamber work, at hotels. See the pale faces, delicate forms, and slender fingers of these men. For what are they fit outside of their vocation? Let them lose that, and to what else may they turn? Having only vegetated they become effeminate, lose their vigor and strength, and acquire all the ways and prejudices of sickly women. Motion and exercise in the open air, are necessary to make men — women may possibly live without. Years ago men would not have engaged in woman's work without suffering the ridicule of their fellow-men, and the contempt of women. For woman's sake it would have been well if it had continued so.

PROVINCE OF WOMEN.

MANY are the virtues and graces that should adorn the home sphere of woman. Woman was intended to be a companion for man — to share with him life's joys and sorrows, and to hold a responsible place in society. And such is generally her station in our fair land. To sew, to read, to think, and visit are among the numberless duties and pastimes of her every-day life.

A woman will find full play for all her powers and talents in the sanctities of home. The Marchioness Ossoli says, "A house is no home unless it contains food and fire for the mind, as well as the body." If people do not get them in one way, they must in another, or perish; for human beings are so constituted that they must either advance or retrograde mentally.

The superiority of woman's moral and social position is supposed by some to arise from a more constant participation in the duties and pastimes of home life. The elements of the heart nature are more cultivated and exercised.

To woman, as mother, is committed the training of the young mind, the sowing of the seed that must bring forth virtue or vice; and consequently to her is intrusted the destiny of our nation. In her hands is the helm of state, in her heart its prosperity or adversity. At the fireside are her charms to be appreciated; and there her influence may give an impulse to be felt when she is in the grave; there her voice may make impressions never to be obliterated.

The spheres of men and women are not so separate and distinct as is generally thought. Yet there is no need that one should trespass on the other. We would not limit woman to any particular sphere more than man, except as her physical strength and modesty should determine that limit. What she now is, is the result of custom founded on arbitrary laws.

Mr. Chapin, in a lecture, said, "If there was a sphere for woman, then, in the same sense, there was a sphere for man. What was man's sphere? It was the realm of being, of thought, of action, which he could legitimately fill — that idea in which all his faculties find employment, and where his entire nature is harmoniously developed." And such, we think, should be woman's sphere.

Said Mr. Curtis, in a lecture on "Woman and her Work," "As honorable men, we must concede that every human being has a natural right to do what God has given him the power to do, within the limits of the moral law."

A man is no more competent, and has no more right, to dictate or say what the sphere of a woman without a family is than a woman has to dictate or say what the sphere of a man without a family is. We are individually responsible to a higher power than either man or woman.

Says Rev. Samuel Longfellow, "As water seeks its level, so talent and energy seek theirs. Let man and woman alone, unhampered, and untrammeled, to find their own spheres. The sphere of a woman is that which her talent, education, and other qualifications, fit her for occupying. But that sphere is, to some extent, determined by herself. If she aspires occasionally to something higher, and uses corresponding exertion, her system will be enlarged and elevated."

How often is the expression arrogantly and presumptuously made by man, "Woman's sphere is at home"! We know home is the sphere for some women. Is it for all? Have all homes? Such men either forget the homeless ones, or never think enough to know such exist. The sphere of married women is mostly confined to home; but for the many thousands of females that have no home ties and home duties, their sphere of action necessarily lies outside of home. We cannot believe that Providence intended them for drones in society; that they are to exist as mummies.

It is the privilege of many single women to soothe the distressed, to comfort the sad, to cheer the lonely, to bless the orphan, and assist the widow. It is their privilege to feed the poor, and clothe the ragged, to encourage the desponding, and draw back the erring into the paths of truth and virtue. Their mission is a holy one. Toil and care may attend it, yet it brings a blessing. But these holy duties and privileges of single women are confined to very few, except those who have means of their own, or live as auxiliaries in other families, for others must earn their own living by labor that consumes nearly, or quite, all of their waking hours.

Those who prate about woman's sphere always speak and act as if all were situated as they should be — provided with food, clothing, and a comfortable home. They think not of the thousands without either. They think not to what many are reduced by the stern, relentless, bitter decrees of fate; that necessity is a severer master than fancy. Perhaps they consider such unworthy of their notice. If so, their want of philanthropy speaks for itself. The crude state of society, as regards women's employments, is not considered, nor the complicated system of the higher and more artificial condition.

A remnant of barbarism still lurks in the minds of those men who think women inferior to themselves. The time is not long past when men declaimed against women for expressing their thoughts by the pen. It was an encroachment on old customs; it did not come within their narrow limit of woman's sphere.

We now and then hear a man complain of what he terms strong-minded women. The inference is that such men prefer weak-minded women. And who are the men? In almost all cases, either narrow-minded men whose prejudices have been imbibed from ignorant parents, or envious men that fear a woman's superiority.

Many people are very ready to pronounce unfavorably on what to them is new, or at all strange. They think, for instance, that a certain occupation would not do for a woman. You ask why. Because women are not so employed. If it is suitable, give the occupation a trial. Do not be frightened by arguments that have no weight in them. Society cannot afford to lose some of its best talents merely because they are woman's. To crush the abilities of the sex by saying they have none, is surely an unfair way of testing the fact.

If you begin to talk to some men about women having a pursuit, they say, or intimate, that all women should marry. Do they say that all men should marry, or urge it upon them? As many men as choose may live single, and heap up riches, but that a woman should have such wages as would enable her to lay by a sum for sickness, and old age, is outrageous! O, no, she should marry — it matters not whom — whether an industrious man, that will be a protector, and help to support her, or a vagabond that she may be abused by, and have to support.

The chivalry of such men as prefer to remain single, and acquire riches, should prompt them to form a fund, from which worthy spinsters and widows, who are paid inadequate wages for their labor, may receive a support.

Could the labor of all womankind be compromised, it might be better for the sisterhood. Some die from too much labor, others for the want of something to do. Enough sympathy is given poor women; but *they need something more substantial — they want remunerative employment.* Give them that, pay them promptly, and thereby prove your sympathy real.

With women, marriage is a more solemn event than with men. A man's sphere of duties is but slightly changed, a woman's greatly. The duties that married life bring her are more fatiguing, more constant, and more lasting. She must endure physical suffering, care, and anxiety. He is comparatively free. Yet, perhaps, her happiness is more intense, more exquisite in parental ties. If she has good health, bright, happy children, and a good husband, in prosperous business, her happiness, as a married woman, is complete.

NEITHER DRUDGERY NOR IDLENESS.

WE have discussed at some length the differences of opinion in regard to what is familiarly termed "the sphere of woman." Some think her place is in the kitchen — her skill to consist in domestic and culinary concerns — to be an expert laundress, or an adept in the ablutions of dirty children — to sweep, dust, scour, iron, and all the thousand and one menial employments connected with house-keeping — in short a slave for her husband and children. These stereotyped ideas are wearing out, as man reflects more, and woman takes her place as a companion for him, — an intellectual and companionable helpmeet.

Labor in the field with men makes women coarse in their manners, and too often immoral. In England, Scotland, Austria, Germany, and France, the effects may be seen. In those countries, women so engaged, lose their modesty, and having no comfortable home to come to, are apt to spend their evenings, and their money, at beer shops, or low groggeries, with vile company.

We repeat, strong, coarse labor is not proper for woman, nor heavy, out-door employment. The labors of the field, and the drudgery of housework, as preparing fuel, drawing water, &c., degrade the better class of women. Few women are men's equals physically, and therefore the mass of women should not perform such labor as calls for an equal strength of body. Neither should they engage in work degrading to their moral or mental nature. The respect due from the other sex forbids it. Everything that is proper in nature, and decent in man, forbids it.

While we condemn one extreme for women, in-door or out-door drudgery, we denounce no less the opposite, that of entire freedom from exertion. It was not designed that woman should spend all her hours in the parlor entertaining heartless fops, reading works of fiction, playing the piano, doing fancy work, dancing, flirting, retailing scandal, and the many other pastimes of fashionable women. God never made her for such a purpose. Neither was it designed that women should be so engrossed in literary pursuits as to have no interest in the scenes of every-day life.

CREEDS OF SOME MARRIED WOMEN.

MANY a woman likes to make her husband and sons think her presence essential in household matters, for the purpose of making herself appear the more important in their eyes. To obey a husband, and conceal his faults, is the narrow formula of some women's creed. To live in style, and be admired by strangers, is another quite in vogue. To marry off her daughters is the sole aim of many a mother; while a small number, taking a religious and higher view of their obligations, endeavor to lead a pure life, and exert a holy influence, that they may thereby help their husbands and children to obtain an interest in the better world above.

ADVANTAGES OF WOMEN MORALLY.

THE courtesy and respect that distinguish American men in their intercourse with the other sex is acknowledged by nations far and near. Ladies receive kindness and attention where men would not. In traveling it is particularly noticeable, except in the street cars of Philadelphia, New York, and Boston, where the majority of men occupy seats while ladies stand.

Delicacy and refinement are imparted to a man by intercourse with virtuous, intelligent, and pious women. Women wield a mighty moral influence. In almost every place some sphere of benevolent action is open to woman. So, if her home duties do not occupy her, she has no excuse for idleness.

Aime Martin says, "The little of true piety which yet exists on earth we owe to women, much more than to theologians."

Women are thought to be more credulous than men. That arises from circumstances. They perhaps have not their trust so often misplaced. They have not so often occasion to test the truthfulness, or reverse, of human nature. If before the fall woman was more credulous than man, surely she was less responsible for heeding the words of the tempter.

The condition of woman has always been a fair index, and standard, of the state of morality among the men of their age. When women were respected, and well treated the men were more correct and humane. It has been said, that women in every age were better than the men of their time.

Women are not exposed to the same kind of evil influences as men. The wickedness of the world in general is not so well known to them. They are not thrown into so great temptations to commit sinful deeds. Man is more engrossed by the objects of sense — more of the earth — earthy — in his nature — than woman. He is more governed by his passions and appetites; consequently he has more to contend with in becoming a spiritual being. Woman's dangers are more from within herself — man's more from without. Woman's are more to be guarded against by a pure heart, a good education, constant employment, and virtuous friends — man's more by external circumstances and moral courage. The character of a man's associates has much to do with these. Women are probably more influenced by passing events than men, and generally find it more difficult to overcome any obstacle arising therefrom. Woman's education should be of a strengthening, not an enervating kind. She needs all the discipline of mind, and force of character, that can be brought to bear upon her earnest every-day life. When woman has been educated for three centuries as man is, her power of thought will obtain as strong a reality. She will think as freely, and execute as well as think.

Since the forbidden fruit was eaten in Eden the race has suffered depression. Woman's physical, moral, and mental depression has been greater than man's. But since by woman came a Redeemer to the world, her condition has gradually improved.

The duties of women are different from those of men, but they are not less arduous or important. Women are the supporters of infant life — the guides of youth — the comforters of old age. Without them home is a desert. They are the refiners of the rude, the softeners of the untamed.

Some writers charge the women of the present day with having less courage than those of the past. They may be physically weaker, but their courage would, no doubt, be found as great, if it were put to the test.

Women are much more patient than men, and it is well, for little events make up the sum of woman's life. This quality of patience, united with perseverance, enables women to succeed well in works of research, and application.

Women are thought to have more lively imaginations, and greater discernment, than men, but inferior judgments. It may be that their judgments are less exercised. The memories of most women are deficient, probably from their being stored with numberless matters of minor importance, but in many cases it arises from poor health.

Scientific knowledge is being more generally diffused among women, and the principles of art better understood, than in past years. Some writer has remarked, "However liberal a man may be, he rarely feels unqualified pleasure in the superiority of a woman. If he does not love, his self-esteem takes offense. If he does, his heart is alarmed by it."

Says Lady Morgan, "As Moses wound up his divine mission on Mount Horeb with his law on female inheritance, so closes the sacred volume of holy writ as it began — with woman — her intellectual influence, and her social importance — a glorious and imperishable record in her favor, to which nature and revelation have both set their seal; and which man, by all his physical supremacy, and by all his artificial combinations, his unjust laws and puerile fictions, cannot conceal or invalidate."

The remark of Mons. Thomas contains a large grain of truth, but we hope it may be left as a myth in the years fast passing away. "It is with women as with sovereigns: they seldom hear the truth, and we estimate them more by interest and by humor, than by justice."

Women usually have more address than men. They are quicker in their perceptions, more acute in their reflections. Pity and benevolence are characteristics of women, and especially noticeable among savage nations, where these qualities contrast strongly with other traits. Under trying circumstances of sorrow, disappointment, and poverty, women have manifested an incredible amount of fortitude. And in sickness, their patience and composure have surpassed those of the other sex.

Women are accused by some of being more gossiping, meddlesome, and unjust than men. The first charge we think unfounded, as men meet each other more frequently in business transactions, public and benevolent meetings, and social pastimes than women, and invariably discuss more or less, not only the news of the day, but their neighbors' affairs.

If women are more interfering, and prying, it arises from their minds being so constantly occupied with trifles, and it may be from a larger share of natural curiosity.

Some young women exhibit a great want of refinement by their coarse jokes, and indecent expressions, when thrown into the society of each other. We believe, however, it is rare. It certainly has a deleterious influence on the advancement of moral growth. There is a respect due to every human being that we should observe, and a respect due to us, that we should require. It is essential to a proper self-respect. Storing the mind with useful knowledge is the best antidote to impure language, for then the tongue has materials at its disposal. Impurity of language, and coarse jokes, generally arise as much from emptiness of head, as impurity of heart.

Women have rather more freedom than in by-gone years. Yet they should remember that public opinion is a severe censor. Suspicion lurks with an Argus eye, and calumny, with her tongue of fire, is ever ready to spread ruin and death.

Women have never had a fair chance in the world. Men impose on them more than they are aware of. They have cramped them in their thoughts and actions, have lowered their moral standard, and made public opinion to frown at any attempt on the part of women to maintain their own individual rights, or those of their sex. "Many women, from the cradle to the grave, scarcely know the exercise of free will, either in the disposal of their own time, or their fortunes, in the choice of pleasures or pursuits, in the selection of friends or acquaintances, or even in determining the spot on which they will reside."

As the motives that govern women are rendered more pure and unselfish, their principles more correct, their words more frank and truthful, their conduct more exemplary, as their moral courage is increased, and their responsibility for the use of time, talents, and opportunities enforced, the race will be elevated morally, and intellectually. But until men become better, and are held, like women, amenable to society for their conduct, progress will be very slow.

MENTAL AND MORAL GROWTH OF WOMEN.

THE comparative freedom of thought, and action, allowed women, by civilized nations, will tend to give both men, and women, clearer views of woman's privileges, and rights. It will open to women plainer, and more decided fields of action. Woman's faculties are cultivated, her powers developed, under the influence of Christianity. It is only where pure vital religion exists that woman, in the capacity of wife and mother, is properly appreciated. Woman now occupies a more exalted position in enlightened countries than since in Eden she made her home. In England and the United States the Christian religion exists in the greatest purity, and in no other countries does woman stand higher. The language of the two countries is the same — the language, that we hope, and suppose, will be universal during the millennium. It is now spoken by a greater number of people than any other. No country is more open to reforms than ours. The general instruction of the masses, the cheapness of books, liberal wages to men, general intelligence, business habits, and social character, added to the deference paid woman, render her ability for engaging in moral reforms, and benevolent objects, superior to all others. M. de Tocqueville attributes the successful condition of America to the superior character of the women. Indeed, most foreigners say the women of the United States are superior to the men.

The sanctity of the marriage tie does much to promote a pure morality in any country. Wherever the marriage tie is disregarded, there exists more or less depravity and degradation.

Adverse circumstances often develop traits and abilities

that the individual was not previously aware of possessing. Favorable circumstances are required for the development of woman's talents. Her sensitive, shrinking nature needs the soil of affection, the dew of hope, the sunshine of encouragement.

There should always be distinct aims in view in the education and training of young people. A difficulty often arises from a proper direction not being given to those aims — not having some one of experience and wisdom to guide them, to assist in forming their characters and minds. It is for the want of a clear and distinct consciousness of what should be done, that so many learned and polished people waste their time and talents.

With the generality of women there is a greater desire to be admired than to admire — to be loved than to love. There is a spice of romance in the young of both sexes, but especially that of woman.

Madame Necker says, "In general, the transition most difficult for women, is that from youth to maturity; and that most so for men, is from maturity to old age." The loss of the senses of sight and hearing, that generally attend old age, may serve to draw the mind and attention from the scenes and events of life. It may lead those so deprived, to fix their thoughts more on things pertaining to eternity. The restraints society imposes on women, if not too great, are beneficial. Now a lady can travel alone from one end of the land to the other, and, if she conducts herself with the dignity and reserve becoming a lady, such attention as is necessary will not be withheld from her.

The judgment, economy, and foresight, shown by women, in the management of their households, proves they have the ability to become competent in other departments of industry. Yet few women, as society now exists, have the qualities that enable them to rise above others of their class. The difficulties they have to overcome are far more than fall to the lot of man.

The powers of the mind become inactive if not brought into exercise by contact with other minds. All the faculties are sharpened by intercourse with others. The strongest mind must lose its vigor, and strength, when confined to loneliness, and solitude.

Literature is with most women a pastime, not a study. Attention has lately been called to the large number of women at the present time married happily, compared with the number of single women, and those married unhappily, at the commencement of the present century. "In Goethe's time, Rehbien observed that the women who had distinguished themselves in literature, poetry especially, were almost universally women who had been disappointed in their best affections, and sought in this direction of the intellect a sort of compensation. It is most certain that among the women who have been distinguished in literature, three fourths have been either by nature, or fate, or the laws of society, placed in a painful or a false position."

"I am persuaded that in the pursuit of knowledge women would never be insulted by sensible men, and rarely by men of any description, if they did not by mock modesty remind them that they were women."

Everything that develops the intellect, taste, and industry of a people should be encouraged. The moral and mental culture of workwomen is much neglected. Nor can it be otherwise while their wages are so scant, their comforts so few, their hours of toil so protracted.

The French working people of Metz are said to be the most polite and correct in their deportment, the best dressed, and best informed work-people of France; and the change in them is attributable to the courses of lectures delivered to them.

It will be observed that in most women of weak characters, and intellects below mediocrity, there is, with a show of amiability and pity, much servility and treachery.

When we see the results of ignorance and a want of judgment in woman, and its wretched effects upon the members of her household, we wonder how any man of thought can, for a moment, say aught against the education and development of woman's talents.

The disposition, the tendencies of education, and the influences of circumstances, render the power of resisting temptation very different in individuals. Various classes of society, and the conventionalities of various countries, also have their effect. One with a cool head, and calculating nature, is not so likely to be led astray, as one of an ardent, impulsive temperament.

In proportion as men respect virtue in women will they be virtuous themselves. The tyranny of the Frenchman in his family, and the jealousy of the Spaniard, do away with much affection.

A certain writer describes men as beings of reason — women as creatures of instinct. He must have had a very weak, silly, ignorant woman for a mother, and have associated with very common women.

Cabarius says, "Woman's eye, if we may so express it, hears every word; her ear sees every motion."

A settled home is necessary for tranquillity of mind. Useless and frequent changes greatly deteriorate the character of an individual, or a nation.

A COMPARISON OF MEN AND WOMEN.

MEN and women may be classed, like the members of the vegetable world, into genera, species, and individuals. There is nearly as marked a difference between the individuals that compose the species and genera. One man or woman may be a mushroom, another an oak, one a vine, another a shrub, &c. It is not sex that makes the difference in their moral and mental natures. One man differs as much from another in disposition, character, taste, and inclinations, as from a woman, and the same may be said to hold true of women, though not in so great a degree, inasmuch as their individuality, as a general thing, is not so fully and distinctly marked.

We cannot assert there is a difference in the moral and mental constitution of the two sexes. The difference in the intellects of men and women is in the difference of expansion, and the nature of the development, not in the original number or quality of the mental powers. Woman's mind is more suggestive than man's. A man will take a subject and revolve it in his mind, until he has educed new thoughts, which he works into an essay, newspaper article, or it may be a volume. A woman will be more likely to take books on the subject that interests her, and read, and have new ideas suggested, or created, which she forms into materials for the benefit of others. And yet women generally have not the power to permeate, to analyze, to appropriate, the thoughts and feelings of a writer, like men. But this difference is the result of cultivation.

Delicacy of organization may possibly tend to promote the growth of some of the mental faculties, such as imagination and observation, and it may retard the growth of others, such as reason and firmness. We doubt whether woman is, by nature, more imaginative than man. That faculty is often developed in her at the expense of her other faculties, and in many cases will prove more of a curse than a blessing. "In comparing the intellectual powers of the sexes, it would be necessary to consider distinctly the philosophical talent, which meditates; the talent of memory, which collects; the talent of imagination, which creates; the moral and political talent, which governs." It is thought by some that women are capable of a greater variety of attainments than men, but do not become so thorough. Few women equal learned men in their devotion to any one scientific pursuit, their constant devotion to study, their thoroughness, and their general information; for the number of women is small indeed, who are encouraged, or have the facilities, for reaching this stand-point. Women who devote themselves to study are less free and lively in conversation than others. They have less time to devote to the accomplishments, and may, therefore, be less acceptable to the other sex. But they generally have stricter ideas of morality and propriety than others, and greater force of character. The majority of married ladies in medium circumstances have a moderate degree of intelligence. Some are above mediocrity, but a large number are below. Married women have less time for reading than men. The cares of their families call for most — in many cases all — of their time. The majority of women in industrial vocations are nearly on a par in intelligence. The mass of women at twenty-five are equal in development of mind, and general attainments, to the mass of men of the same age; but at fifty, men are superior; and why? Because, while women have been giving life and nourishment to their young, and engaged in household duties that occupied their time and attention, men, by the contact, and conflict, of mind with mind, by the exercise of thought, the general information obtained by observation, conversation, reading, and experience, have been rising higher and higher in the scale of intelligence.

There is a greater variety in the attainments, mental culture, and original thought, of men than of women.

Beauty of character is marred in some women by venting their bitterness, littleness, and prejudice, against individuals. A corresponding class of men are more given to generalizing, and spout forth their invectives against societies, church sects, and political parties, of which they are not themselves members.

Few women have that firmness of purpose which most men have, and which can only be acquired by business experience. Men are more gregarious than women; even boys are more so than girls. Women are not capable of as much gratitude as men, nor so courageous in the expression of it. With women it is an impulse — with men it is a principle — a part of their code of honor. Among men every grade of humanity is represented, from the lowest biped in the scale of reason to the most exalted intellect. The chasm that now exists between men and women intellectually we would see bridged. In some of the lyceums of the Eastern States, the ladies, as well as gentlemen, take a part in the discussion. We think it a more sensible way of meeting than in some of the social gatherings where gossip, nonsense, silly plays, and indifferent music, occupy the hours. Women independent in thought and action, are sneered at by some men as strong-minded, because they do not like that a woman should have a will or an opinion that does not coincide with their own. If women have the same native talent as men, and the same cultivation of that talent, why have they not the same right to form and express opinions? How often is man represented as the head, woman as the heart! We advocate a union of head and heart, in both man and woman — a happy blending of the two. Women are more impressible than men. Men have stronger nerves and more muscular power. The nervous organization of woman produces a desire for peace, and hatred of bloodshed, that it is hoped will tend to diminish the frightful ravages made by war.

Most women have quick, perceptive powers, and are more sharp-witted than men. The Creator has made the sensibilities of women finer; consequently they receive impressions more vividly than men. Their likes and dislikes are often formed, as it were, by intuition. They are closer observers, and have more penetration. Consequently they are, with the same facilities for learning human nature, better readers of character. The judgments of women are more reliable, and sooner formed, than those of men. Some say they arrive at their conclusions by a more rapid course of reasoning — others that it is more the result of a natural sagacity, or instinct, than by a course of reasoning. Let the cause be what it will, the fact is not altered. There is a want of mutual appreciation by the sexes. They know but little of each other's tastes and pursuits, temptations and encouragements. This arises partly from the difference of education, and prospects, in the sexes.

Love and religion have been the strong impelling forces of women for ages; power and wealth, of men. Women often receive kindness and attention where men would be passed by. Women are more sensitive than men. Pity is a soul-impelling power, and one which women largely possess. The charge has been made that women are more indolent than men. We deny the charge. Women are not naturally more indolent, and when habitually so, it is confined to women of wealth, or those whom the customs of society seem to justify in being so. The majority of women work longer, and more continuously, than men. Women have more regard to order, and are more economical than men. Misbehavior is more rare among women than men.

Men are much more natural and child-like in their manners and conversation than women. They plunge right into a subject, while women wind about like a crystal stream in a meadow. The minds and actions of men are more practical than those of women. Women are more fond of dress, and fine houses, and elegant furniture, than men. They have more time to devote to the ornamental. In some places there is much rivalry between women of fortune in their styles of living.

The passions and appetites of men are stronger than those

of women. There are in all large cities, both demons and angels, in the form of men. One class is luring to destruction, while the other is trying to save. Besides, there are all intermediate grades — every class and condition. The dominion of woman, even when arbitrary, is rarely cruel. It is rather a disposition of caprice, than of oppression.

Men generally have more uniform tempers than women, but it is because they have better health, not so many annoyances, and more things of a pleasant and interesting nature to occupy their minds. Men have more expanded views and better judgment. They also excel women in business qualifications. Women may beg more successfully for a benevolent object, but men give more largely. It is not that women are less generous than men, but most of them have less to be generous with.

The customs of society have done much to abolish the original characteristics of the sexes. The qualities for which men were once noted as men, and the qualities that gave grace to women, are less confined to the sexes. The line of demarcation has become less distinct. As a general thing the qualities have become modified, and blended, in most people. Bravery, courage, and firmness, are not confined to men, nor tenderness, fortitude, and patience, to women. There may exist more stamina in the character of men, but there is less delicacy. Men excel in humor, women in wit.

Women lead a more sedentary life than men. They are more quiet and contemplative. A woman's resources for beguiling thought are more limited than a man's. Women's minds are less strengthened by exercise than those of men. The views of men are generally less superficial. One reason is, they mingle more with each other. They learn much by such intercourse. They mix indiscriminately. There is not the same reserve between those of different positions in social life.

I make one exception in regard to the liberality of men's views. It is that the *mass of men* have not very liberal, just, or correct views, of what women may, and can, do with propriety. They would limit her duties entirely to home, whether she has one or not. They would not permit women to enter the store, the workshop, the counting-room, nor even the more exalted and refining atmosphere of the study, or the *atelier.* They would exclude her more especially from the professions.

The attachments of men for women are thought to be more short-lived, but more fervent and ardent, than those of women for men. The friendship of women for each other is more gentle and soothing, less deep and stirring, than that of men for men. The coquetry with which the female sex is charged is fast becoming a characteristic of the other. Women are generally more tender in all the relations of life, and the performance of their duties, than men. Women have more delicacy of feeling, and a keener appreciation of the good and beautiful, than men. Being more moral, on an average, than men, they make the best instructors of youth. Women are thought by some to have less moderation than men — to be more subject to extremes. Women have more fortitude, men more courage. Man was made to act, woman to endure. The differences in men and women arise more from the difference in training, education, influence, example, and association, the circumstances arising from a difference in business pursuits, and pecuniary matters, and other contingencies of a similar nature, than from any marked characteristic peculiar to the sexes — any native-born antagonistic elements.

Says Mrs. Hale, "Of all the sinful deeds done on earth, nine tenths are committed by men, or caused by their wickedness. More than three fourths of the professed followers of Christ, are women. In judging between the sexes, Jesus has left his record, that man is the greatest sinner; and hence Christian lawgivers should take warning and example, restrain their own passions, and make laws to punish their own sex, while carefully protecting the honor, safety, and happiness of women. I anticipate the time when wise and good men will consider this subject of providing for the well-being of the female sex, as their most important earthly duty. Hitherto the mass of men, in Christian countries, may be said to be at enmity with any improvement of women that does not gratify their own sensuous properties. Women are free to adorn their persons; but if they seek to cultivate their minds it is treason against the prerogative of man. The source from whence this jealousy of female intelligence springs is not fear that the sex will excel in learning; it is hatred of the moral influence the sex would wield, were they better instructed. Sensuality and selfishness always dread enlightened women."

If truth is eternal, and if men and women are both endowed with reason, why must they have different codes of morals? Works for the moral improvement of the race are especially adapted to women; those more intellectual, as well as those requiring greater physical force, are best adapted to men.

Says Mrs. Child, "The character and condition of women are always in correspondence with those of men; and both sexes have always furnished about an equal number of exceptions to the general character of the age in which they lived. There were liberal-minded women, as well as men, during the bigoted times of Cromwell, and many an English matron, of stainless character, educated her pure-minded daughters far from the corrupting court of Charles II. The excellent Lady Russell, who was perhaps the very best woman in the world, lived in those profligate times."

WANT OF DEFINITENESS.

WITH a boy, the question, *What shall I be?* suggests itself in the early hours of childhood. In the more thoughtful days of youth it comes with startling earnestness, and still later, as manhood approaches, it becomes one of momentous importance. The joys and sorrows, and hopes and fears, the misfortunes and success of life, depend much upon the decision. The youth and his friends ponder the matter day after day, and week after week. The question bears the stamp of sober reality. Such is the early part of a man's career. You may see the little cadet lift his miniature sword, and declare his intention to be a warrior. The noisy lad in his merry gambols assures his mother he will some day be a gentleman, quiet and sedate. The indolent school-boy declares his design of forsaking his idle habits, and becoming a learned physician, or pleader at the bar. The gallant youth seems anxious to cast the veil from dark futurity, to read his destiny, hoping to acquire celebrity as a great man, and leave

> "His hope, or love, or truth, or liberty,
> To be a rule, and law, to ages that survive."

But what are the early dreams of a woman's life? What bright visions does the future offer to her? Perhaps she thinks she will marry, and live as her mother does. If not, the life of a teacher is most likely to present itself. The whole round of occupations is not before her to choose from. No hope of future glory excites her. No prospect of rising in the world by her own exertions comes to cheer her pathway. Her infancy is soon gone, her girlhood past, and youth's pleasant seasons ended. Then come the cares and anxieties of womanhood. The woman either marries or remains single. If she remains single, unless she has an income of her own, she must either be supported by relatives, or earn a subsistence for herself. Often she lingers on in the family of some relative until life begins to wane. Then the memories of by-gone days come to mind. All the bright joys of the past have fled. The lightning was not more swift, nor a meteor more brilliant. Her life is like a flower which in the morning lifts its head unseen on the mountain top, but ere noon droops and withers beneath the burning heat of midday. She considers what she is, and what she might have been. She contemplates misspent hours, and golden opportunities lost. She had been the delicate object of parents' care. A mother's tender hand had shielded her from the cold and chilling winds of a selfish world. Her affections had been cultivated, her sensibilities cherished, until like the sensitive plant she shrank from any save the gentlest touch. She had not been taught to brave the difficulties that might beset her. She had not been disciplined for the battle of life. She had not been fitted to encounter the loneliness, the effort, the struggle that must be made to supply the physical wants. And in her hour of need she finds herself pressed down in the scene of action, and driven far back by the current of competitors. Amid the temptations of an evil world she wants a safeguard. In the purity of her thoughts, the benevolence of her feelings, and the nobleness of her soul, she finds her *only* safeguard. But she looks back to feel that if she had been furnished with an occupation, and passed through the discipline necessary to obtain one, she might have been among the foremost in the race of life. Her condition and circumstances might have been different. She might have had a home won by her own exertions, and not exist a dependent on some one's bounty, or caprice.

Of the hundreds and thousands of women that struggle, and labor, their whole adult lives, how few rise to any but a subordinate position in business! A few cannot succeed from want of native ability, a large number from want of early training, and a still larger number from the exclusion of women from the higher branches of industry. If a better class of occupations were opened to women, the same stimulus, to become intelligent and energetic, would be given as to men.

Far more can be accomplished where some definite pursuit is kept in view — some distinct aim. Then one's reading can be directed in that way, one's thoughts and energies all bent in the same direction. The hundreds of poor women in large cities that live from hand to mouth do so from the want of some definite occupation, or not being thoroughly qualified to perform any one branch of labor. They do house-cleaning, wash by the day, sew, knit, go errands, &c., &c., just as an opportunity offers; but the subsistence is so precarious that they may often suffer. Their parents are to blame for not having given them trades. They were brought up to be dependent, and then left without any one to lean upon. No individual has a right to become a parent without having definitely in view the means of providing for, and properly training, his children. It is a sin in the eyes of God.

A common deficiency is the want of some one of experience, and judgment, and proper moral tone, to guide and advise the young, to properly cultivate their hearts, and train their minds. How many even learned, and polished, men and women, waste their time and talents, from the want of a clear and distinct consciousness of what should be done, and what they can do. Besides, they are frequently drawn away from the attainment of some great aim, the accomplishment of some noble work, by caprice, passion, or self-interest. A chaotic mass of learning is not rare among the women of our country; but the want of discipline, and distinct aims, make it of comparatively little avail. Pleasure may be derived from its possession, but too often it is not applied to any practical purpose. The time, talent, wealth, and strength, wasted by idleness, inefficiency, and misguided effort, since our Saviour's advent, would, combined, have regenerated the world.

The work now done by women in non-domestic employments requires but little skill, consequently women are not paid as men are who have skill and experience. So there is little competition between skilled and unskilled labor. The wages of middle aged, and old women, fall to those of the young, instead of those of the young increasing with the maturity, and experience, of years, as with men. A man with a family receives double, or treble, as high wages as a single man. A man can lay by money, and make for himself a home, and a reputation — a woman cannot. She can barely earn a support while she labors.

WHAT A WOMAN SHOULD BE.

SOME women are by nature gifted with more refinement of feeling, more delicacy of thought, than others. Education, or training, makes a still greater difference.

A woman's virtuous counsels are a beacon-light to save from the rocks and quicksands of this stormy world, but the evil counsels of a woman lead to ruin and misery.

There are a thousand little courtesies that woman alone is capable of performing; volumes could not contain all the delicate minutiæ that form a true lady. The feeling that makes one must be native.

Order and harmony should prevail in all the arrangements of a lady. In the adjustment of her dress — the furniture of her room — her studies — her pastimes — her hours for rest, — in all, order, system, and harmony, are important.

A kind consideration for the comfort of others is one of the most lovely traits of female character. A woman that does not discharge her duties, as wife and mother, does not deserve the name of woman.

Gentleness, tenderness, and decision should characterize a woman. A cheerful, contented, and forgiving disposition should mark her temper. Nothing is more to be admired than modesty, humility, and consistency. They form bright jewels in the crown of virtues. A warm heart, and refined manners, command admiration and love; but a cultivated intellect will add a greater charm, and enable a woman to accomplish more good. It is surprising how much more information some people impart than others. It is like the soil that appropriates mineral and vegetable properties, produces a change in them, and sends them forth under new forms and aspects, animate with life and beauty. Just so individuals take in facts and principles, by the operations of the brain and heart, and stamp their own impress. Then by the gift of speech, or the use of the pen, they impart those facts and principles, modified by their own idiosyncrasies.

Happiness depends as much on the condition of the mind as on extraneous circumstances. Like the lonely flower that exhales its sweetest perfume when crushed, so the best traits of woman's heart are often developed by privation, sorrow, or some other unfavorable turn of fortune. It is as well to let the living spirit seek and find companionship — to pour forth its warm, gushing feelings — to love, even if that love prove a false dream, a delusive phantom.

"How continually in retirement, and in the world, is the lesson of submission forced upon woman! To suffer, and be silent under suffering, seems the great command she has to obey, while man is allowed to wrestle with calamity, and to conquer or die in the struggle."

We think the position so long sustained by woman as the slave, and then the angel, of man, and her subsequent dependence, have made her too subservient to him in her opinions. Not that we would depreciate the most unbounded reverence for the opinions of good, wise, and unselfish men; but women have so long had men to think for them, that we fear the mass of women do not think freely enough for themselves. They do not form opinions of their own, through the clear medium of reason. They are too likely to rely entirely on the opinions of the men with whom they are associated, whether husband, brother, or father, without considering whether he is a man of sound sense, good principle, and devoid of prejudice in his judgments.

"The reason men are not generally so much given to trifling as women, is, they have some object for thought beyond dressing and eating. They dress and eat, but their larger intercourse with society furnishes some food for thought, even while engaged in those necessary avocations. Women require something to think about, as well as men."

Woman is physically, mentally, and morally, more delicately organized than man. In excess this delicacy is apt to render women nervous, languid, and indolent. Indeed some think it excites an interest, and under that impression even affect an infirmity. We must acknowledge, we are so old-fashioned in our views, as to delight in seeing a woman active and energetic. In our eyes such a one looks as if created for some purpose. A large-hearted, free-spoken, sensible, earnest woman, we like. Such a woman can work and rest, can think and feel, can reason and be reasoned with. A woman that will strengthen virtuous principle by a judicious influence, is one to be prized.

The exercise of all the powers, mental, moral, and physical, is necessary for a harmonious and complete development of woman's, as well as man's, character.

There is more, with the majority of people, in the manner of doing things than in the acts themselves. You must let a person know, without seeming to do so, that you are doing him a favor if you expect his thanks. Constant sacrifice, and unremitting exertion, may not receive any hearty expressions of gratitude, but the individual will be likely to recall such sacrifice and exertion when needed again. In some cases, your indignation is likely to betray a consciousness that you expect a reasonable degree of appreciation, and your words to that effect may lead the recipient to better understand both you and himself. A true woman asks no other triumph than that of a just and honorable kind. Her triumph will be in winning the evil from error, sustaining those that do right, and cheering the pathway of the lonely, in being blessed by blessing others.

Of all jewels that adorn woman's character, truth is one of the brightest. It casts splendor over all the others. Woman has been charged with being deceitful. If more so than the other sex, which we doubt, has not man done much to cause it by his tyranny and injustice? Nothing is more alien to the nature of a perfect woman than boldness and selfishness.

Woman's potent influence socially has long been acknowledged. Supremacy in moral worth is generally conceded to woman by the other sex, but with it let her combine mental power, and then may she stand still higher.

When women consider their destiny, the question arises in their minds, For what were we created? Was it to make an idol of pleasure, of fashion, of wealth, or honor? The worldly woman may answer in the affirmative, but not so the Christian. She turns to the Bible, the treasure-house of earth's richest gems, the depository of life's noblest gifts, the casket of peace, of hope, and happiness.

That which sheds a lustre over all woman's virtues is true, unaffected piety. It forms the topmost jewel in her crown, shedding a magic beauty over the rest. It is a halcyon light about her path, giving a charm to her every thought, word, and action. It confers energy and nobleness of mind. It is a stimulus to support woman in her unceasing round of duties. In times of affliction it cheers her drooping heart. In hours of adversity it opens to her view a brighter and happier world. It gives woman a higher sense of her influence and responsibility. It fits her better for the duties of daughter, sister, wife, mother.

POOR HEALTH OF AMERICAN WOMEN.

THE want of health in Americans is fast becoming proverbial. A gentleman of intelligence once told me that the belief originated with the English, and is without just foundation; but I am convinced, by ocular demonstration, that the tender and fragile nature of American women is not a myth.

The want of physical exercise by American girls, while growing up, is one cause of their premature old age. Much of the insanity that affects our land is attributed by physicians to the want of bodily out-door exercise in childhood, and the precocions development of mind. With the ancients physical culture first received attention, then moral, then mental. The American girls have a fairer, fresher appearance from sixteen to eighteen years of age than foreigners, but fade earlier.

The loss of health and dejection of spirits, of single women, in the middle and higher classes of society, arise mostly from the want of some regular occupation, some definite aim, some high and elevating pursuit. We believe it is Alexander Walker who says, "It would be easy to show that disease, as well as deformity, is an inevitable result of the neglect of active duties." Dr. Combe says, "Inactivity of intellect and feeling is a very frequent predisposing cause of every form of nervous disease. For evidence of this we have only to look at the numerous victims to be found, who have no call to exertion in gaining the means of subsistence, and no objects of interest on which to exercise their mental faculties. The intellect and feelings, not being provided with interests external to themselves, must either become inactive and weak, or work upon themselves, and thus become diseased. The most frequent victims of this kind of predisposition are females of the middle and higher classes, especially those of a nervous constitution and of good natural abilities. The liability of such persons to melancholy, hysteria, hypochondriasis, and other varieties of mental disease, really depends on a state of irritability of the brain, occasioned by imperfect exercise."

The health of women that work in the fields is generally excellent — and why? because of their exercise in pure out-door air. O that I could impress on my countrywomen, in the higher walks of life, the necessity of more exercise in the open air. It will give women clearer thoughts, firmer principles, more patience, self-reliance, and stability of character. It will give vigor and freedom to both mind and body. Especially would we recommend this panacea to the consideration of young mothers. Since the hydropathic system has become fashionable, we think more attention has been paid to the general health of the body. A prudent diet, out-door exercise, relaxation, and freedom from the use of strong medicine, are tending to restore strength and vigor to many shattered constitutions.

The early entrance into society of most American ladies has its bad effect. The night is devoted to fashionable gayeties, and the day to rest. This accords with the fast and sanguine character of our people. The dissipated, unsettled state of mind it engenders, the intense love of excitement, and fondness for admiration, are certainly disadvantageous.

Women marry too early and live too secluded. Many are scarcely out of school before they have settled down as wives and housekeepers. The cares of a family are devolving on them before they have the strength and nerve to perform them. One reason that our female ancestors lasted longer and had better health was, that their minds were not so much taxed, nor the nerves so highly strung. They had the full use of their powers. Their physical health was better — their constitutions stronger. Those that had much mental activity generally had sufficient physical exertion to counterbalance it.

Most women know not enough of the laws that govern health, and of the diseases incident to their sex and children. How often do we see peevishness and impatience manifested by a sickly wife and mother, that, by a knowledge of the laws of health, and strict observance of them, might be strong and healthy, and fitted for her responsible and arduous duties! The majority of married women, with families of small children, need more relaxation, and a greater variety of innocent recreations. Many of them become so chained down in body and mind, by the minutiæ of household cares and labor, that their health and spirits sink beneath the load, and in appearance, strength, and feeling they grow prematurely old. Some housewives suffer much annoyance from bad servants, and some perform drudgery for which they are unfitted. The amount of indoor labor performed by American women, especially in the Northern States, is astonishing. What affects the body influences the mind, and vice versa. When either is worn and irritated, it acts on the other. English women usually have better servants and more of them. They walk and ride more, marry later, and have by nature better constitutions.

Most American men are so absorbed in business they have not time to relieve their wives at all of domestic cares, and fail to give them encouragement and friendly advice. The want of congeniality in the dispositions of husbands and wives, and the customs of social life, often produce a discord in the home-circle that is detrimental to health. The readiness of American women to make any exertion for the good of those they love is highly commendable, yet, in justice to themselves, they should not make sacrifices that will involve their soundness of mind or body.

Another source of discomfort, and even of ill health, is occupying imperfectly-ventilated rooms. Especially is this the case with the poorer classes of people.

Another cause of ill health is want of sufficient sleep, and another is anxiety of mind, caused by uncertainty of obtaining the means of living, and the fear of want in the future.

The general use of flour bread, and constipating food, are fertile sources of indigestion, with its train of ailments. In addition is the excess of food, in which Americans indulge. They eat even more heartily than the English, and indulge more than any other civilized nation in the use of warm, liquid, oily substances.

The quantity, quality, and nature of food should depend somewhat on the occupation of the individual, as well as constitutional tendencies to special diseases. Another cause of the poor health of American women, is the want of thoroughly educated and experienced female physicians, to whom they may explain their diseases, and from whom they may receive relief. Quack medicines have done much to bring about the present low state of health. They will account in many cases for weak nerves, aching bones, and shattered frames.

A lady of foreign birth spoke to me of Americans being so nervous, and attributed it partly to the climate. She thought it marvelous that Americans have such good forms as they do, when they grow so rapidly, but attributed it to their restlessness, which prevented their being long in one position, so that any defect was not likely to become fixed. Much of the ill health of shop-girls is brought on by their standing so long and constantly, and the employer who will not allow his store-women to sit down and rest when they can, deserves to lose his patronage.

Another cause of premature decay and increase of disease is, the adoption of certain fashions. Fashion has ever been a tyrant, and those who yield to her behests must pay dearly for the homage. One form of disease, so common among ladies for a few years past, has been attributed, by some of our best physicians, to the wearing of too many and too heavy skirts; and some who saw the terrible effects rejoiced at a remedy in the introduction of lighter and stiffer materials for skirts, as crinoline and whalebone. A more healthy style for the make of women's apparel would be to have the skirts shorter, as is now the case in some places, and the weight of the clothes to press more on the shoulders — less on the waist and hips. I suppose that there are none who will read this but have learned from hearsay or observation — perhaps experience — something of the injurious effects of tight lacing. By wearing heavy skirts, and lacing, the vitals are compressed, their action retarded, and eventually disease ensues. Though the fashion is done away to a great extent, its bad effects are not entirely gone. Fashion is so arbitrary that often in midwinter the clothing of a lady does not shield her chest. The searching blasts of winter are not guarded against. The sudden changes of the American climate are severe enough on the constitution at best. Most American women, in easy circumstances, are like hot-house plants, chilled by the fresh, bracing air, that is intended to strengthen and invigorate them. Their slightest exposure to cold or dampness is sure to be followed by catarrh. What traveler that observes the silk hose and kid slippers still worn by some American women in the rigors of winter, or the sacrifice to appearance of comfort in their clothing, can form a favorable opinion of their judgment and taste, or be surprised that so many are annually carried off by that lingering and insidious disease — consumption?

One fertile source of disease is getting the feet wet. An umbrella and gum shoes should be used by every individual, when exposed to the inclemencies of out-door weather. Dressing so as to injure the health is suicidal. We find, as a general thing, that women live longer in southern climates. Never in my life have I seen so many invalid women, in so short a time, as I have met with in traveling during the last three years. The war that distracted and desolated our country, was the principal cause of it. The loss of friends, and the loss of property, have broken the hearts and ruined the health of many. The anxiety attending the absence and the uncertain fate of fathers, brothers, husbands, and friends, has made the nation one of prematurely old, sad, and invalid people.

The peculiarities of our institutions, the nature of the

people, the mode of government, and other circumstances, have combined to develop in earlier life, more fully and more rapidly, the capabilities of women than in any other country.

Pure air, out-door exercise, sufficient light, wholesome food, frequent bathing, and clean, comfortable clothing, are the best preventives of disease. Girls growing up and just reaching womanhood particularly need them. Light and fresh air, in some cases, prove not only preservatives of health, but a restorative to those out of health. Dark rooms and solitude tend to produce mental as well as bodily diseases.

The poor health of American women has done much to bring about that deplorable fashion so detrimental to domestic economy and happiness. I refer to the plan of families boarding, instead of keeping house. The domestic virtues of men suffer by it. The moral influence of the wife is lost, to some extent, and the temptations to be out late at night, in dissipating and expensive amusements, are increased. Parents also lose much influence and control over their children, and are apt to neglect an oversight of their minds and morals.

Without health no useful purposes can be attained — no vast schemes for good accomplished.

Some one has said, "He who is not a physician at thirty is a fool — a physician to his mind as well as to his body, acquainted with his own moral constitution — its diseases, its remedies, its diet, its conduct."

PECUNIARY, PHYSICAL, INTELLECTUAL, AND SOCIAL ADVANTAGES OF MEN.

AFTER leaving school there is a much greater difference between the conditions of young women than young men. The former associate freely together at school, but when they enter into society, dress, education, and the thousand etceteras that go towards making up a woman, stamp her position — and very often falsely. With men it is different. They can, to a great extent, win a position for themselves. They are not so much trammeled by the laws of society and custom. The republican feeling that exists among the majority of men is unknown to most women. If circumstances or relations are unfavorable to a man's advancement, he can go to a new place, and gain for himself a home, character, and influence. It is more difficult for a lady to do so, particularly if she is without gentlemen acquaintances, to whom she can apply for guidance, and letters of introduction. Indeed, a woman cannot forever cut herself off from her relatives unless she marry, and then she is not certain of doing so. A woman with an unhappy home deserves sympathy and consideration. It seemed to me, during the war, that nearly one half the men and women I met with were partially crazed, from losing their trust in God, and having more labor, trouble, anxiety, sorrow, and disappointment, than they could endure. The revolution of the times has cast a large portion of educated and refined people from the topmost round in fortune's ladder to its foot, while it has raised the coarse and ignorant to the highest rounds. Blind fortune has been as senseless as unjust in the turnings of her wheel. The aristocracy of the present day, in the United States, is of a mushroom growth — it sprang up in a night — it has not been forming from one generation to another, of the best material of the land. Many a man, with but little effort of his own, has sprung from poverty and obscurity, to wealth and distinction, without the requisite intellectual culture for the position. Money is an excellent friend, and it is a *sad* fact, that it will carry us through the world more easily, comfortably, and cheerfully, than any other unconnected with heaven. Yet the question sometimes arises, Do not people lose their humanity in proportion as they acquire riches? If so, are they worth exhausting toil, and the sacrifice of pleasure, and health, to acquire? Many a poor being on the high road of life hammers, and breaks, the rocks into stone, over which the proud, scornful, hard-hearted, rich usurper is driven. Said usurper looks down upon the hand laborer as at an immeasurable distance below him. There is a vast amount of selfishness and egotism in the world. Stony, flinty grit is the business experience of every-day life to some of the poor. Thereby the draught obtained by personal exertion is often turned to wormwood and gall. Men who gain wealth by their own exertions are usually more vain of it, than when it is left to them.

We have referred elsewhere to the want of proportionate profit resulting from the exercise of equal talents and attainments in men and women. Men are educated for professions, or trades, and generally make a comfortable living. A woman's education may cost as much; but how rarely can she turn her education to the same pecuniary advantage! Men receive such compensation for their services as enables them to lay by something for emergencies. So they have not occasion to suffer, as many women do, from apprehensions of want, and loneliness, in sickness, through declining years.

Men have more strength than women, their style of dress is not so injurious, they are more accustomed to being on their feet, in the open air, and are not subject to the physical exhaustion of women. These, with their naturally stronger frames, and more active occupations, tend to render life more agreeable to them. They can more easily cast off care, and brace themselves under adverse circumstances.

Men have over women also the advantage of intellectual pleasure. Usually a woman of superior attainments must, with the generality of her own sex, confine her conversation to the subjects of dress, fashion, and the every-day incidents of life, or, if literature is dragged in, it must be of a light kind — love stories, and sentimental rhyme. With gentlemen she may converse. Yet many of them, however interested and profited they may be by such conversation, have a feeling of restraint towards such a lady, as if they thought she had stepped from her " sphere," and in so doing excited their pity, and yet their gallantry would endeavor to put her at ease. Why is it? Is it that such men fear to recognize equality, or superiority, in a woman? Is it that they fear criticism? Is it that such women are rare, and men fear that they cannot interest them? Or is it that the want of self-reliance, sensitiveness, and a fear of criticism, are likely to render such women reserved and ungenial? We know not, but rather think it may, in most cases, arise from a combination of these causes.

We think ladies and gentlemen are both to blame, to some extent, for such a state of affairs. If ladies, whose male relatives and friends would love to see them educated and intelligent, would only become so, gentlemen would not entertain such ladies with light and frivolous talk — it would be different. Yet we would make some honorable exceptions to these statements, for there are educated men who enjoy the society of cultivated women, and do what they can to promote strength of mind, and dignity of character, in the female members of their own families, and among their lady acquaintances.

Mind in woman, as a general thing, is not brought fully into exercise. Men are in the world meeting with their friends and aquaintances every day. Their conversational powers are brought into play, their wits sharpened, and their faculties of course more exercised. Their information is brought more constantly and practically into use. As face answereth to face, as iron sharpeneth iron, as diamond cutteth diamond, so the contact of mind with mind brings out its beauty and strength.

A large majority of men make their business, or something connected with it, the topic of conversation. As few women have anything of the kind to interest them, it is not strange that many are often at a loss for improving topics, or indulge freely in such as are trifling.

A woman, with a family of young children, becomes so absorbed in providing for their material wants, that she finds little time for the improvement of her mind. Her husband should endeavor to supply that want, as he has leisure for reading, and is thrown with other men, from whom he gains, or should gain, much intelligence. The conversation of intellectual and refined men is a rich treat to most women of education.

In the present day the power in an intelligent community lies in thought, not in physical force.

We sometimes see those characteristics considered as belonging to one sex exhibited by the opposite sex. We occasionally see women with reasoning powers, breadth of comprehension, aud mental attainments, equal to the most superior men, while now and then we meet with men possessing all the sympathy, fineness of feeling, and poetry of sentiment, common to the fairer sex. Men can be brave and courageous, and yet possess all the finer, softer, gentler qualities of woman. Our Saviour is an example.

Most people are whatever it is their interest to be. The majority are devoid of moral courage, and without originality of thought. A gentleman once remarked to me, that he thought a smart woman could get along better in the world than a smart man; but an ordinary woman could not get along so well as an ordinary man.

The natural wants of man are greater than those of any other animal. As an equivalent, nature has afforded greater natural and artificial means for gratifying them.

Most men are ambitious. That makes them discontented. An acquaintance remarked to me, it is more excusable that men should struggle to acquire wealth than fame, for fame is very unsatisfactory, while wealth brings with it many comforts. Yet the heart craves something higher and better than either wealth or fame. It will not be satisfied. There is in the never-dying soul a longing for something more satisfactory than earth can yield.

People of a warm, impulsive nature rarely have uniform tempers. Such tempers are more often possessed by cool, selfish, calculating people, who study only their own interests, or by those who have acquired them by a careful watchfulness and self-control. The ignorant are as rarely amiable, and uniformly kind, as the learned; but there is greater ability with them to throw off care, a negligent indifference, and a docility, the result of submissive inferiority, that with some people acquires the name of good temper. Men have more control of their tempers than women, owing to their better health, and their freedom from the little annoyances that beset a woman. Besides, their work is such as to more pleasantly, and fully, occupy the mind. In addition they have more encouragement by looking forward to an advancement in their business, to the acquisition of wealth or fame, to a desirable establishment in life, and to an old age of ease and competency.

Men have the advantage of women in selecting from a large number of the opposite sex one to love, and in making that love known. A woman, even if her affections are deliberately won by a man, is not expected to manifest her attachment until he declares his. Or if he chooses he may deliberately leave her without explanation to perish in wretchedness and intense suffering. Among many cases that have come under my observation I will mention one. A man occupying a high and responsible civil office, who sits in judgment upon men and women, for trivial offenses, pronouncing a severe penalty for such, coolly and deliberately, yet with passion and fervor, by looks, manners, and attention, though not in words, won the affections of a highly respectable, worthy, cultivated woman (in every respect his equal, if not his superior), and then without explanation, or known cause, neglected her, and wounded her feelings before others. That man stood high in the world as a gentleman, and in the church as a Christian. Was he in reality either a gentleman or a Christian?

WHAT A MAN SHOULD BE.

OF course no one is responsible for what he is by natûre, or education, but he is for his deeds of omission and commission, so far as they are the result of opportunity for learning what is right and wrong. "Mothers often endeavor to dwarf the masculine life down to the standard of the feminine one — to narrow under the name of refining, to weaken and call it purification. It would be better if men were more influenced by reason — less by instinct — were more earnest and sincere."

The selfishness of a majority of American men is surprising. They collect, and talk, and go to places of amusement, but they do not often take their wives and daughters. In that respect, the Germans are a model for all nations. Their amusements differ from those of Americans, but if they were the same, no doubt they would make the same efforts to have their families enjoy their pastimes with them, while if Americans participated in those of the Germans, they would continue to confine them to their own sex.

The leisure afforded in the United States, by a fair compensation to men for their labor, leaves them without an excuse for ignorance. Mankind are mentally dependent, as well as physically.

A woman's character and station depend somewhat upon herself, but not so much as a man's. Circumstances, and domestic relations, have a strong bearing upon the destiny of women. The majority stand higher in a moral point of view than men. Compare the number of idle men with the number of idle women, in a village, or town. Compare the number of dissipated men and women. Compare the number in a country neighborhood, or in your city circle of acquaintances. Then tell me what comparison the sexes bear each other morally. Compare the number of working hours of men and women everywhere; compare the amount of work accomplished in proportion to their physical strength. Then say in whose favor the scales sink.

Men with strong wills and bad dispositions, united, are likely to trample on the weak. Their wives and children are in danger of suffering from their ungoverned passions and imperious wills. If they do not control their tempers they blight the prospects of their children, and domestic misery is the fate of their wives. Such a man ceases to see the injustice and oppression of his course. In the pride of his soul he feels himself a demigod, and forgets his responsibility, and relation to the Maker of heaven and earth. No man has a right to govern the soul of his wife. She owes duties to her God, as well as her husband, and she should never sacrifice the first to the last. The harsh and arbitrary conduct of some men, in their families, is such, that the mental faculties of their wives and children become weakened, and their dispositions irritable.

"Cowards only are the unnatural enemies of woman; and the man who pursues her with private calumny, or public hate, is, if all were known, but *one of nature's monsters*."

When a man ceases to repose confidence in, and give his affections to, his own family, but attaches himself to strangers, he perils his own happiness and good, and that of his family. When such is the case with a woman it is a sad and equally perilous thing—sad that it is, or must be so, and equally perilous in its consequences.

Nothing in life is more beautiful than the strong love and confidence existing in a happily united man and wife. If congenial in taste and disposition, if living with an earnest desire to fulfill their duties as Christians and members of society, supporting and being supported by each other, with an earnest desire to afford their children every advantage of a moral and religious as well as temporal character, they are indeed blessed. Their principal aim and great hope is a reunion in the world above — "a united family, not a wanderer lost."

Motion is a more natural state to man than quiet. Nature has given man more strength than woman — therefore greater ability for physical labor. It is obligatory on a man, so far as he can, to aid his helpless or infirm female relatives. A man that does not provide for his family is unworthy the name of man.

Of what use are riches to a man without education or cultivation, unless he has judgment and goodness of heart to make them available in the education of those with whom he is associated, or by benefiting the destitute and afflicted?

MUTUAL INFLUENCE OF THE SEXES.

"CIVILIZATION ameliorates the condition of woman, because it lessens the influence of physical strength in proportion to that of mind; and because woman is more nearly equal to man in the power of intellect, than in strength of limb."

"It is obvious that whatever develops mind, and augments its ascendency in the world, must add to the responsibility of woman, who depends for her social relation upon the moral and intellectual influences she exerts over man. Accordingly, though chivalry has ceased to exist, the moral dignity and social equality of the female sex continue to be distinctive of Christendom."

The ability of men to concentrate their thoughts and energies exclusively on any one object of thought, or pursuit, arises principally, but not exclusively, from a business education. The engrossing nature of boys' amusements and studies serves to draw the whole soul into action. At school they are required to have fewer books, and learn them better, than girls. The thoughts of girls are more diverted, and their time more divided by music, drawing, and other accomplishments. The separating line in the education of boys and girls is too strongly marked. Indeed, none should exist. In early and later life their spheres approximate less closely than they should. As society exists, men and women are mutually dependent. They should, therefore, be mutual helpers. Life's duties and labors ought to be more nearly divided. Women are taught to regard with too much anxious solicitude the opinions of men, and too little their accountability to God.

The ignorance of the women of a community is a drawback upon the intelligence of the men, while general intelligence among the women of a community elevates man and renders his affairs more prosperous.

"The two sexes," says Thomas, "always follow one another (though at a little distance, by imitation), and are elevated or improved, or weakened or corrupted, together."

For the most perfect condition of society all the mental faculties and moral attributes of its members must be fully developed. The qualities, which, by education and the customs of society, are made to some extent peculiar to each sex, must be mutually reflected.

The social, moral, and intellectual condition of woman has much to do with the honor and standing of a nation. The glory of a nation and its intellectual advancement sink together. The general diffusion of knowledge in France in 1792 has been attributed to the social intercourse that had long existed between the sexes. A reciprocal influence is exerted on the minds and manners of men and women. As the virtues of women decrease, it is a pretty sure indication that the government is in a fair way to decline — that the effeminacy of voluptuous ease is making clear the descent to ruin. Ignorance and depravity of the female sex are often the first indications of the downfall of a nation. In a corrupt state of society women are the greatest sufferers. The intercourse between the minds of men and women is mutually beneficial, and detracts not from the strength of the one, nor the beauty of the other. What woman is not conscious of the information she gains from the society of intelligent men? of the spirit and power given her intellect by such intercourse? If men are bolder and stronger than women, let them endeavor to do right, and by their example encourage women to do so. Where is the man that does not experience a reforming influence from the society of a true woman? In the hours of darkness she is a cynosure leading to light and happiness. Most men prefer to see women happy, because a cheerful face is always most pleasant. A man's virtue and refinement of feeling can be determined, to a great extent, by the kind of women he associates with, and by his opinion and treatment of women.

Hitherto the dependence of woman on man, in the marriage relation of civilized life, has been too great, and that of man on woman too small. There needs to be a more nearly equal balance for the good of both. It has arisen from man's selfishness and woman's depression. Women are not angels, but by nature the equals and companions of men. Women should be treated as rational beings, not as slaves, nor as silly children. In some tribes of North American Indians, women were formerly elected members of the council, and did much to influence its proceedings. "In many of the black tribes of Central Africa, the women rule; and they are as intelligent as they are amiable and kind."

A fear of losing the good opinion of those men by whom they are surrounded, has prevented thousands of women from speaking freely and honestly their thoughts. The more independent of the other sex women (whether married or single) can be, the better for them. Mary Wolstonecraft says, "It is vain to expect virtue from women till they are, in some degree, independent of men. Whilst they are absolutely dependent on their husbands they will be cunning, mean, and selfish, and the men who can be gratified by the fawning fondness of a spaniel-like affection, have not much delicacy." Says Mrs. E. Oakes Smith,* "Take one of the other sex, surround him with restrictions, fetter him with petty claims, hold his intellect in abeyance, because knowledge is power; compress his movements, condemn him to ungenial companionship; and make the labor of his body and the action of his mind all subservient to a routine, and he is false, crafty, petty, sullen, degraded, and irresponsible. The case is analogous. Make a woman nobly free, and she is the companion of sages and philosophers, a helpmeet for man; confine and dwarf her, and she is subtle and

* See "Woman and her Needs."

dangerous, both to herself and others. The worst crime is the betrayal of trust; and now, as the world is, this instinctive loyalty must either die out of a woman's soul, as a useless manifestation of the divine element, or it is violated, overwhelming her with remorse, and throwing her whole being into discord. She must use mean weapons because the nobler are denied her; she cannot assert her distinctive individuality, and she resorts to cunning, and this cunning takes the form of cajolery, deception, or antagonism in its many shapes, each and all as humiliating to herself as it is unjust to man."

The wisest and best men are invariably those who treat women with most respect and kindness. A man of good character, and extended influence, can do much to elevate and establish, in society, the female members of his family, if they are virtuous and educated.

"Presence of mind, penetration, fine observation, are the sciences of woman; ability to avail themselves of these is their talent." "The gay vivacity, and the quickness of imagination, so conspicuous among the qualities in which the superiority of women is acknowledged, have a tendency to lead to unsteadiness of mind; to fondness of novelty; to habits of frivolousness, and trifling employments; to dislike of sober application; to repugnance of grave studies, and a too low estimate of their worth; to an unreasonable regard for wit, and shining accomplishments; to a thirst for admiration and applause, to vanity and affectation. They contribute likewise to endanger the composure and mildness of the temper, and to render the disposition fickle through caprice, and uncertain through irritability."

What is the motive that inspires a number of gentlemen when in company with the lady they admire? Is it to pass time? or is it a rivalry among themselves of their own merits and superiorities? or is it a desire to make a favorable impression on the lady by comparison? And why, when the circle is broken by the exit of one or more, do all soon withdraw? That depends on the nature of the lady's attractions. If it is superiority of intellect or attainments, are all men so conceited that they think they cannot learn anything from a woman? Such may be the opinion of some men, but certainly not that of all. Is it personal attraction? youth, beauty, vivacity? If so, it is strange that more men do not linger longer — or is it the homage of fashion? — or, to view the matter in a more charitable light, does it arise from consideration of the lady's feelings — fearing to fatigue her by too great a tax of her entertaining powers?

A modest reserve should ever be observed between not only individuals of different sexes, but of the same sex. A pure, high-toned intercourse should be kept up between the sexes. It is beneficial to both parties. It cultivates the moral nature of man, and the intellectual of woman. The advantage is reciprocal. How rare to find a hearty, earnest, whole-souled interchange of thought and feeling between individuals of opposite sexes! The difference in their education, their pursuits, their tastes, and habits, tends to bring about, and continue, this want of affinity. This difference is most marked among people of middle station, in which woman is free from definite employment, and depends on relatives for maintenance. This can be done away to some extent by such women entering respectable and remunerative occupations. Such women are educated above their station, and aspire in most cases to what is unattainable.

By studying moral and mental science, women would better learn to appreciate themselves and other people, and place a more correct estimate both on their own value and that of others.

Observation teaches us that men and women are more obliging to members of the opposite sex, than to those of their own sex, even when there is no partiality for the individuals. If a woman conducts herself with courtesy and dignity, she need not fear rudeness or insult from men, for fifty would fly to the rescue, where one would venture to insult her.

I think, where men and women meet most naturally, and become most attached, women are more likely to share in the public duties of men. In France and Great Britain, the ablest statesmen, and wisest philosophers, have the friendship of virtuous and sensible women, outside of their families, and from them often derive hints that quicken slow-footed reason, and inspire to noble and generous deeds. The French women have always taken an active part in the politics of their country.

Mrs. Jameson says, "Might we not, in distributing the work to be done in this world, combine and use in a more equal proportion the working faculties of men and women? Have we lost the true balance between the element of power and the element of love? and trusted too much to mere mechanical means for carrying out high religious and moral purposes? It seems indisputable that the mutual influence of the sexes — brain upon brain, life upon life — becomes more subtle, and spiritual, and complex, more active and more intense, in proportion as the whole human race is improved and developed."

Rev. J. H. Fox writes, "The weal of the world depends upon the rectitude and sanctity of the female character in the *humble spheres of life*. The few who are elevated above necessity for toil, into pomp and plenitude, separate themselves too assiduously from the great human family to exercise over it any lasting control."

Young women do not check as they should what is immoral in men. Indeed, I am sorry to say, some young women rather encourage what is evil in their associates, from a want of moral courage. For instance, a young man may laughingly refer to some acquaintance "being tight," or "carrying a brick in his hat." A young lady friend might perhaps do good to that young man, by expressing, in free, unqualified measure, her disapproval of intemperance. But she thinks her friend may sometimes patronise freely the wine cup, and she fears to do so, lest she lose his admiration, or attention. And so in regard to gambling, and other such sins. A woman will not lose worthy associates by shunning those who are immoral. Were all the young women of the land to make, and execute, the resolution to decline the attentions of any young man who uses ardent spirits, or is known to be guilty of any other immorality, how long do you think it would be before the majority of young men would prove themselves in every way worthy of respect? Let young women require that high-toned morality from young men, that young men require from them, and I can assure you a mighty and glorious revolution would dawn.

A man is in no way more improved than by the society of virtuous and cultivated women. It ennobles a man, increases his respect for the sex, and renders him more just and liberal in his views. New ideas are suggested, plans of benevolence are brought forward, and an interest elicited, and counsel obtained. The influence will cause men to render women their dues, and to elevate instead of depressing them. It will rejoice in a wide and whole-souled freedom of judgment, speech, and action. Men and women are so intimately associated, that what elevates one must elevate the other. It cannot be otherwise. One sex cannot be independent of the other. It was never so intended. "We are not sufficiently sensible of the fact that sometimes a simple word can save a man, and raise him up, and teach him to respect himself, and give him an abiding strength, which until then he had not."

Love and duty are the strong, impelling forces of woman. Power and avarice are the mainsprings of action with men.

In life a continual warfare is waged between spiritual and animal force. When the former predominates, there will be virtue and wisdom; when the latter, ignorance and depravity.

The erroneous idea is common that a woman should not concern herself with what belongs to the business and political views of men. The war that has been going on in the United States was calculated to create a sympathy, and intelligence, connected with political matters, and engender a spirit of patriotism, that has had, and will continue to have, a beneficial effect on women, and society. The war came to their homes and hearts. The same dangers threatened all, and the same hopes of success animated them. Political corruption and intrigue will hereafter be more readily exposed, and we hope gradually overcome. It may lead women to encourage men in being honest and faithful in the discharge of their duties, particularly those duties that pertain to their country's welfare. It will lead women to enter more into the every-day lives of men, to be less governed by emotion, more by reason. Women will investigate more thoroughly, and feel more interest in, the laws and institutions of their country. And we doubt not but it will lead to the making, and amending, of laws that will have more at heart the welfare of woman. If conversation was more elevating in general society, women would make more effort to be posted on such subjects as would inform, as well as entertain.

AMERICAN CHARACTERISTICS.

THE active, restless spirit of Americans is proverbial. Their temperaments, their fast way of living and transacting business, and the poor health induced thereby, will mostly account for it. Their excitability, and their proneness to excess, are to be lamented, and the effects are being seen in the rapid increase of lunatic asylums.

The Americans are too sensitive in being told of their defects. It seems to be an individual and national failure. It reminds one of spoiled children.

The Americans are prone to hero-worship, as is evinced by the erection of costly monuments. As a trading people the Americans have become famous, and the American flag is known in all waters.

The ideas of liberty, with foreigners in our country, are inconsistent and false — their ideas of justice extremely vague and undefined. The freedom that exists in our country increases the responsibility of individuals. It calls peremptorily for the acquisition of valuable knowledge. But more particularly does it demand that deep-rooted principles of virtue be implanted in youth — such virtue as will lead them not only to consult their own welfare, but observe strict justice in their intercourse with others. Their government lies almost entirely in self. Therefore let them be trained to govern themselves with firm and positive reins. Their own happiness and that of others will depend on it.

The independence of American character is favorable to bring about reforms that take place more slowly in older countries, and require the wealth and rank of those countries to indorse.

The pride and vanity of Americans have become proverbial with foreigners. It has brought about an extravagance that at times has threatened to overturn our government. It has introduced a fondness for display that is not unfrequently gratified at the expense of all that is good and honorable. I would refer the reader to Mrs. Graves's "Woman in America," pp. 103–105. Wealthy Americans have indulged in luxury to a fearful extent. Their houses are furnished with velvet cushions, tapestry carpets, and French mirrors, and they sink into effeminacy, trying to follow in the footsteps of the old, aristocratic nations of Europe. The vices of the European nations are likely to be introduced with their refinement. Mr. Sedgwick says, in his "Public and Private Economy," "Much finery is made in Paris, and in other parts of France, principally for our market, in the same way as we buy and make beads, and other trinkets, to send to savage nations." Fashionable ladies in the United States pride themselves on their excessive delicacy. But little pride is attached to learning by those who possess it. Yet it is of all prides the most excusable. The American women of the middle classes are charged with being not only proud, but frivolous. We do not know what comparison they bear to those of other countries; but where the qualities exist, they generally arise from the want of proper home-training, and the fast and extravagant way of living common in the United States.

The fashion of giving frequent and costly entertainments, by those not able to afford it, is sometimes a source of embarrassment. We think, if the German plan of reunions could be adopted in our country, it would tend to advance the intellectual, and retard the growth of animal, appetites.

Dress was given to Adam and Eve in their shame and guilt. It betokened the displeasure of the Almighty. Yet now it is a source of pride to many, and occupies most of their thoughts and time. If the means of parents are ample, or even moderate, they should not restrict their children in dress so as to make them appear odd, or out of place in any assembly. A feeling of meanness and inferiority follows such restriction, and has bad effects.

On the other hand, we would not encourage an extravagant, wasteful, or silly expenditure of time, or money, on dress. But good materials made up in the prevailing style, so as not to render the individual conspicuous in any way, are most desirable.

Few Americans are satisfied with what they acquire. The more they accumulate, the more they toil. As a general thing they devote too much time to the acquisition of wealth. The consequence is, men and women are too much estimated by pecuniary circumstances, not enough by intrinsic worth. I fear we tread in the footsteps of our ancestors, the English, in permitting riches to exert so great an influence, and command such an ascendency. Much pride of birth and wealth is felt in American society, by those who think they have a claim to precedence so founded. Dissipation and its enervating effects generally attend wealth. The minds and hearts of men are so engrossed in the great struggle for honor and wealth, that they are in danger of neglecting the moral and mental, social and religious, training of their children.

The Americans cannot tolerate a want of chastity in women. It is well. But why should not as severe and lasting a condemnation rest on men that lack purity? Why may the seducer be received in society when the seduced is forever branded with infamy? The North American Indians are more just. A guilty man is abhorred by them, while a woman is more lightly judged. We think justice would mete out a like penalty when both are equally criminal.

There are two kinds of character in most society of civilized countries — positive and negative. The positive are those of strong, determined will, with energy, enterprise, fearlessness, and courage. The negative are those possessing patience, meekness, fortitude, submissiveness, and all the tame qualities that belong to a passive mind. The negative usually possess a great deal of cunning and servility, which they use to attain their ends. There is a vast number of people that feel, and a comparatively small number that think.

LABOR OF AMERICAN WOMEN.

THE physical energy exerted by women in other countries may not be exercised to the same extent by American women, but we incline to think it is by wives in moderate or contracted circumstances. American women, *en masse*, may not perform as much drudgery as the same number of women in foreign countries; but we think they probably labor just as hard in proportion to their strength and health. American women that superintend their households generally have considerable care; particularly have those had who depended upon slave labor. We think the poor health, the constant pressure of home duties, and the want of agreeable recreation, shortens the life of many a married woman. The wife and mother who faithfully attends to her house duties, who conscientiously trains her children in the ways of virtue and industry, does as much as her husband to support her family. Her work is indispensable and important.

Street sweeping, and, indeed, all such laborious employments, when performed in this country by women, is mostly done by foreigners — not by American women. The foreign population in New York city is very large.

Some account for the inefficiency charged against workwomen in American cities, by the reckless idea of freedom that prevails. But we think it arises from not being thoroughly trained when girls, and many not expecting to make it a life-long business. The tendency to engage in regular employments will increase as our country becomes more thickly populated. In England, for instance, there is a greater diversity of employments, and the masses of the people are more generally raised with a view to pursuing some occupation steadily. We strongly advocate the acquisition of some practical business pursuit by every woman. In doing so it is far, very far, from being our wish to encourage the making of woman a piece of soulless machinery. That would be bringing her back to her past condition, when the loom and the knitting-needle occupied most of her working hours. No, let mindless machinery perform this labor, guided, where women see proper, by their own careful hands. I rejoice that in the middle and upper walks of life machinery is doing the labor formerly executed by the fingers of woman. It will give her more time for self-culture. A nobler purpose, a higher aim, a more exalted destiny, are placed before her. I hear the famishing call to her for food, the suffering for aid, the desolate for comfort. I hear the pleadings of the orphan, and the moans of the dying. Woman turns from her labors to comfort and console. She leaves her other duties to administer to the needy. She is awakening to a sense of her high mission. A blending of labor and thought is needed — all labor will not answer — neither will all thought in this business age.

The labor of the two sexes is, and to some extent should be, different. Woman's labor is more perishable in its nature than man's. Those stores, factories, workshops, and saloons, where women are employed are more quiet and orderly than where men of only the same experience are employed. In all labor, save that of a literary kind, the most mechanical part, the mere drudgery, is given to women.

A false pride has existed, and does exist to some extent, among the higher and middle classes of American women in regard to labor. To this may be added a fondness for dress. The two combined have no doubt proved the downfall of a number.

Some travelers have charged the young women of this country with idleness. Some of them are idle, but, we are inclined to think, not more so than those of other countries. Until the war commenced, a larger number of women and girls were maintained by their parents or relatives than in England, but the majority of those so maintained were not idle. The proportion, too, of single women was not so great. Added to this, more money was afloat, and more easily got by those women that did work. The gulf between wealth and poverty was not so wide. But now that the war has ceased, the public debt is enlarged, and taxes are increased, the necessaries of life are higher, unskilled labor finds a market more difficult to secure, business in the South remains confused, and thousands of women and girls suffer in every way.

The uncertainty and inconstancy of obtaining work differ but little in our cities. The supply of labor is generally much greater than the demand, while in many parts of the country there is really a call for labor in the domestic branches. The question arises, Why do not women go from the city to the country to seek labor? The majority have not the means, and those that have, fear they may expend all in getting where work is offered, and there be uncomfortably situated or overworked, and not have the means to return, while many are too proud to engage in domestic service, or feel unwilling to give up the varieties and excitements of a city life.

Women coming to this country from Europe to seek work, are liable to be shamefully treated in New York, if they are without friends. It is said that men go to ships, professing to be runners from boarding-houses, and take the unprotected women landing, up to houses which they leave less pure than when they enter. Sometimes these men pass themselves off to the captain as uncles, or cousins, if the women have so forgotten, by long absence, their relatives, as not to recognize them, and not unfrequently the captain has to stand guard when his vessel lands, to protect these homeless strangers. If the captain is a bad man, he will sometimes join in the unprincipled schemes of others. This infamous imposition is being done away to some extent by the establishment of emigrant agencies.

AMERICAN WIVES.

AMERICAN women are considered more faithful and devoted wives than those of any other nation. We met with a newspaper article some time ago that so well defines the characteristics of females among different nations that we cannot forbear transcribing it.

"The Englishwoman is respectful and proud; the Frenchwoman is gay and agreeable; the Italian is passionate; the American is sincere and affectionate. With an Englishwoman love is principle; with a Frenchwoman it is a caprice; with an Italian it is a passion; with an American it is a sentiment. A man is married to an Englishwoman; is united to a French; cohabits with an Italian; and is wedded to an American. An Englishwoman is anxious to secure a lord; a Frenchwoman a companion; an Italian a lover; an American a husband. An Englishman respects his lady; the Frenchman esteems his companion; the Italian adores his mistress; the American loves his wife. The Englishman at night returns to his house; while the Frenchman goes to his establishment, the Italian to his retreat, the American to his home. When the Englishman is sick, his lady visits him; when a Frenchman is sick, his companion pities him; when an Italian is sick, his mistress sighs over him; when an American is sick, his wife nurses him. The Englishwoman instructs her offspring; the Frenchwoman teaches her progeny; an Italian rears her young; while an American educates her child."

The intelligent, warm-hearted, sensible wife can make a little heaven of home, on condition that she has a good man for a husband, that assists in rendering home pleasant. The home of the virtuous and good is dear to all. If it contains a well-regulated family, bound in heart and interest by mutual esteem, confidence, and affection, it proves indeed a shelter from the pitiless storms of life, a covert from its dark and stormy tempests.

It is a great disadvantage for a woman to be closely confined at home with her family, year after year. Her range of thought becomes limited. Her mind wants nutriment, and it is the place of the husband to furnish it. He has time for reading and opportunities of mixing with those who talk over the latest intelligence. Domestic obligations rest as much on the husband as on the wife. When we consider the neglect and indifference of many husbands, their absorption in self, and sinful pleasures, we only wonder and feel grateful that more wives are not insane, or tempted to go astray.

An important position is accorded woman in the home department. Obedience from servants, and a kind yet decided manner with the mistress, will generally make the lower departments of household machinery move smoothly. But fretting and scolding make the wheels of the machinery work very roughly. The long, wearing toil of servants might in some cases be diminished by consideration and management on the part of the mistress. Domestics should be treated with kindness. Much of the comfort of a family depends on them. They labor hard. If industrious and well behaved, they should at least receive our kind words and sympathy. They should be taught to read, and furnished with good books to enjoy in their leisure hours. Do not accuse, or suspect, those in your employ of having done wrong. A friend related to me a circumstance that came to her knowledge, which illustrates, in one instance, the evil consequences. An Irish girl, in one of our western cities, was accused, by a lady for whom she sewed, of taking a breastpin, and immediately dismissed. The accuser was visiting not long after at the house of a friend, and was invited into the bed-chamber to see a dress she was having made. The maker was the Irish girl she had dismissed. As Mrs. A. left the house, she told Mrs. C.

that her seamstress was dishonest — that she had stolen from her a breastpin. Mrs. C. went up and told the seamstress she did not wish her services any longer, and paid her what was due. The girl inquired the cause. Mrs. C. related what Mrs. A. had said. She protested her innocence, but all in vain. The seamstress, feeling her reputation was blasted — the all upon which her prospects in life depended, went to her boarding-house, took poison, and was found dead in her bed the next morning. Subsequent events, a few months after, led to the detection of the real thief, in the person of a servant girl, employed at that time in the house. Be careful of the reputation of others, particularly that of dependent females.

CHANGES OF FORTUNE.

TO die and leave children without property and business qualifications, is like setting them adrift in a rudderless boat, on a strange ocean. But in the possession of a pursuit it is different. It will prove a real Aladdin's lamp — a talisman that will ever make them independent.

Those that have been tenderly and delicately cherished, are more frequently thrown upon their own resources for a livelihood, in new, than in some of the older countries, where property is entailed. So it is desirable that the people of the United States be prepared for emergencies. It is not an unusual sight to witness the daughter of affluence to-day, penniless to-morrow. And between the extremes of fortune we see almost every day some fluctuation. A lady should, therefore, be educated to adorn the highest ranks of society, or, if necessary, earn a livelihood by her acquirements. Prepared for both extremes, she will be enabled to pass through the world comfortably and creditably.

Sudden revolutions in financial affairs come not with such serious import to our male, as to our female population. Men generally find no difficulty in turning their talents and acquirements to account. The wheel of fortune may place a man at a different point to-morrow from the one he occupies to-day. But when women are cast helpless and alone upon the world, their timidity, anxiety, feeble constitutions, and the limited number of occupations that offer employment, are likely to render them very helpless.

The changed circumstances occasioned by the late war, are opening to the eyes of both men and women, the necessity for women to be prepared to take care of themselves, in the most trying and straitened circumstances. No one can tell what the future will bring forth. Men will now have more occasion to think what is for the good of their families, and more time to do so, if the females of those families, in the middle ranks of life, help bear the burden of the day, and assist in the labors and cares of life. Such men will be less oppressed by labor, and have more cause and inclination for seeking the good and happiness of those with whom they are connected. Uneducated men in the lower walks of life, may be changed in their views also. Instead of making beasts of burden of their wives and daughters, they will endeavor to lighten their labors, and the money they have been accustomed to spend in their own self-indulgence, will be appropriated to the good and comfort of their families.

VALUE OF EMPLOYMENT.

BY want of occupation, idleness is engendered, discontent produced, envy and jealousy aroused, and the individual either becomes listless and idle, or fault-finding and morose. It causes depression of spirits, and brings about a moral inertness that prepares the mind for vain or wicked thoughts. Without employment both mind and body become enervated. It is essential to the preservation of health, and with health comes moral and physical beauty.

Employment is the best promoter of happiness and morality. It is the greatest preventive of evil, the surest restorer of the wicked to morality. We are so constituted that if not engaged in something good, we shall be in something bad. Employment drives away discontent. By it the sorrow that would become a giant, to crush and destroy, is banished. The despair that would prey upon the heart gives way to a cheerful hope. People, we all know, are more lively when actively employed. They have not time for hard feelings, and bitter thoughts, or morbid sensitiveness, to corrode the heart. It creates a feeling of friendliness that engenders confidence, and obtains an influence. It also gives force to character. Occupation is the great pillar of support. It tends to develop the threefold nature of man — to make him stronger, wiser, and better.

An individual had better work even for low wages, than be idle, unless engaged in some plan for the general increase of wages, in his or her trade. What is lost in money will be gained in character.

Work, with an anxious, overtasked brain, may destroy that brain. It is best to be as free as possible from care when at work.

Without labor, nature would be comparatively unproductive, and her productions would be almost useless.

God did not intend that man or woman should live for self alone. All of us are beings dependent in some way. If we have means to live without remunerative work, we should employ ourselves to give to those physically, or mentally, incapacitated for work.

Action is necessary to develop the faculties of a human being. Diet for the mind must be of a kind to suit its strength and growth. If the mind has been fed on light or unwholesome food, it will be in a faint and sickly condition; if on strong, substantial aliment, it, of course, will be strong and healthy. And such a mind will desire and seek reading of a solid and profitable kind. Jotting down notes, opinions, suggestions, and incidents, will impress what one reads and hears on the memory, and render the mind more fertile and suggestive.

"Some positions," says Legouvé, "attract by their ease; but it is work that purifies and fills existence. God permits hard trials; but he has appointed labor, and we forget them all. A serious comforter, it gives always more than it promises, and dries the bitterest tears. A pleasure unequaled in itself, it is the salt of all other pleasures."

ALL MADE TO WORK.

THE birds warble their sweet notes, the flowers smile in their beauty, the stars twinkle merrily, the waves chase each other playfully, the fountains cast their jets sportively — all, all tell of activity, save here and there a human idler, more gifted, more favored than all — possessing the faculty of speech, intellect, heart, and hands. What do you suppose the angels think when they look down upon an idle, useless mortal? And what do you suppose the great and good God thinks? Does he view with satisfaction a useless creation of his hands? Of all pitiable objects a know-nothing, do-nothing kind of man or woman is the most so. Uneducated people, without a trade, or a profession, know nothing of the value of time. And here I would suggest not merely to supply the poor with contributions, — many of them will become idle and make no exertion of their own, — but furnish them with employment, and pay them well for it.

Instead of the activity of the great mass of people being of an intellectual kind, sin has made it to consist in activity of body, with the object mainly in view, of contributing to the necessities of the physical nature.

No one is wholly exempt from labor, or entirely free from duty. Who can suppose that a human being was created for no purpose but to seek his or her own comfort, or amusement. Surely such a one is not fulfilling the end for which he, or she, was made. Without labor we should gradually fall back into the condition of savages.

Indolence is the bane of happiness and usefulness, and always brings a curse. Nothing is more contagious than indolence. The languid condition of mind and body produced by years of idleness unfits an individual for the exertion necessary to earn a comfortable livelihood. It is natural to be occupied in some way, but I think few are by nature fond of work. A fondness for close and constant application is, usually, the result of cultivation.

It would be well if the thoughts and efforts of women did not so often center in the one condition of matrimony; if parents and teachers would consider that some of the girls in their charge will certainly not marry, and therefore should fit all, by the bestowment of an honorable employment, to work their own way through the world. Who of a given number of girls will remain single we do not know. Therefore let all be prepared by each one having a vocation to rely upon. They will so better understand their positions, and their capacities.

A woman must, and does, exert an influence, whether she will or not. Woman's great influence demands of her a holy activity. Most wives do housework and sewing — those engaged in trading, and the manufacturing and mechanical employments, perform other labor; those in professions work mentally, and to some extent manually — so these all work, but there are thousands that do nothing useful.

Some women do not work because it is not fashionable to do so; some because they are not qualified by education and training; and some from the want of health. Everybody has to work, or somebody else must do their work. If we believe that God does all things right, we must decide that there are not more women on earth than there should be, and exactly enough work for their varied strength and different abilities. That each one cannot find her own work in the vineyard, and the proper place to perform it, ought not to be charged to the Owner of the vineyard.

Every individual has his or her part to perform in the machinery of nature — in the great drama of life. "He alone," says Seneca, "can be truly said to live who devotes himself to some purpose of usefulness and activity." Cicero says, "It is action only that gives a true value and commendation to virtue." Remember that one of the three things that Cato repented, was, to have spent a day inactive.

Idleness is the mother of mischief. It creates physical, moral, and mental disease. The inefficiency and imbecility it produces are not confined to the idle merely, but transmitted to offspring.

A sense of mingled pity and contempt is felt for a man that lives in idle repose. It is not so with woman in the higher and middle classes of society, but it would be better if it were. Though man was doomed to hard labor as a punishment, yet in it lies his greatest good. In all labor there is profit. Prov. xiv. 23. In some countries, all classes and conditions of men are expected to know how to labor.

Professional men and women should be paid better than industrial or domestic workers, because of the long time, and great expense, attending a preparation, to say nothing of the superior mental ability required. But as matters now stand, some people work sixteen hours and are paid for eight, and some work eight and are paid for sixteen, while others experience all the intermediate gradations of work and pay.

RECREATION.

"A HARMLESS, cheerful laughter," says Miss Bremer, "is certainly the most effectual means of reconciling one to life and mankind." Some one has said, "The noisy mountain brook puts its broad shoulder to the wheel of a mill, and shows that it can labor as well as laugh."

We would not advocate the doctrine of unceasing labor for any, for recreation is as necessary as labor itself. The mind must not be cramped by oppression, the body worn out by fatigue. Occupation furnishes us with a capability of appreciating rest, of enjoying recreation. We believe in a medium — neither all work, nor all play. Excessive fatigue calls for relaxation, and should receive it. It is better for those who can, to work but six days and rest the seventh, as one, on an average, gets the same pay; because by constant work one has not the strength to accomplish more, and so the employer pays the same for seven days labor as for six.

The body will suffer if the brain is overtasked. Some resort to a change of employment. If this is of a light and cheerful kind it may answer the purpose. But the consequences of over-taxation are so deleterious that I would warn my young friends against it. More is lost than gained in the long run. A better preservation of health, and consequently greater power to labor, are gained by moderation. For when the energies of mind, or body, cease, life becomes dull even with its comforts at command.

WORK APARTMENTS OF MEN AND WOMEN.

SOME people think the mixing of men and women in business operations has a tendency to make the women coarse in manners. We think it tends to equalize — to diminish the refinement of women, and increase that of men.

Their indiscriminate mingling in workshops is thought to be detrimental to morals, as well as manners. That depends altogether on the character of the work-people, their supervisors and employers. If they have moral principle and self-respect, there will not be much danger; but the misfortune is, that many are without that decorum and sense of propriety that arise from proper training. Some women and girls do not conduct themselves properly in their work-rooms, and on the street, and that gives rise to the frequent want of respect felt for them by the mercantile and professional classes.

Moral and honorable employers, and foremen, can do much by establishing regulations that will enforce a becoming demeanor, in the work-rooms at least. They can do much to inspire feelings of decency and self-respect, by having a proper arrangement of their work-rooms, and the necessary appurtenances.

To reach work-rooms in the great metropolis, New York city, where women were employed, we have climbed up dark, narrow, dirty staircases; some with the planks loosened and broken; some without planks at the back; some of cast iron; and some located almost over the hatchway, so that the individual was liable to break her neck, or have her whole person exposed. It will not do to deny this, for we can point out the places our own eyes have seen, and our own feet trod; places where women must go daily to labor for their bread.

In many of the workshops that we visited, the females, owing to the arrangement of the rooms, and want of necessary conveniences, with the employing of workmen in the same apartment, or having a foreman instead of a forewoman to superintend, necessarily made a great sacrifice of their health. Most of them remained in the same room from the time they came in the morning until they left in the evening. None can estimate the amount of suffering, and the number of diseases induced by such thoughtlessness, cupidity, and cruelty.*

A pert young clerk in New York said to me, that a nice and sensible girl would not be willing to work in a room with men. Poor fellow, he is very ignorant not to know that many women in New York must either do it, die of hunger, or sell their souls for bread.

The foreman in a knitting-machine factory remarked, if girls are too free with men, they ought not to be permitted to work with them; and if men are too fond of the society of women, the same restriction should be put on them. He added, if a girl is inclined to be immoral, she will be so, let her be shielded from temptation as much as she will. We are not so strongly predestinarian. The foreman told me he judges of girls, that apply for work, by their conversation and appearance, and says he has never failed to judge correctly but once in four years.

Pride deters some women from being seen wending their way to and from workshops, and for this reason they prefer to work at home, while others do so because of the greater privacy and protection afforded.

Of the metal manufactories in England, Home says, "As to illicit sexual intercourse, it seems to prevail almost universally, and from a very early period of life; to this conclusion witnesses of every rank give testimony." We know

* I would call the attention of employers to an excellent book entitled "Heads and Hands in the World of Labor," by W. G. Blaikie, D. D. For sale by Routledge & Son, New York.

from statistics, and the accounts of travelers, that a much larger proportion of work-people are corrupt in England than in the United States. We doubt not, some immorality, but not all, may be traced to the indiscriminate blending of men and women of every moral cast, in the labor of the field, workshop, and manufactory. Therefore, so far as practicable, it may be best that men and women, *where such a variety is employed, and as society now exists*, should occupy separate rooms, while engaged in their various employments. Perhaps if women would qualify themselves for suitable occupations now closed to them, men who are liberal, desire their advancement, and are willing to secure their services, would furnish them with a separate apartment to work in.

Barbara Leigh Smith says, "If women were in active life, mixing much with men, the common attraction of sex merely, would not be so much felt, but rather the attraction of natures especially adapted to each other."

I have been told by some employers that their men do better when a few women work in the same room. Other employers have complained that their workmen do not accomplish so much, because they will talk to the women, while a number told me that their workmen complained of the restraint produced by the presence of women.

We doubt not but the most expedient plan would be to employ *forewomen* in the female department, and to have men and women labor in separate rooms, when their work will admit of such an arrangement.

TEMPTATIONS.

ACCORDING to Michelet two fifths of the crime in France is committed by the French people in *towns*, the entire population of which constitutes only one fifth part of the population of the whole country.

Crime is increasing to a fearful extent in England, Ireland, and Scotland. In 1830 it had increased in England within the thirty years previous *five fold;* in Ireland *five and a half*, and in Scotland, *twenty-nine fold.* In this country, immorality and vice have increased with astonishing rapidity, during the last few years.

The pauper laws of England do much to encourage an illicit intercourse of the sexes, by supporting pauper children, and allowing the mother a pension.

In a work by Reynolds called "The Seamstress," I read as follows of a work-girl in England: "Sad were the experiences which her contact with the young women who worked for the same establishment brought to her knowledge; sad and mournful were the social phases which she was too often forced to contemplate! She saw that the earnings of honest labor were so poor, so wretchedly small, that the oppressed needlewomen were goaded, by famine and desperation, to have recourse to the earnings of shame. Many — O, how many! — of these unfortunate beings loathed and abhorred the base idea of walking in the paths of error; but their choice lay between starvation, suicide, and infamy. They dared not beg, the police laws hung in terror over them; they shrank from the thought of self-destruction; and yet they could not starve. What were they to do? Reader, spurn not away the unfortunate girl who accosts you in the streets; but pity her and give her alms. Perhaps she belongs to the class of needlewomen that would be virtuous, if they could, but who are made the victims of all the tremendous tyranny of *capital*, *monopoly*, and *competition*. Yes; let there be pity and compassion for those who err, not from any impulsive love of profligacy and vice, but in obedience to the stern necessity, which breaks down the strongest defenses that women may set up around their virtue."

The starving child of toil, who preserves her chastity amid the temptations to which she is exposed, well merits the respect of those who possess superior advantages. When we hear of the poverty, misery, and degradation of thousands — yes, thousands of our own sex, in the cities — we feel that none who are good need be idle for the want of benevolent and reformatory work.

How much training and discipline, both of mind and heart, girls need! As I have sometimes been overtaken by the shades of evening, and hurried home, I have seen girls pass out from their work-rooms, and O, how my heart sunk as I thought, evening after evening it is so with them! To how many temptations are they exposed! Perhaps many live a long distance off, and no fellow-worker lives in the same direction — so such must go entirely alone. Some, that are young and thoughtless, linger along, glad to get into the comparatively fresh air, and gaze in shop windows. Rowdy boys jostle, and look them in the face. They are glad to be noticed, and soon a leer, and a jest, carry them on, until they are lost in the stream of vice. Or bad men may be waiting to lure them to ruin. Many are the snares and pitfalls that beset even the most favored.

It is a sad fact, that for the last few years, those that fill the ranks of prostitutes in New York are, according to published reports, very young girls, and not, as formerly, women beyond the prime of life. A large number of street-walkers in that city are said to be educated women, who have taught music, and the languages, and resorted to this practice because unable to obtain employment by which to keep from cold and starvation.

Tait says, that "the permanent prostitution of any city bears a recognized numerical relation to its means of occupation. You ask for proof. Out of two thousand cases in the city of New York, five hundred and twenty-five pleaded destitution as the cause." According to Mrs. Dall's statistics, seven thousand eight hundred and fifty abandoned women walk the streets of New York, which is doubtless the most corrupt city on the western continent.

My feelings have occasionally been saddened by seeing ladies of cultivation and refinement, intrenched, by their wealth, friends, and position, from temptation to do wrong, curl the lip, when the fallen of their sex are spoken of, and with a sneer say, "I have no patience with such women." Think not, selfish woman, that you are free from all obligation to aid and rescue such. The unhappy outcasts may not be punished in this world according to their sins. You certainly are not. For have you not sorrows and afflictions of some kinds, the *causes* of which you cannot account for. The most sensitive and refined woman should not shrink from inquiring, How can I, in any way, stop this evil? Can my influence, wealth, position, or sympathy, devise any plan to check this terrible vice? The true woman, the Christian philanthropist, will not shrink from making an effort to reform the erring wanderer. When the interests of an immortal soul are at stake, who may innocently neglect that soul? Many women sink into irremediable helplessness after they have committed the unpardonable sin. Any man that seduces a woman should certainly be required to support her and her children. "The Mohammedan law, that legitimate and illegitimate children should share equally in the division of their fathers' estates, shames the narrow and cruel prejudice, which prevents a just distribution of property among us."

A fertile cause of prostitution is, that men have taken from women those occupations which rightly belong to them. Were better occupations opened to women, and women of a more improved class in them, it would be a safeguard to the less favored class of workwomen. Women have not that encouragement from their superiors that workmen have. The sins of women are more the result of circumstances over which they have no control, than they are of the natural depravity of human nature.

The principal causes of the loss of chastity of women in the cities of this country are probably the following: —

1st. A majority of females being raised without acquiring any pursuit by which to earn an honest livelihood. 2d. The low wages paid for female labor. 3d. The inability to obtain remunerative employment. 4th. Poverty from sickness. 5th. Loss of relations. 6th. Slander, or bad treatment from those that should protect and sustain. These, no doubt, furnish a key to the problem in most places.

"When, indeed, we are told that the various kinds of seamstresses yield the largest quota to the ranks of prostitutes in Great Britain, it needs no prophet's eye to detect the hand of Poverty in the act of beckoning them on to sin. Poverty, poverty, we repeat, is often the principal, and pleasure the second, in these cruel woundings of girls' souls. Whether it shall be theft, or dishonor, to the exhausted frame, and the weakened, hunger-maddened mind, seem the only points left, for choice, and may depend somewhat upon the natural passion or appetites of the various women. Next in number to seamstresses follow the race of inferior servants, who have the hardest places and the worst pay. The next class are the families of seafaring men in the various ports. The higher classes of workwomen, the young girls in notable milliners' establishments, also swell the stream of guilt. Once let persons be forced to outride their strength, and exceed that sentence of toil which is upon Adam's family, and we must expect, either early decay of bodily powers, or demoralization, or both."

"Some *pretended* moralists, and politicians, tell us openly that one fifth part of our sex should be condemned as the legitimate prey of the other, predoomed to die in reprobation, in the streets, in hospitals, that the virtue of the rest may be preserved, and both the pride and passion of men gratified." The men that teach or assert such a thing are doubtless immoral, yes, guilty of this heinous wickedness.

REFORM OF FEMALE CONVICTS.

THE treatment of female criminals in France is deplorable, on account of their exposure, and the wretched condition of the branch prisons, in which most are confined. The number of convicts is small compared with that of male convicts — "a remarkable fact," says Madame Mallet, "seeing that women earn much less than men, and are, therefore, more tempted by poverty."

She continues, "The true and frequent cause, which drives these women to vice, and even crime, is the *ennui* and sadness of their lives. Virtue, for a poor girl, means, to sit fourteen hours a day making the same stitch for ten sous — her head down, her chest bent, her bench hot and tiresome. Add to this, in winter, that miserable charcoal pan, (the cause of many diseases,) all the fuel she has — though shivering with cold."

And when we read her examination into the causes of these crimes, we find that as crimes the number is greatly diminished. Her view of reform for prisoners is admirable. "Her *remedy* is to tear down the walls, and to let in fresh air and sunshine; for light moralizes. Another remedy is labor, under very different conditions — severe, but somewhat varied, and enlivened with music. (This plan has been successful in Paris, through the liberality of some Protestant ladies.) Imprisoned women are crazy for music; it soothes them, restores their moral equilibrium, and calms their heart-burnings. Leon Foucher has wisely said that prisoners from the country, men and women, should be put to field labor, not immured within horrible walls, which are only consumption factories. Yes, set the peasant to tilling the earth again, in Algeria, at least. I could add that even the working woman can be very profitably colonized under a semi-agricultural system, where several hours in the day she might do a little gardening, which would contribute to her support." Madame Mallet remarks that, "in general, passionate women, who, excited by rage and jealousy, have committed a criminal act, are not at all depraved. Place them where they may healthily expend their energy, and they would concentrate it in love and a family, and become the veriest lambs of gentleness. And those martyrs who have yielded to wrong from filial piety or maternal love — who will believe them irremediable? Even the truly guilty, if they are sent out of Europe and placed under a new sky, in a land which knows nothing of their faults — if they feel that society, though a mother that punishes, is still a mother — if they see, at the end of their trial, forgetfulness of the past, and love perhaps, their hearts will swell, and in their abundant tears they will be purified. The silence imposed upon them in the central prison is torture to the woman — many become insane from it."

The French government is now *practically* carrying the suggestion made above into operation by sending female convicts to Cayenne, and marrying them there to male convicts who behave well. The plan is reported as working a change for the better, in both parties.

PREVENTIVES OF EVIL.

SUFFICIENT measures are not taken for preventing suffering and crime. How few virtuous young women are aided in preparing themselves for remunerative labor, or obtaining such labor when qualified, while efforts are very extensively made to rescue those that have fallen. Must a woman commit the unpardonable sin before her condition is attended to? Is sin to be thus encouraged? a premium paid to vileness! God forbid that such a course should long continue.

If a girl has a talent for drawing and painting, let her learn to paint portraits, or large, handsome landscapes, in oil; if no taste for this, let her become a good translator of languages, or if talent enough, an authoress, or if partial to music, become proficient in it, or if possessing a mathematical mind, pursue that branch extensively; or any science to which fondness or nature directs; if without inclination or taste for pursuits of this kind, let her acquire some industrial branch. Every facility for obtaining a knowledge of various branches of business should be rendered to children. Parents would find it to the interest and advantage of their children to take them to see the operation of printing, telegraphing, the manufacture of textile fabrics, the working of metals, &c. Give your daughters independence of character, but found it on a correct, womanly sense of propriety. Impress upon them the fact that in the possession of an education and a practical knowledge of some employment, they will possess a treasure that may be highly useful in case they ever become dependent on their own resources. Teach them to look upon the acquisition of such knowledge not as a task, but a privilege.

24

Some parents object, that daughters will lose much of the home-feeling by this training; such parents may rest assured that the love of home is so strong in woman's nature that such fears will not be realized. They will not love their homes the less, and they will not be less willing to accept a home of their own; at the same time will not be tempted by a sense of dependence to sacrifice themselves. No; home and its endearments will ever be uppermost in their hearts and minds. They can better appreciate their own individual worth as wives. They can better understand the holy and responsible duties connected with marriage, its privileges and sanctities. If you give your daughters a pursuit you need not then toil to secure fortunes for them, which may prove a bait to idle or worthless spendthrifts, that will squander what you have toiled to accumulate. Nor will your daughters be so likely to barter their affections and independence for the wealth of a coarse-souled man. How often do we see young ladies defer their marriage until their affianced have accumulated wealth by their own exertions, while they live idly and uselessly during the time! To such ladies I would say, you had better marry, and assist your husband in making a home. You will be more contented in doing so, and feel more entitled to it when obtained. Such marriages are usually the most happy. That which we earn by hard labor becomes endeared to us.

Some say, Why give a girl a trade or profession, when she will be sure to give it up after marriage? It will not be lost. The knowledge, and discipline of mind gained will help her to rear her children as she should, and impart to them useful knowledge, and form business habits in them. Her husband, though a good man, may fail in business, or she may become a penniless widow; her acquaintance with business will then be invaluable. Parents, when they look upon their daughters, young, gay, and happy, think not of the changes in feeling and disposition that may take place in the course of ten or fifteen years, if they have nothing to employ their time and talents. If your daughters do not marry, they will be discontented if idle and unemployed; but if engaged in active employment, in benevolent works, and doing good as they have opportunity, they will pass through the world respected and beloved. If they marry they will need industrious habits even more. Rich people are apt to raise their children in idleness, a habit that can never be entirely overcome.

In years of childhood and youth cultivate industrious habits in your children, impress upon both boys and girls that if they live they will have to be employed; and tell them the cold philosophy of the world, "He that helps himself, I am ready to help, but he that cannot help himself may get assistance where he can." It is inhuman, cruel, to raise children so tenderly, so effeminately, that when the biting winds of later life sweep over them, they are chilled, frozen. Parents should certainly assist their children in selecting some one channel for the exercise of their thoughts, talents, and energies. We would not have parents put their dull or lazy children to pursuits requiring study, for exercise of the mind requires more perseverance and industry than exercise of the body. Children of weak bodies and active minds are better fitted for professions, those with strong physical frames are best suited to mechanical and out-door labors. We doubt not but the most healthy vocations are those in which there is a happy blending of mental and physical labor. Sometimes the mind is stinted in its growth by too constant and unchanging exercise of mental faculties. Encourage children inclined to sedentary habits to take exercise in the open air; let it be gradually entered into and regularly continued; then may your children have strength to contend successfully with the various giants that beset the journey of life.

In addition to giving your daughters a practical business education, we would advise those with means to purchase a house and ground for each daughter, that may serve as a home, or the income of which may be a maintenance in case of reverse of fortune; or invest means in the land of newly-settled countries, or purchase stock in mines or railroads, or, as Miss Parkes suggests, secure them a living by life insurance.

We would urge upon those people engaged in benevolent works the fact that girls whose parents are poor or trifling, as much want something to look forward to, as a pecuniary support, as boys do. If some branch of industry is opened to their energies, and they are properly encouraged, they will be likely to display quite as much patience, industry, and perseverance, as individuals of the other sex. Give them some definite employment. Why should not the minds and hands of girls be trained just as well as those of boys? Are the thoughts of girls less susceptible of a wrong direction if left to idleness? Or are there more ways in which they can earn an honest livelihood? I was told by a New York city missionary that many of the abandoned women of New York are highly accomplished, and a few even thoroughly educated. I asked this excellent man why this was so. He replied that it was mostly owing to the death of relations, the loss of property, unfitness by education to labor, and failure in obtaining such employment as they were accustomed to and able to execute. I thought of the words of a lady writer, "As long as fathers regard the sex of a child as a reason why it should not be taught to gain its own bread, so long must woman be degraded."